T0389740

Collections and Books, Images and Texts : Early Modern German Cultures of the Book

Chloe

BEIHEFTE ZUM *DAPHNIS*

Founding Editor

Prof. em. Dr. Dr. h.c. Hans-Gert Roloff

Chief Editor

Tobias Bulang (*Universität Heidelberg*)

Editorial Board

Prof. Dr. Miroslawa Czarnecka (*Uniwersytet Wrocławski*)
Prof. Dr. Inga Mai Groote (*Universität Zürich*)
Prof. Dr. Didier Kahn (*Université Paris-Sorbonne*)
Prof. Dr. Ursula Kocher (*Bergische Universität Wuppertal*)
Prof. Dr. David H. Price (*Vanderbilt University, Tennessee*)
Prof. Dr. Elisabeth Rothmund (*Sorbonne Université*)
Prof. Dr. Robert Seidel (*Goethe-Universität Frankfurt am Main*)
Prof. Dr. Stefanie Stockhorst (*Universität Potsdam*)

VOLUME 49

The titles published in this series are listed at *brill.com/chlo*

Collections and Books, Images and Texts: Early Modern German Cultures of the Book

Edited by

Mara R. Wade

BRILL

LEIDEN | BOSTON

Cover illustration: Jost Amman and Hans Sachs, "Der Buchdrücker," *Eygentliche Beschreibung aller Stände auff Erden, hoher und nidriger, geistlicher und weltlicher, aller Künsten, Handwercken und Händeln, ...* Frankfurt am Main 1568. This work is in the public domain.

The Library of Congress Cataloging-in-Publication Data is available online at https://catalog.loc.gov
LC record available at https://lccn.loc.gov/2023028512

Typeface for the Latin, Greek, and Cyrillic scripts: "Brill". See and download: brill.com/brill-typeface.

ISSN 0168-9878
ISBN 978-90-04-68172-9 (hardback)
ISBN 978-90-04-68224-5 (e-book)

Copyright 2023 by Koninklijke Brill NV, Leiden, The Netherlands.
Koninklijke Brill NV incorporates the imprints Brill, Brill Nijhoff, Brill Schöningh, Brill Fink, Brill mentis, Brill Wageningen Academic, Vandenhoeck & Ruprecht, Böhlau and V&R unipress.
All rights reserved. No part of this publication may be reproduced, translated, stored in a retrieval system, or transmitted in any form or by any means, electronic, mechanical, photocopying, recording or otherwise, without prior written permission from the publisher. Requests for re-use and/or translations must be addressed to Koninklijke Brill NV via brill.com or copyright.com.

This book is printed on acid-free paper and produced in a sustainable manner.

Essays in Honor of Gerhard Dünnhaupt

Contents

PART 3
The Organization of Knowledge: Case Studies from the Herzog August Bibliothek, Wolfenbüttel

Illustrations

Notes on Contributors

Victoria Gutsche
is a research fellow at Friedrich-Alexander-University Erlangen-Nürnberg. Her research centers on early modern literature, editorial studies, literature of the 19th and 20th century, German-Jewish literature, and diversity in literature. In addition to book chapters and articles she has published *Zwischen Abgrenzung und Annäherung. Konstruktionen des Jüdischen in der Literatur des 17. Jahrhunderts* (2014) and *Die Romantrilogie. Zur Geschichte einer großen Form von ihren Anfängen bis zur Mitte des 10. Jahrhunderts* (2023); her edition of Julius Wilhelm Zincgrefs *Deutsche Kleinschriften* (with Werner Wilhelm Schnabel and Dirk Niefanger) is forthcoming.

Peter Hess
is a Professor of German and European Studies, teaching early modern cultural history at the University of Texas at Austin. He recently published *Resisting Pluralization and Globalization in German Culture, 1490–1540: Visions of a Nation in Decline* (2020) and *Violent First Contact in Venezuela: Nikolaus Federmann's 'Indian History'* (2021). A book-length study on German conquistadors in Latin America in the first half of the sixteenth century is in progress. He currently also is editing a volume entitled *Managing Pandemics in Early Modern Germany*.

Cornelia Niekus Moore
is Emeritus Dean of the University of Hawaii's College of Languages, Linguistics and Literature, where she was also a longtime faculty member (1971–1999). Her research has concentrated on the reading and writing practices of women in early modern Germany, especially their interest in and writing of devotional literature (*The Maiden's Mirror* 1986) as well as the genre of the Lutheran funeral book as part of the development of biography in early modern Germany (*Patterned Lives* 2006). She has recently changed her focus from devotional texts to the accompanying illustrations and the interaction between word and pictures.

Matthias Roick
is a Marie Skłodowska Curie Fellow at the Institute of Philosophy and Sociology of the Polish Academy of Sciences. He specializes in Renaissance philosophy with a focus on ethics, early modern literary culture, and book history. His current research concerns scholarly writings on friendship.

Jason Rosenholtz-Witt

is Assistant Professor of Musicology at Western Kentucky University. He specializes in music and geopolitics in the Venetian Republic during the sixteenth and seventeenth centuries, extending into German-speaking lands and England. Additional interests include American experimentalism (1960s–80s) and jazz during the Civil Rights era. He has published on topics ranging from musical life in early modern Bergamo, English viol consort music, music printing, and avant-garde cellist Charlotte Moorman. His research at the Herzog August Bibliothek was supported by the Dr. Gudrun Busch Stipendium für Musikwissenschaft and the American Friends of the HAB.

Sara Smart

is Honorary Associate Professor of German, University of Exeter. Her research focus is on Protestant courts of the Empire in the early modern period with particular interest in the stylization of the ruling dynasty in the court's print culture. Currently she is working on representations of the consort at the Hohenzollern court in Berlin. Publications include: the co-edited volume with Mara R. Wade, *The Palatine Wedding of 1613: Protestant Alliance and Court Festival* (2013), and with Benjamin Marschke, Daniel Riches, and Alexander Schunka, *Religious Plurality at Princely Courts: Dynasty, Politics, and Confession in Central Europe, ca. 1555–1860* (forthcoming, Spektrum).

Kathleen M. Smith

is the subject specialist for the Germanic Collections & Medieval Studies at Stanford Libraries. She received her MLIS from the University of Texas at Austin and her PhD in Germanic Languages & Literatures from the University of Illinois at Urbana-Champaign. Prior to Stanford, she worked in the Research and Development Department of the State and University Library in Göttingen, Germany.

Dwight E. Raak TenHuisen

received his PhD in comparative literature from the University of Illinois at Urbana-Champaign. As professor at Calvin University, he teaches a range of language, culture, and literature courses in Spanish and German. He has written on the hagiographic discourse in Cabeza de Vaca's *Relación*, Staden's *Wahrhaftige Historia*, and Mendes *Pinto's Peregrinação*, as well as on the transformations, domestication of alterity, and elimination of self-representation in the reception of these authors in the context of early modern confessional geographies. His current project examines Calancha's *Crónica moralizada* in the context of early modern Augustinian evangelization strategies and global networks.

Janette Tilley

is Associate Dean of the Faculty of Language, Literature, and Performing Arts at Douglas College in New Westminster, British Columbia. She earned a PhD in musicology from the University of Toronto. Her research focuses on the intersections of music, gender, and pious practice in German Lutheranism of the seventeenth century. Her current research examines musical engagement with the Song of Songs and mystical love metaphors from the late sixteenth to the mid-eighteenth century. She is editor of the Web Library of Seventeenth-Century Music, an open-access collection of modern scholarly editions published by the Society for Seventeenth-Century Music.

Mara R. Wade

is professor emerita of Germanic Languages & Literatures at the University of Illinois at Urbana-Champaign and earned the Ph.D. at the University of Michigan under the supervision of Professor Gerhard Dünnhaupt. Her research focuses on emblems, digital humanities, court studies of Germany and Scandinavia, gender, and early modern German literature. She is the past president of the Renaissance Society of America; she holds a senior research prize from the Alexander von Humboldt Foundation. As a fellow at the Swedish Collegium for Advanced Study, Uppsala, in 2023 she continues work on the monograph *A Social History of the Renaissance Emblem*.

Gerhild Scholz Williams

has published widely on German and French literature and culture from the Middle Ages to the Early Modern Period (1100–1700), specializing more recently in the sixteenth and seventeenth centuries. Williams has been working in translation theory and practice, the early modern witch phenomenon, the early modern *Volksbuch*, the development of the novel, and Ottoman Eurasia in German literature. She has explored the impact and influence of newspapers and other early modern media on the production of novels.

Enrica Zanin

is senior lecturer in Comparative Literature at the University of Strasbourg (France). An alumna of the Ecole Normale Supérieure (Paris), a Humboldt Fellow, and an honorary member of the Institut Universitaire de France, her research focuses on ethical issues in early modern European literature. As a fellow at the Duke August Library, she became deeply interested in the Ethica section and the literary books it contains. She has worked on ethics and theater in the early modern period (*Fins tragiques*, 2014) and is currently preparing a book on ethics and the novella (working title: *Ethique du récit*).

Introduction

1 The Scholar

The honoree of this volume Professor Gerhard Dünnhaupt is both a celebrated scholar and a beloved teacher. (Fig. 0.1) Many of the contributors to this volume also count him as a friend. His accomplishments include the annotated three-volume *Bibliographisches Handbuch der Barockliteratur* that evolved into the six volume *Personalbibliographien zu den Drucken des Barock* with 4,000-pages,[1] as well as many editions and articles. Among his many honors are the International Prize in Bibliography (1985). As a retiree he remains an active and enthusiastic patron of early modern studies at the University of Toronto, funding travel fellowships for graduate student research in musicology.

Gerhard Dünnhaupt (born 1927) is well known to readers of this series. A prolific scholar, he is best known for his *Personalbibliographien zu den Drucken des Barock*, which in a single stroke established a canon of German Baroque authors with short biographies and exhaustive bibliographies of their works, editions, and secondary sources. It remains the definitive work in the field, cited by scholars, auction houses, and collectors. For this monumental publication he was recognized with the *Prix Triennal de Bibliographie* by the International League of Antiquarian Booksellers (ILAB). His scholarship remains influential to the present day, and scholars of seventeenth-century German literature continue to cite "Dünnhaupt" as their authority. His recognitions as both an honorary life member of the Modern Language Association of America and as a Fellow and Life Member of the Royal Society of Canada confirm the high estimation of his peers and colleagues across all areas of humanistic study. Decades after his retirement, his impact endures in his areas of expertise that include German literature of the Renaissance, Reformation, and Baroque, the history of printing and publishing, the cultural history of the early modern period, comparative Renaissance studies, and, of course, bibliography.

Born in Berenburg in Anhalt as the son of a printer and newspaper publisher, Professor Dünnhaupt entered the family business, earning his *Meisterbrief* as a printer in 1949 in Leipzig. He worked in the publications department at the University of Giessen until he emigrated to Canada. Beginning in 1964, Dünnhaupt received his undergraduate education at the University of Toronto and then earned the PhD at Brown University in 1972 with a dissertation on the German translations and adaptations of the epics by Torquato Tasso and

---

1 (Stuttgart: Hiersemann, 1990–1993).

© KONINKLIJKE BRILL NV, LEIDEN, 2023 | DOI:10.1163/9789004682245_002

FIGURE 0.1   Professor Gerhard Dünnhaupt celebrating his birthday on his Toronto balcony
PHOTO GREGORY JOHNSTON, TORONTO

Ludovico Ariosto. His first academic position was at the University of Washington, Seattle, followed four years later by an offer from the University of Michigan where he taught German and Comparative Literature. Professor Dünnhaupt was a visiting professor at the University of Illinois Urbana-Champaign, Cornell

University, and Universität Göttingen. In 1992 he became emeritus at the University of Michigan and an Adjunct Professor at Queen's University in Kingston, Ontario.

In addition to having published the two editions—one in three volumes and one in six volumes—of "Dünnhaupt," Professor Dünnhaupt has published widely in a number of areas of early modern German literature in its European contexts, with particular focus on members of the seventeenth-century literary society, the Fruchtbringende Gesellschaft. His book, *Die fürstliche Druckerei zu Köthen* (1979), explores the printing and publications endeavors of the Society, while his monograph, *Diederich von dem Werder: Versuch einer Neuwertung seiner Hauptwerke* (1973), remains the definitive work on this author. His early articles anchored the fledging journal *Daphnis* and include studies such as "Ein unbekannter Druck der 'Friedensrede' Diederichs von dem Werder" (*Daphnis* 3), "Das Oeuvre des Erasmus Francisci (1627–1694) und sein Einfluß auf die deutsche Literatur" (*Daphnis* 6), "Die Übersetzungen Fürst Ludwigs von Anhalt-Köthen: ein Beitrag zum 400. Geburtstag des Gründers der Fruchtbringenden Gesellschaft" (*Daphnis* 7), and "Altes und Neues zur Opitzbibliographie" (*Daphnis* 11).

Among his many academic accomplishments, Gerry, as he is known to his friends, served as the series editor for the reprint series *Rarissima litterarum*.[2] Before the age of digital libraries, this series produced high quality reprints of rare seventeenth-century literary texts that were no longer easily available, often by little known authors worthy of closer acquaintance. The series reflects his vast bibliographic knowledge of rare German books and his literary acumen concerning texts that deserve(d) further study. These authors include Abraham a Sancta Clara, Johann Ludwig Prasch, Gabriel Rollenhagen, Johann Vogel (with Georg Philipp Harsdörffer), the pseudonymous Perseus Sperantes, Johannes Riemer (likely), Johann Joseph Beckh, and Conrad Vetter. He also produced respected popular Reclam editions of the comedies *Horribilicribfax Teutsch. Scherzspiel* and *Absurda Comica oder Herr Peter Squenz Schimpfspiel* by Andreas Gryphius. The commentaries from these editions frequently served as the basis for work by other scholars and editors. Continuing his enduring interest in comparative studies, he edited and introduced Diederich von dem Werder's translations of Torquato Tasso's *Gottfried von Bulljon* (Niemeyer 1974) and Giovanni Franceso Loredano's *Dianea oder Rähtselgedicht* (Lang 1984). For several years he also served as the book review editor for *Michigan Germanic Studies*. In 1983 he organized the international conference held in Ann Arbor

---

2 https://www.hiersemann.de/reihen/rarissima-litterarum.

observing the Luther year and edited the volume of its proceedings, *The Martin Luther Quincentennial.*[3]

While his monumental bibliographic achievement often overshadows his significant literary and editorial accomplishments, these many editions have stood the test of time and made German Baroque literature available to wider audiences. Professor Dünnhaupt justly earned widespread recognition as a book collector, amassing a collection of early German and European books that reflected his extensive knowledge of literature, printing, and collecting.[4] His *ex libris* depicts the tree of wisdom growing from an open book. (Fig. 0.2) Perhaps more than any other scholar, Prof. Dünnhaupt established the canon of seventeenth-century German literature.

One measure of the impact of a scholar's work is the impetus it provides to new research. In a forward-facing digital initiative, the Herzog August Bibliothek (HAB), Wolfenbüttel, began to exploit the "Dünnhaupt" scholarly ecosystem and established *dünnhaupt digital.*[5] As a test case for digital humanities, this project demonstrates how print metadata can be repurposed for new projects that contribute to semantic web technologies. Funded by the Deutsche Forschungsgemeinschaft (DFG), the HAB digitized c.2,000 works from its holdings of seventeenth-century literature from "Dünnhaupt" and provided them with additional metadata from VD 17[6] and the GBV.[7] As a testbed for future research, *dünnhaupt digital* demonstrates how print and electronic resources can be combined and repurposed to produce a curated digital resource of immense scholarly value. It speaks literally volumes for a scholar who retired from academia when the internet was in its early stages, that his well conceptualized print project can provide the foundations for digital innovation and national data infrastructures. The smooth transition to a digital project that requires consistent metadata attests to the intellectual organization and guiding principles that informed the original development of the "Dünnhaupt" literary corpus. His bibliographic accomplishments continue to inform digital research concerning the Fruchtbringende Gesellschaft.[8]

---

3 Detroit 1985.

4 His collection was auctioned at Bassenge in Berlin 9–10 May 1996. See the catalog of the auction *Europäische Literatur der Spätrenaissance und der Barockzeit meist aus der Sammlung Prof. G. Dünnhaupt, Literatur und Buchillustration des 18.–19. Jahrhunderts.* Berlin: Bassenge, [1996].

5 https://www.hab.de/duennhaupt-digital/.

6 Das Verzeichnis der im deutschen Sprachraum erschienenen Drucke des 17. Jahrhunderts. http://www.vd17.de/en/home.

7 Gemeinsamer Bibliotheksverbund https://www.gbv.de/gsomenu/?id=home&ln=de.

8 See Thea Lindquist, "The Publication Patterns and Networks of Fruchtbringende Gesellschaft (Fruitbearing Society) Members based on the VD17." A foundational corpus for Lindquist's

FIGURE 0.2 Ex libris of Professor Gerhard Dünnhaupt
PHOTO MARA R. WADE

In recognition of his generous support of our research, the contributors to this volume, some known to Gerry for many years, celebrated him at a special reception held at the annual meeting of the Renaissance Society of America in Toronto in March 2019. Gerry has lived in his *Wahlheimat* Toronto for over seventy years and is a proud citizen of Canada. It seemed only appropriate to

research is Dünnhaupt. (Based on scholarly discussions at the Herzog August Bibliothek, Wolfenbüttel, July 2022.)

FIGURE 0.3   Reception honoring Professor Gerhard Dünnhaupt at the 2019 annual meeting of
the Renaissance Society of America, Toronto. Pictured from left Elio Brancaforte,
contributors Mara Wade, honored guest Gerry Dünnhaupt, Peter Hess, Dwight
TenHuisen, Cornelia Moore; contributors above from left Jason Rosenholtz-Witt,
Gregory Johnston, Janette Tilly, Gerhild Scholz Williams and from right above
Matthias Roick and Victoria Gutsche
PHOTO MARA R. WADE

celebrate him in his hometown. The conference event was sponsored by the
American Friends of the Herzog August, Bibliothek (AF HAB), Wolfenbüttel,[9]
and the AF HAB would particularly like to acknowledge the generous support
of Professor Gerhild Scholz Williams in hosting the reception for Gerry and
of the RSA for including this event in its program. (Fig. 0.3) It is also fitting
that these panels, specifically in honor of Professor Gerhard Dünnhaupt, were
organized by the American Friends of the Herzog August Bibliothek. Professor
Dünnhaupt has a special connection to the HAB and in 1975 was one of the
library's very first *Stipendiaten* during the tenure of Director Paul Raabe. The
contributors to this volume also have many intersecting points of association with the HAB, with the RSA and, of course, with Professor Dünnhaupt
himself. Both as a person and as a scholarly resource, he has fostered new

---

9   https://www.hab.de/doktoranden-und-nachwuchsfoerderung/.

generations of the research community. Senior scholars, members of the Executive Committee of the AF HAB, have written pieces for this collection, while a former Toronto recipient of a "Dünnhaupt fellowship," Janette Tilley, is also a contributor.[10] Several others were recipients of travel grants funded by the AF HAB. All contributors, who now have academic careers in the US, Canada, Germany, UK, Poland, Italy, and France, spent time at the HAB working in the collections that grounded Professor Dünnhaupt's own research, relying on his work as a guide. The research presented here would be unthinkable without him.

As the due date for submission of the papers loomed, covid struck and the editorial process was delayed by all manner of issues resulting from the global pandemic. I am most grateful to the contributors for their patience with one another and with me, as everyone experienced illness, slowdowns, and all the problems associated with a worldwide shutdown. I also want to thank the editors of this series for their patience and for publishing this volume. Most of all, we all want to thank Gerry, whom we honor with this publication. Thank you, Professor Dünnhaupt.

2 The Volume

This volume presents twelve essays by established and emerging scholars who explore early modern German book culture from a variety of interdisciplinary perspectives, including literary studies, book history, translation studies, musicology, early modern globalization, text/image/media studies, and collection studies. The contributors investigate the processes by which books and collections were created and maintained over time; in which individual texts and images circulated and evolved; and by which the broader scope of knowledge was organized in early modern Germany and beyond. The authors also show how these interactions and processes were critical for personal and corporate identity formation, at court, in town, and in the transatlantic world.

The core of this volume centers on six papers presented in two panels at the annual conference of the Renaissance Society of America when it was held in Toronto. The sessions in honor of Professor Gerhard Dünnhaupt were

---

10   Professor Dünnhaupt established a fellowship for graduate student of early modern musicology at the University of Toronto, where he worked closely with Professors Gregory Johnston and Mary Ann Parker to identify students whose dissertations required travel funding for field research in libraries and archives. His support of the next generations of early modernists has had tangible, enduring impact on the future of early modern scholarship.

entitled "Transitions, Translations, Transformations" with papers by Peter Hess, Victoria Gutsche, and Gerhild Scholz Williams, and "Text and Image at Court and in Town" with papers by Cornelia Moore, Mara R. Wade, and Sara Smart. His former students and colleagues chose this opportunity to honor him with these panels signaling their respect and gratitude for his generous advice, assistance, and collegiality, which continues to distinguish him even many years after he retired. Owing to Professor Dünnhaupt's extraordinary standing in German Studies, the papers were of an extremely high quality as all contributors wanted to present him with their best possible work as he sat in the audience.

The editor also invited papers from other AF HAB panels to complete the volume. These are written by Matthias Roick, Jason Rosenholtz-Witt, Dwight TenHuisen, Janette Tilley, and Enrica Zanin. As his doctoral "grandchild," Kathleen M. Smith, Curator, Germanic Collections & Medieval Studies, at Stanford University Library, was also invited to contribute. These papers complement the core selections, and all contributions reflect cutting-edge research in the field of German and Comparative Studies broadly conceived. All of the research presented was conducted, at least initially, at the Herzog August Bibliothek and thus constitutes research that engages directly with primary sources. This methodological foundation was a key component in the conception of this volume in honor of Professor Dünnhaupt. In this way we present the best interdisciplinary and comparative research in honor of both the person and the institution that has fostered our work.

The volume is divided into three Parts:

> Part 1: Transitions, Translations, Transformations
> Part 2: At Court and in Town: Text, Sound, and Image
> Part 3: The Organization of Knowledge: Case Studies from the Herzog
> August Bibliothek, Wolfenbüttel

The research presented in this volume contributes to new perspectives in the study of early modern books, with its focus on the material culture of texts, music, and images from original sources and collections. In their desire to honor Professor Dünnhaupt, the contributors follow his considerable legacy, presenting new insights and approaches as well as exhibiting a broad comparative and interdisciplinary range. The methodological focus on original research based on the primary study of texts and collections integrates this volume into a cohesive whole.

Acknowledgements

At an early stage of this volume Kathleen M. Smith provided valuable editorial assistance, while Jeffrey D. Castle copyedited the entire volume. Professors Gregory S. Johnston and Dwight E. Raak TenHuisen also contributed to the final shape of the volume. All of the contributors appreciate their work.

Mara R. Wade
University of Illinois Urbana-Champaign
November 2022

PART 1

Transitions, Translations, Transformations

∴

CHAPTER 1

From Villain to Jokester: The Early Reception of the Ulenspiegel Figure

Peter Hess

Dil Ulenspiegel, or Till Eulenspiegel, is the most influential and lasting German literary figure of the sixteenth century. He first appeared in the prose narration entitled *Ein kurtzweilig lesen von Dyl Vlenspiegel* [A diverting reader about Dyl Ulenspiegel], presumably authored by Hermann Bote (*c.*1450–*c.*1520) and published in Strasbourg in 1515.[1] This work tells us the life story of Dil Ulenspiegel in 96 loosely connected stories. Only the first seven and the last eight chapters create something of a biographical frame, while the remaining chapters present episodes that are cumulative rather than sequential in character.[2]

The Eulenspiegel figure became important in German children's literature in the nineteenth and twentieth centuries, most notably in the narration by Erich Kästner, from 1938. In these stories, Eulenspiegel was pitched as a benign, folksy, funny, and congenial prankster who unmasks the stupidity and selfishness of his contemporaries.[3] In much of secondary literature, Ulenspiegel similarly is represented as a wise yet sometimes subversive figure who unmasks society around him as egotistical and dysfunctional.[4] I argue here that the original Ulenspiegel figure was designed as a mean-spirited villain who posed a threat to social order and to the common good. Furthermore, the

---

1 I cite from the 1515 edition, except where noted otherwise. Honegger (1973) claimed Hermann Bote as the author of a low German version of the text, whose existence cannot be verified. This authorship attribution has been questioned in more recent scholarship. The first known text is a fragment of a High German version that was published in Strasbourg in 1510 or 1511.

2 Honegger, 1973: 101–16, proposed a different sequence of the stories and a different numbering system. As this is highly speculative, I follow the numbering of the 1515 edition and quote from it, unless stated otherwise.

3 Wunderlich, 1984: 106–10. According to Ivanov, 2014: 102, the Ulenspiegel figure appeared in more than 250 texts of children's and youth literature in the nineteenth century, typically as an entertaining jokester.

4 Bachorski, 2000: 277; Classen, 2008: 485; Schwarz, 2011: 102. Bässler, 2005: 294–95, points to a contradictory reception of the Ulenspiegel figure as both villain and harmless jokester without discussing it further. His explanation is that Ulenspiegel is a "flat" character, which remains without consequence as plot, not character, drives the narrative. For similar interpretations see also Schwarz, 2010: 498–99, and Solbach, 2019: 119.

© KONINKLIJKE BRILL NV, LEIDEN, 2023 | DOI:10.1163/9789004682245_003

reinterpretation of the figure is not a product of the Romantic imagination but, rather, a development that took place within the first few decades after the text was published.

In the preface of the early work, Ulenspiegel is introduced as "ein behender listiger vnd durchtribener eins buren sun." [a quick-witted, sly and cunning son of a peasant.][5] In chapter 31, the narrator states, "IN allen landen het sich Ulenspiegel mit seiner boßheit bekant gemacht." [Ulenspiegel had become well-known in all lands because of his wickedness.][6] The German uses the word "boßheit" meaning wickedness or malice. Ulenspiegel is also referred to as "schalck," in the sense of an evil rogue or villain, consistently throughout the narrative. The beginning of chapter 32 serves as an illustration: "Vlenspiegel was künstlich in der schalckeit/ als er nun mit den hopt weit vm gezogen wz/ vnd die lüt vast betrogen het/ da kam er gegen Nürnberg." [Ulenspiegel was a master of malice. After he had traveled far and deceived a lot of people he went to Nuremberg.][7] After some time, Ulenspiegel gets bored and restless: "Da kunt er von natur nit lassen er müst da auch ein schalckheit thůn." [He could not resist by nature; he had to do an evil deed here as well.][8] It is evident that performing evil deeds is part of Ulenspiegel's nature—a pathological urge, even. This assessment is shared by his many victims, who invariably see him as a malicious person.

Bote's understanding of the term *schalck* was in line with the common definition of the term at the time. The Strasbourg preacher Johannes Geiler von Kaysersberg defined the term *schalck* as a rogue:

> Aber der heisset ein schalck (homo nihili) den man dannen oder neben uß schaltet/ der nüt wert/ noch nyenen zů nütz ist/ weder zů syeden/ noch zů broten/ ein unmensch. Ein ding das man neben uß schaltet/ das ist ein schalck/ und heißt im latin nequam/ quasi nequicquam/ ad nihil utilis. [He is called a rogue (worthless man) whom one pushes away and aside, who is worth nothing nor is useful to anybody, neither to simmer nor to fry, a brute. A thing that one pushes aside, that is a rogue, and it is called in Latin wretched, without purpose, useful for nothing.][9]

---

5 Bote, 1515: fol. 2r.
6 Bote, 1515: fol. 42v.
7 Bote, 1515: fol. 44v.
8 Bote, 1515: fol. 44v.
9 Geiler, 1522, fol. 101v.

To Geiler's mind, there was nothing alluring or amusing about a *schalck*; rather, he was a useless human being whose sole purpose was to harm others.

Bote also used the term *schalck* to designate the heinous rebels in his *Schicht boick* [Chronicle of uprisings], written between 1510 and 1514.[10] Here he compared the rebels to boys on horseback,[11] just as young Ulenspiegel, in the second chapter of *Dyl Ulenspiegel*, performed his very first trick on horseback. By bringing the Ulenspiegel figure into the proximity of the evil rebels in his native Brunswick, Bote marked him as a transgressor and villain, even in early childhood. The frontispiece of the 1515 edition of *Dil Ulenspiegel* also shows young Ulenspiegel on horseback. Apparently, this was lost on the editor of the 1532 edition, where Ulenspiegel is shown as an old, bearded man in the frontispiece and in many of the illustrations.

At the center of each episode stands a malicious trick or deceptive action, typically at the expense of another individual. Sometimes Ulenspiegel's actions lampoon the greed, pride, or narrow-mindedness of others—in particular, members of the clergy. But in most other instances, they target innocent people for no good reason, with a particular focus on craftsmen who just want to earn an honest living and have the misfortune of taking Ulenspiegel into their employ. In 55 of the 96 chapters, Ulenspiegel's acrimony is directed against craftsmen[12] who had done him no harm and who, in general, had not transgressed against social or moral norms.

From the beginning of the book, it is clear that Ulenspiegel refuses to conform to any kind of social order. His criminal energy aims at disrupting the communal order and solidarity—an idea on which social cohesion in German cities around 1500 depended. We never learn what social class he was born into. In two separate chapters Ulenspiegel rejects his mother's urging to enter an apprenticeship, despite the fact that his mother is impoverished and in need of support after his father's death. Ulenspiegel prefers engaging in mischief over working; he also does not want to be tied down and locked into a position. Ulenspiegel is a transient figure, who is constantly on the move. He does not have geographic roots or a secure social identity. Ulenspiegel is a mobile person who lives at the margins of society.

Ulenspiegel begins most adventures with an act of masquerade. Among the fake identities he creates for himself are as a doctor, an apprentice, a merchant, and a court fool, to name a few.[13] Invariably, he changes clothes to support his

---

10   For examples see Hayden-Roy, 1993: 566.
11   Bote, 1880: 451.
12   Lindow, 2001: 294.
13   Hayden-Roy, 1993: 570.

chosen role. In chapter 31, the narrator states that Ulenspiegel and his malice were so widely known that he could not return to a place where he had been "es wer dan das er sich vercleidet dz man in nit kant." [unless he disguised himself so that one would not recognize him.][14] In chapter 83, Ulenspiegel puts on different clothes to inflict further abuse on a woman he had abused in the previous chapter. Inflicting hurt is a conscious objective, and changing clothes is a strategy to achieve it. This unstable relationship between his clothes and his body signals the protagonist's unstable identity and projects an insecure body image. Ulenspiegel leads a sexless life; while he recognizes and plays on sexuality in others, he never expresses desires himself.[15]

Ulenspiegel's transgressive and destructive behavior manifests itself primarily in two ways: taking language literally and instrumentalizing fecal matter.[16] Ulenspiegel consistently exploits the space between the literal meanings of words, on the one hand, and the figurative and idiomatic meanings, on the other. Ulenspiegel's abuse of language is his literalism.[17] From the beginning, there is evidence that Ulenspiegel consciously creates misunderstandings that play to his advantage. The narrator wants us to know that Ulenspiegel's play with the meanings of words is conscious, calculating, and subversive and, thus, has to be interpreted as a transgressive act.

It has been claimed that Ulenspiegel breaks up rigid language and opens up new layers of meaning.[18] In fact, the opposite is the case: it is Ulenspiegel himself who deprives language of its dynamic range and interpretive openness by diminishing it through his own rigid use of language. Taking things literally reduces the meaning of words to a most basic, primary level and dismisses figurative, metaphoric, and allegorical usages.[19] Communication—and, by implication, the underlying social order—can only function if all participants honor its conventions. Ulenspiegel subverts conventional norms of communication on which the corporate social order depends, and he undermines the societal interest in creating mutual understanding and consensus through verbal communication.[20]

Early on, Ulenspiegel's strategy of taking things literally was identified as a source of humor. In his *Von schimpff vnd ernst* [Jest and earnestness], from 1522, Johannes Pauli retold the story of Aesop, who cooked one lentil when told

---

14   Bote, 1515: fol. 42v.
15   Wailes, 1991: 129.
16   Kirschner, 1996: 95.
17   Wailes, 1991: 131.
18   Rusterholz, 1977: 20.
19   Kirschner, 1996: 95.
20   Kirschner, 1996: 96.

to cook a lentil dish. In his mocking commentary on the art of taking things literally, Pauli referenced Ulenspiegel:

> Also sein vil menschen, die thůn mit fleiß was man sie heißt, vnd wie man sie heißt, das sol nit alwegen sein, man sol ein ding thůn nach der meinung vnd dem willen des gebieters. Der verirten vnd seltzamen historien findestu in dem Vlenspiegel, der thet was man in hieß. [Thus there are many humans who do on purpose what one tells them to do and how one tells them to do it, but one shouldn't always. One should do things according to the intent and the will of the master. Such drifting and strange stories you find in Ulenspiegel who did what he was told.][21]

Pauli picks one aspect of Ulenspiegel's disruptive and transgressive communication strategy and reframes it as a prank and a benign source of humor. Pauli's example makes evident that the idea of Bote's Ulenspiegel subverting communication to create discord was lost even on contemporaries.

Ulenspiegel's use of fecal matter is a mode of body language that is part of his overall communication strategy. It is an extension of the lack of complexity of his communication system and of his inability to communicate. Like Ulenspiegel's words, defecation directed at others only has a simple literal meaning: it has no pretense to be something other than a sign of dislike, disrespect, and disapproval of another human being. Fecal matter serves as an extension and completion of his verbal abuse and provides a medium for trickery, punishment, and revenge. Applications of fecal matter, as well as other obscene acts, are forms of bodily communication that extend and replace verbal communication and point to dysfunctional social interactions. Bote tells us that it is not the impurity of society that is unveiled through the acts of defecation; rather, it is Ulenspiegel's own transgressive contamination of society. Just like his use of language, his use of fecal matter is a subversive tool designed to dislodge the order of the world. Ulenspiegel's world is not intrinsically topsy turvy; it is Ulenspiegel's dysfunctional communication and social interactions that make it so.

Martin Luther was one of the few contemporaries who viewed the Ulenspiegel figure in this manner. He likened the actions of the Papists to Ulenspiegel's crude and evil deeds: "Vnd es gemanet mich solcher vnverschampten buben/ gleich als wenn ein grober Vlespiegel mitten auff dem marckt für ydermann sich auffhübe vnd seinen mist machet." [This reminds me of such outrageous rogues, just as if a rough Ulenspiegel rose in front of everybody in the middle of

---

21   Pauli, 1866: 336.

the market and did his crap.][22] By pulling Ulenspiegel into confessional polemics, Luther aimed to defame his confessional adversaries through association with Ulenspiegel, whom Luther viewed as rogue and villain.[23]

While it is evident that Bote conceived the Ulenspiegel character as a rogue and a villain, the next generation of writers recast it in a much more benign and even jocular framework. Ulenspiegel is a negative role model in Kaspar Scheidt's *Grobianus* (1551), where bad manners and habits are praised. Alluding to Bote's chapters 75 and 76, *Grobianus* recommends that one should drop one's snot into serving platters so others would not be tempted to eat from them:

> Thus you'll so disgust the others that no one will want to eat; then the dish will be yours alone, because you've produced such revulsion. That's written of Ulenspiegel: he did this little trick, too; everyone holds him high and worthy and they follow his book much more than all the lives of the philosophers. You too should follow this rule.[24]

In spite of the comment's irony and sarcasm, the inversion of the argument reveals the humor of the situation. While it is understood that his deeds represent bad manners, the thought of enacting them evokes laughter rather than disgust.

The Nuremberg writer Hans Sachs (1494–1576) played a key role in the transformation of the Ulenspiegel figure. He was not only a prolific writer but also the most productive adapter of episodes from *Dil Ulenspiegel*. Sachs focused on Eulenspiegel in at least thirty-eight mastersongs that according to convention could not be printed. Of these, he reworked and printed seven as *Schwänke* [short verse narratives] or *Spruchgedichte* [didactic poems] with almost identical lines and verses. Furthermore, Eulenspiegel is the protagonist in four carnival plays written between 1553 and 1557.[25] Sachs wrote all texts with Eulenspiegel references in this time frame.[26] Sachs owned the 1532 Erfurt edition of the book,[27] so it is not surprising that he started to write about Eulenspiegel in 1533. Among the episodes Sachs used were chapters 97 and 99 from the 1532 edition, both of which were not in the 1515 edition.[28]

---

22 Luther, 1528: sig. A4v.
23 Tenberg, 1996: 90.
24 Scheidt, 1551: sig. D2v; translation by Correll, 1996: 150.
25 Tenberg, 1996: 97.
26 Tenberg, 1996: 97.
27 Sachs, 1870–1908, vol. 26: 179.
28 I will limit the discussion to chapters 17, 38, 63, and 71 from the 1515 edition and chapter 97 from the 1532 edition.

The very first *Ulenspiegel* text used by Sachs in 1533 was a mastersong simply entitled "Der Ewlenspiegel," which implies that Sachs at that time had no intention of drafting additional texts on the Eulenspiegel figure; indeed, Sachs did not revisit Eulenspiegel until 1538. In Bote's corresponding chapter 17, Ulenspiegel advises a hospital on how to heal patients and, thus, to relieve overcrowding and the related financial burdens. He tells each patient individually that all patients who feel well must leave the hospital. The last remaining patient, presumably the sickest one, would be burned and the ashes used as a remedy to heal the others. As all the patients leave the hospital in a hurry, Ulenspiegel receives his reward and skips town quickly, before the ailing patients return to the hospital one after the other. The key point is that Ulenspiegel makes an agreement with each patient individually and convinces them not to act in solidarity with the hospital community but, rather, to pursue their self-interest. As someone who privileges individual interests over the common good, Ulenspiegel is a threat to the social order.[29]

In Sachs's version, the basic story is the same, although it now is set in Nuremberg. Sachs's conclusion is quite different, however. While Bote's story ends with a bitter complaint by the hospital administrator about the loss of funds and the deception of the patients, Sachs's version ends in benign laughter, as the hospital chief learns how he has been tricked. Sachs ends with the administrator's conciliatory remark: "Als er vernam den gůeten schwanck, | Můest er der schalckheit lachen." [When he learned about the good farce, he had to laugh about the craftiness.][30] Here, the term "schalckheit," craftiness, loses the entirely negative connotation it had in Bote's text; in Sachs's use it refers to a funny prank.

Right at the beginning of chapter 38, Bote notes that Ulenspiegel acted with "BOser schalckheit," with evil craftiness.[31] In this episode, the Duke of Brunswick covets a priest's horse. Ulenspiegel visits the priest and stays at his house, pretending to be indigent. During confession, he claims that he slept with the priest's maid. The enraged priest challenges and beats the maid, breaking the seal of confession in the process. Ulenspiegel threatens to report this to the bishop unless the pastor gives him the horse. The pastor has no choice in the matter, and Ulenspiegel brings the horse to the duke and gets his reward. While the priest misreads Ulenspiegel as a sexual being, the reader knows that the protagonist has rejected all previous sexual opportunities. Ulenspiegel uses the priest's assumption for his deception, and he uses his lack of human

---

29   Kirschner, 1996: 94.
30   Sachs, 1893–1913, vol. 3: 110, v. 59–60.
31   Bote, 1515: fol. 53r.

connection as a wedge callously to hurt the maid and the priest, both of whom had done him no harm.

Hans Sachs based the carnival play *Ewlenspiegel mit der pfaffen kellnerin und dem pfert* [Eulenspiegel with the priest's servant and the horse] from 1553 on this chapter. In both versions, the plot unfolds in a similar fashion, although Sachs provides more detail. Yet there are subtle but significant differences between the two versions. Sachs's play opens with a monologue by Eulenspiegel in which he talks about his poverty and lack of shelter in the middle of a cold winter, and a plan to gain access to free housing—a ploy we find in all four Eulenspiegel carnival plays and in a number of his other Eulenspiegel texts. While Ulenspiegel in Bote's original is marked as a villain, Sachs's framing is designed to generate empathy for and a positive attitude toward the protagonist.

Johannes Pauli also retells this episode in his *Von schimpff vnd ernst* [Jest and earnestness], with subtle but important differences.[32] In Pauli's version, Ulenspiegel is described, in rather positive terms, as an adventurer who is eager to fulfill the duke's wishes—or, in Pauli's text, the count's wishes—rather than a villain who victimizes people. The priest is a good man, who does not beat the maid, and the maid does not leave the pastor's household at the end. Thus, the damage to the priest is limited to the loss of his horse, which does not leave his existence in tatters. This allows us to laugh about Ulenspiegel's clever trick.

The key difference is that to Bote, the duke's wants are unjustified, and Ulenspiegel's rogue actions to obtain the horse are unfair, even malevolent. The pastor is the innocent victim, who is tricked into breaking confidentiality and who loses both his horse and his maid as a result of Ulenspiegel's mischief. For Sachs, however, the duke's desire to have the horse is legitimate, which turns the pastor into the main culprit of the story because he resists the righteous wishes of his sovereign. To make this more evident, Sachs also taints the pastor's character with the maid's accusation that he was a philanderer. In his closing monologue, the duke asserts that the pastor deserved to lose his horse because he had refused to sell it and that he earned both mockery and the damage he suffered. As Hans Sachs signed off the final monologue of his carnival play with his own name, as he did in most texts, we can assume that this represents his point of view.

The role and perception of Eulenspiegel shifts accordingly. In Bote's text, Ulenspiegel is his own agent, who does not subject himself to anyone—which marks him as an outcast and as a transgressive figure. The tricks he plays on the pastor and the maid are censored. For Pauli and Sachs, Eulenspiegel becomes the duke's servile subject, who willingly fulfills the duke's wishes. While

---

32   Pauli, 1866: 358–59.

Eulenspiegel as adventurer still lives in the margins in Pauli's text, he moves from outcast to insider, from a transgressor against the order to a supporter and enforcer of authority in Sachs's play. The world still is in disarray and its social order under siege, but Eulenspiegel now has switched sides.

As noted earlier, Bote's *Ulenspiegel* in the 1515 version was without sexual or any other human relations. That changes in one of the chapters that were added to the 1532 Erfurt edition. In chapter 97, Ulenspiegel has a wife who cheats on him with the village priest. The priest is bragging to Ulenspiegel about his sexual exploits and promises to identify all the women he has slept with. On church holidays, women pass by the altar to make an offering. Each time a woman passes by whom the priest had slept with he says "brems."[33] Of course, when Ulenspiegel's wife passes by he says "brems," which upsets Ulenspiegel: "Vlenspiegel sprach es ist mein fraw. Der pfaff sprach es ist dein fraw odder nicht/ sie ist brems/ ich wil dir nicht vnrecht thun." [Ulenspiegel said, this is my wife. The priest responded, whether it is your wife or not, she is *brems*. I do not want to do you wrong.][34] The priest inflicts his spiteful injury on Ulenspiegel in the disguise of honesty and truth-telling. Ulenspiegel flees town immediately, leaving his wife behind.

This episode, from the 1532 edition, represents a significant shift in the representation of Ulenspiegel's personality from the 1515 version. First, the editor departs from the earlier concept of a sexless protagonist. He misunderstands how important Ulenspiegel's self-chosen celibate life and sexlessness are both as a narrative device and as yet another marker of his transgressive outcast existence. Second, Ulenspiegel is the true victim here, as is the case with several other episodes added to the 1532 edition. While the priest assumes the role of malicious *schalck*, Ulenspiegel as innocent and helpless victim is emasculated. While others scored victories over Ulenspiegel in the 1515 edition, they always were temporary in nature, as Ulenspiegel invariably managed to exert his cruel revenge. In this episode, Ulenspiegel is left without recourse and without a response. It appears that the editor of the 1532 edition no longer understood Ulenspiegel as rogue and villain who lives outside of society.

Hans Sachs transformed this story into a mastersong in 1539, entitled *Ewlenspigel mit dem prems* [Eulenspiegel with the muzzle].[35] Here, too, Eulenspiegel has a wife who sleeps with the priest, causing him to flee without her

---

33 *Brems* has two distinct meanings. In its meaning of "horse bit" it could serve as a metaphor for taming or subduing women. A *Bremse* also is a horsefly; its sting might reference sexual relations. The first is a neuter noun, the second a feminine one. Bote, however, avoids revealing the grammatical gender, which creates the ambiguity.

34 Bote, 1532: sig. V4r.

35 Here, the word *prems* or *brems* is marked as a neuter noun, in the sense of horse bit or muzzle. As a result, the more overtly sexual reference of the sting of a horsefly is lost.

when he learns of the transgression. However, Sachs's ending gives the story a completely different spin:

> Scham, zuecht vnd er ist worden klein,
> Den estant wil nimant zw herczen fassen.
> Des ist der epruch gar gemein,
> Man fint in laider schir in allen gassen
> Die weil man in nicht heftig straft,
> Thůet er sich teglich meren.
> Derhalb, dw raines pider weib,
> Phůet hercz vnd leib
> Vor epruch, halt dich an dein mann,
> So tregst ein kron der eren.

[Modesty, discipline, and honor have become worthless. Nobody wants to take to heart the marital estate. Because of that, adultery is all too common; unfortunately, one finds it almost in all streets. As one does not punish it harshly, it multiplies daily. Therefore, you pure and honest woman, safeguard your heart and body against adultery. Stick to your husband, so you will wear a crown of honor.][36]

Here, Eulenspiegel is not ridiculed, nor is the pastor scorned for his misdeeds. Instead, Sachs added a discourse on the decline of fidelity in marriage. In a misogynist twist, Sachs made it the wife's responsibility to safeguard marriage, not the priest's. Sachs disregarded the obvious point that the pastor is the true perpetrator, who habitually seduces women in his parish, and instead admonished women to stick with marital fidelity. Sachs thus added a didactic twist to this episode that does not relate to the Eulenspiegel figure at all.

Hans Sachs wrote well over half of the mastersongs with an Eulenspiegel theme between 1546 and 1548.[37] Sachs's mastersong "Der prillen macher" [The maker of eyeglasses], an adaptation of Bote's chapter 63, is indicative of how he repurposed Bote's texts. Bote's chapter 63 is unique in two ways. First, this is the only chapter that focuses on imperial politics, rather than urban affairs or individual transgressions. Second, Ulenspiegel actually learns the craft of making eyeglasses in spite of the earlier assertion that he was not willing to learn a trade—unless we read his purported identity as a craftsman as a mask. While

---

36   Sachs, 1893–1913, vol. 3: 220, v. 51–60.
37   Tenberg, 1996: 97.

this is one of a number of inconsistencies in the narrative,[38] Ulenspiegel's unsteady lifestyle does not change as he is unable to find work, which is the point of the episode.

Chapter 63 focuses on the discord among prince-electors in the empire that was seen as a source of instability, not only diminishing the power of the emperor but also threatening the independence of cities like Bote's native Brunswick—or Strasbourg, where the text was edited and printed. This theme was central in the writings of Bote's contemporary and Strasbourg native Sebastian Brant. While Bote did not directly refer to contemporaneous politics, this can be read as a hidden critique of the disunity within the empire under Emperor Maximilian I. As imperial politics are only ancillary to the plot of chapter 63, we have to read this as an extraneous comment on an issue that was important to this urban author.

On his way to Frankfurt, Ulenspiegel encounters the archbishop and elector of Trier, who takes an interest in Ulenspiegel because of his odd clothing. Ulenspiegel identifies himself as a maker of eyeglasses from Brabant who is wandering around because he cannot find work. The bishop replies that there should be opportunity in this craft as people are increasingly afflicted by health issues and poor eyesight. Ulenspiegel responds that there is one problem with this theory, and, with the permission from the archbishop to speak freely, he engages in a monologue, the longest in the book. In Ulenspiegel's analysis, there are two factors that spoil his craft. First, princes of the church and secular leaders turn a blind eye to what is right, often motivated by gifts of money. The ruling classes, from the pope down to city-council members, fail to provide justice because bribes make them disregard the law. In contrast, rulers in the good old times read and studied the law books in order to administer equitable justice. In order to do so they needed eyeglasses: "Aber vor alten zeiten find ma[n] geschriben. Dz die herre vnd fürsten als vil ihr seint/ in rechte pflegte zů lesen vn[d] studieren/ vff dz niema[n]ß vnrecht beschehe vnd darzů hette sie vil brillen vnd da wz vnser hantwerck gut." [However, one finds written of old times that the lords and princes, you being one of them, used to read and study the law so that no one would suffer injustice. And for that purpose, they had many eyeglasses, and our craft was doing well.][39] Second, Ulenspiegel makes the point that clerics no longer read because they just purchase books and put them on the shelf: "darzů sie ir bůcher i[n]. iiii. wochen nit me dan eins vff thůn." [Furthermore they do not open more than one of their books in four

---

38   The Strasbourg editor of the 1515 print added several episodes, which accounts for some inconsistencies. Several episodes were added from other sources, such as Der Stricker's *Pfaffe Amis* (c. 1240). For a discussion of this aspect see Tenberg, 1996: 59–65.

39   Bote, 1515: fol. 88r.

weeks.][40] He concludes that clerics who no longer read do not need eyeglasses anymore. Ulenspiegel has the last word here, and, more importantly, he challenges an important political leader without consequences.

In Sachs's version, the mastersong "Der prillen macher" [The eyeglass maker] from 1546, the idea of political authorities succumbing to corruption is toned down. Sachs instead blames clergy for the decline of the craft of making eyeglasses: young monks running away and old monks knowing everything by heart, thus having no need to read.[41] However, this plot change does not lead up to anti-clerical or anti-Catholic polemics. The bishop and elector is quite amused by Eulenspiegel's speech and treats him like a jester rather than a renegade. In fact, Sachs's anticlerical polemic is quite restrained and less stinging than Bote's, which is surprising given that Sachs was an ardent follower of Luther's teachings. It appears that Sachs offered his views on large political issues only reluctantly after the Nuremberg city council reprimanded and censored him, in 1527, for his anti-papal polemics.[42] Similarly, the mastersong "Ewlenspigel mit dem pabst" [Eulenspiegel with the pope], from 1548, which is based on Bote's chapter 34, treats a visit with the pope in Rome as a surprisingly normal event without even a hint of criticism of the pope or his church. Likewise, Sachs pitched confession in the carnival play *Ewlenspiegel mit der pfaffen kellnerin* (1553), discussed above, as a normal event.

Sachs returned to the plot of Bote's chapter 63 in a verse narration (*Versschwank*) in 1554, entitled *Ewlenspiegels disputation mit einem bischoff ob dem brillenmachen* [Eulenspiegel's disputation with a bishop about making eyeglasses]. Here, Eulenspiegel encounters a bishop who is on his way to the diet in Worms:

> Alda solt werden ein reichßtag,
> Und mancher fürste darzu lag.
> Solten betrachten gmeinen nutz,
> Römischem reych zu hülff und schutz.

> [There a diet was going to be held, and many princes stayed there. They should consider the common good, to aid and protect the Roman Empire.][43]

---

40   Bote, 1515: fol. 88r.
41   Sachs, 1893–1913, vol. 4: 63, v. 19–28.
42   Hess, 2007: 401–2; Bernstein, 1997: 246.
43   Sachs, 1870–1908, vol. 9: 256, v. 12–14. In Bote's text, the diet takes place in Frankfurt. At the time of Sachs's writing, the most recent diets took place in Worms (1535, 1544, 1545).

In contrast to the earlier mastersong, this version focuses on the discord within the empire and, thus, brings out the political dimension of Bote's text.

In Sachs's text, the bishop has the opportunity to respond to Eulenspiegel's political charges. He blames wicked courtiers and shifty civil servants. Eulenspiegel counters that violent crime and infractions against the political and social order are common in Germany and mostly directed against the free cities and their citizens. He repeats his appeal to the princes:

> Solch unrecht soltn die fürsten wehrn
> Und untersthen bey iren ehrn
> Und dem römischen reych beystehn,
> Es nit lassen zu drümmern gehn.
> So sitzn die fürsten still mit rhu
> Und sehen durch die finger zu.
> Derhalb dürffens kein prillen nicht,
> Zu behalten ein gut gesicht.

[The princes should fend off such injustice and take care of it on their honor, and they should support the Roman Empire and not let it be ruined. Now the princes sit still and in silence and look through their fingers [turn a blind eye]. That is why they do not require eyeglasses to maintain good eyesight.][44]

Sachs adds that crime and injustice happen when the empire is threatened by self-interest. However, the bishop laughs it off and invites Eulenspiegel to accompany him to the diet, just like in Bote's chapter, but also concedes that the diet needs to act to restore justice to German lands.

The ending of Sachs's narrative poem differs from Bote's chapter in significant ways. Sachs gives the bishop the last word, allowing him to adjudicate the conflict and formulate a final statement. Thus, the authority of the sovereign is maintained, and Eulenspiegel ultimately must subject himself to it. Furthermore, Sachs's texts focuses on building a consensus that castigates vices and transgressions, with the aim of promoting the common good. The protagonist criticizes the authorities more openly than in the earlier mastersong. However, just like in all other Sachs texts, he does not have full agency; rather, he must subject himself to the compromise proposed by the authority figure.

---

44 Sachs, 1870–1908, vol. 9: 260, v. 5–12.

In his chapter 71, entitled "Wie vlenspiegel. xii blinden. gab. xii guldin" [How Ulenspiegel gave twelve guilders to twelve blind men], Bote developed one of the most twisted and complex plots. Ulenspiegel encounters twelve blind men outside the city gates of Hanover on a cold winter day. He promises to give them twelve guilders so they can lodge at the inn until the weather gets warmer. The blind men happily accept. When it is time to settle the bill, the blind men notice that Ulenspiegel has not given the money to any of them. As they are unable to pay, the innkeeper locks them up in the pigsty. When Ulenspiegel arrives, he asks the host why the blind men are locked up. Ulenspiegel promises that he will find someone to settle the tab, whereupon the innkeeper releases the blind men. Ulenspiegel then visits the priest and tells him that the host was possessed by evil spirits and that he will bring by the host's wife to confirm it. He goes back to the host and tells him that the priest is going to pay the bill, and then takes the wife back to the priest. The priest confirms that he is going to help her husband. In Ulenspiegel's clever setup, both have a different idea what is involved. Ulenspiegel leaves town, but the wife returns to the priest on the third day to demand the money. The priest responds that her husband was possessed by evil spirits. The wife goes back to her irate husband who returns with her, heavily armed. A number of peasants intervene and barely can prevent bloodshed.

The conflict remains unresolved. The enmity between the host and the priest endures, the priest believing that the host is possessed and the host believing that the priest is a swindler. Peace and harmony in the community are disrupted and communal order disturbed. Ulenspiegel is the root cause for all the turmoil. The narrator tells us that at the beginning of the episode Ulenspiegel went on a stroll just outside the city walls without a particular purpose, as if he were looking for trouble.[45] None of the participants—or, for that matter, the community of Hanover—have done Ulenspiegel any harm, and, prior to Ulenspiegel's involvement, there was no conflict among community members. Ulenspiegel created upheaval and disrupted the order out of malice.

Hans Sachs reworked this plot twice: in his mastersong from 1547, entitled "Ewlenspigel mit den 12 plinden" [Eulenspiegel and the twelve blind men] and in the carnival play from 1553, entitled "Der Ewlenspiegel mit den blinden" [Eulenspiegel with the blind men]. In both versions, Bote's plot remains essentially unchanged, although the emphasis and conclusion shift. In the short mastersong, Sachs stresses how excessively the blind men indulged while staying at the inn. But at the end, Sachs presents all three parties—blind men, innkeeper, and pastor—as Eulenspiegel's victims, labeling Eulenspiegel

---

45   Bote, 1515: fol. 100v: "Dar reit er ein zeit für das thor ein acker leng wegs spacieren."

a "schalck" in the last line. This conclusion contradicts Sachs's own storyline, where the innkeeper is the sole victim, as it is left to him to absorb the financial losses.

As mentioned above, there is evidence that the meaning of the term *schalck* has shifted in Sachs's usage, like in the 1533 mastersong entitled "Der Ewlenspiegel," where Ulenspiegel's "schalckheit" is engendering pranks that provoke laughter. In his monologue at the beginning of the 1553 carnival play about the blind men, Eulenspiegel introduces himself as follows:

> Ewlenspiegel bin ich genandt,
> Im gantzen Teudtschland wolbekandt.
> Mit meiner schalckheyt umbadumb
> Bin ich gar schwindt, wo ich hin kumb.

> [I am called Eulenspiegel, well-known in all of Germany. With my mischief all around I am very shrewd, wherever I go.][46]

He describes his own quality as "schalckheyt," which can be translated as "craftiness," but also, more benignly, as "mischieviousness." In his monologue, Eulenspiegel cheekily presents himself as a jokester or trickster while flirting with the language of villainy. Furthermore, the blind men—the victims in this story—are described as "schelck" in the sense of poor fools.

The carnival play paints a richer picture than the mastersong of the environment within which the story occurs. The three blind men—the smaller number making the staging more manageable—complain to Eulenspiegel that they are shunned by peasants and outright abused by the inhabitants of the city. Eulenspiegel expresses regret for their situation and promises to help. Here, Eulenspiegel is a more neutral figure, and the other protagonists are presented in a more differentiated light. Since business is going poorly, the innkeeper's wife who is in charge of household and inn decides to lodge the three blind men over his objections. The peasants are stingy with their offerings for the priest as he holds lousy sermons, and the priest, in turn, dislikes the peasants and is not motivated to deliver riveting oratory.

In the carnival play, the core conflict is between the innkeeper and the priest, who have a pre-existing conflictual relationship. The priest describes the innkeeper as a greedy and dishonest man who dilutes the beer he serves. The innkeeper, in turn, refers to the priest as a penny-pinching, stingy dog. Eulenspiegel feeds off this animosity between the two:

---

46   Sachs, 1870–1908, vol. 14: 288, v. 4–7.

> Weil ich thet an einander knüpffen
> Den wirdt unde diesen dorffpfaffen,
> Hab ich gemachet beidt zu affen.

> [Because I am linking together the innkeeper and this village priest,
> I turned both into monkeys.][47]

In other words, the community is in disarray before Eulenspiegel arrives, and he merely takes advantage of existing antagonisms.

The three versions have remarkably different endings. In Bote's version, violence erupts, and the cohesion in the community comes undone. Sachs's mastersong portrays the three parties as victims of Eulenspiegel's prank, but there are no further consequences for the communal order. In Sachs's play, the peasants try to calm the innkeeper. At the insistence of the priest, they tie him up and take him away, presumably to be exorcized. The play ends with the priest's monologue, in which he sharply censures the innkeeper's greed. By blaming the disruption on the innkeeper, a semblance of peace and order in the community is restored, although the priest's shortcomings are not addressed. In contrast to Bote's version, Eulenspiegel's intervention does not disrupt the communal order; rather, it helps unmask the innkeeper's failings, thus helping to restore the order.

Sachs's four carnival plays that are based on the Eulenspiegel figure give us clear insight into how Sachs processed Bote's plots and reinterpreted both characters and moral lessons. They are much longer than the original episodes and therefore offer opportunities to add material. The dramatic form allows for a better development of the characters and requires the dialogues to be expanded in order to add plausibility; at the same time, it reduces the role of the narrative voice. As in other Sachs texts, Eulenspiegel is not the unruly transgressor, who embodies moral decay and social disruption through his personhood and his actions. Instead, he becomes an agent of change by revealing transgressions committed by others and by generally diagnosing political and social disorder. Sachs added a moral lesson to his poems where Bote offered none. The key difference is that for Bote Eulenspiegel is a villain, transgressor, and agent of disorder, while in Sachs's versions Eulenspiegel serves to unmask moral failings and, in so doing, repair the social fabric.

The reception of the Eulenspiegel figure in the first half of the sixteenth century reveals broader cultural developments. The larger context is that the generation around Hermann Bote, Sebastian Brant, Johannes Geiler von Kaysersberg, and others shared a bleak view that saw the world under pressure,

---

47   Sachs, 1870–1908, vol. 14: 299, v. 26–28.

existential threats emanating from globalization and pluralization, strife and disorder in the empire, economic pressures from large merchant bankers, and a perceived loss of the common good. These writers expressed a yearning for a static and permanent vision of history, where the social and political order remained stable. They viewed the rapidly changing world around them with a great deal of anxiety because they read innovation as a sign of decline that followed a period of constancy and strength. The order and stability their German forefathers had fought for and achieved was under attack—something they perceived to be the fundamental crisis of their time. In their vision, the empire represented the end of history, and Brant in particular stylized the rule of Emperor Maximilian I into an ideal period that ushered in the end of times.[48] This is the context within which Ulenspiegel's transgressive acts disrupted and threatened the existing order, which is why he is presented as a malicious protagonist in Bote's text.

Later writers, like Sachs, Pauli, and Scheidt, framed Eulenspiegel as a relatively benign prankster, as opposed to Bote, who pitched him as a rogue and a villain. None of them picked up on Bote's point that Ulenspiegel used language to offend, control, and inflict damage, and that his tricks were mean-spirited and malicious with the intent of hurting innocent artisans, servants, and shopkeepers. In Bote's world, Ulenspiegel himself was at issue because his mischief and unwillingness to integrate into society were the key destabilizing forces. Bote saw Ulenspiegel as a corrosive force posing a threat to the social fabric. As Bachorski argues, Ulenspiegel moved through different layers of society and sought to destroy them by setting free latent egoisms.[49] To Bote, Ulenspiegel was not a figure that exposed the threat to society; rather, he himself was the threat.

The later writers, in contrast, disengaged from the large political and social questions of the day and withdrew into a tranquil and private urban sphere. They did not share the bleak outlook of the generation of Bote and Brant and instead focused more empirically on small-scale communal issues and individual shortcomings. The writings of Hans Sachs are exemplary for this. They no longer perceived Eulenspiegel as an existential threat, and they displayed a more relaxed attitude toward Eulenspiegel's transgressions. The misdeeds were now treated as individual foibles that needed to be exposed and modified. Hans Sachs's Eulenspiegel figure, for instance, was a more integrated member of society, who often collaborated with state actors. While often pushing boundaries, his actions were not evil and did not pose systemic threats. Rather, they were designed to unmask the moral and social shortcomings of

---

48   For a detailed argumentation see Hess, 2020: 11–124.
49   Bachorski, 2000: 277.

those around him. Sachs turned evil deeds in Bote's text into harmless jokes and used the stories to add his own invective, with a heavy emphasis on individual behavior. This gave Sachs the opportunity to close with his own moralizing musings, which often diverged substantially from the points established in the template.

It is interesting to note that the illustrations of the 1532 edition show Ulenspiegel in a fool's costume, in the tradition of Sebastian Brant's *Ship of Fools*. A case can be made that the reception of the figure of the fool underwent exactly the same transformation as Ulenspiegel. Both figures were conceived as immoral and evil figures who threatened the social and moral order and who created a great deal of anxiety. In the more benign world of the 1530s, both were reinterpreted as jokesters who unmasked the foolishness and immorality of others.

Bibliography

Bachorski, Hans-Jürgen. "Wie der Narr ins Irrenhaus kommt. Diskursdifferenzierung im 16. und 17. Jahrhundert." In *Das Berliner Modell der Mittleren Deutschen Literatur*, eds. Jörg Jungmayr and Christiane Caemmerer (Amsterdam: Rodopi, 2000), 273–98.

Bässler, Andreas. "Eulenspiegel erzähltheoretisch. Vladimir Propps 'Morphologie des Märchens' und der 'Ulenspiegel.'" *Fabula* 46 (3–4) (2005), 291–304.

Bernstein, Eckhard. "Hans Sachs (5 November 1494–19 January 1576)." In *Dictionary of Literary Biography, vol. 179: German Writers of the Renaissance and Reformation, 1280–1580*, eds. Max Reinhart and James Hardin (Detroit: Gale Research, 1997), 241–52.

Bote, Hermann. "Das Schichtbuch. 1514." In *Die Chroniken der niedersächischen Städte. Braunschweig, 2. Band*, ed. Ludwig Hänselmann (Leipzig: Hirzel, 1880), 269–493.

Bote, Hermann. *Ein kurtzweilig lesen von Dyl Vlenspiegel geboren vß dem land zů Brunßwick. Wie er sein leben volbracht hatt. xcvi. seiner geschichten* (Strasbourg: Johann Grüninger, 1515).

Bote, Hermann. *Ein kurtzweilig lesen von Dil Ulenspiegel geboren vß dem land zů Brunßwick. Wie er sein leben volbracht hat. xcvi. seiner geschichten* (Strasbourg: Johann Grüninger, 1519).

Bote, Hermann. *Von Vlenspiegel eins bauren sun des lands Braunschweick/ wie er sein leben volbracht hat/ gar mit seltzamen sachen* (Erfurt: Melcher Sachse, 1532).

Classen, Albrecht. "Laughter as the Ultimate Epistemological Vehicle in the Hands of Till Eulenspiegel." *Neophilologus* 92 (2008), 471–89.

Correll, Barbara. *The End of Conduct: Grobianus and the Renaissance Text of the Subject* (Ithaca, NY: Cornell University Press, 1996).

Geiler von Kaysersberg, Johannes. *Doctor keiserszbergs Postill* (Strasbourg: Johann Schott, 1522).

Hayden-Roy, Priscilla. "The Masquerade of History: Herman Bote's *Schichtboik*." *Daphnis* 22 (4) (1993), 561–80.

Hess, Peter. *Resisting Pluralization and Globalization in German Culture, 1490–1540. Visions of a Nation in Decline* (Berlin, Boston: De Gruyter, 2020).

Hess, Peter. "German Poetry, 1450–1700." In *Early Modern German Literature. Camden House History of German Literature, vol. 4*, ed. Max Reinhart (Rochester, NY: Camden House, 2007), 395–465.

Honegger, Peter. *Ulenspiegel. Ein Beitrag zur Druckgeschichte und zur Verfasserfrage* (Neumünster: Wachholtz, 1973).

Ivanov, Cristina Dogaru. "Ambivalenz und Vielseitigkeit der Eulenspiegel-Figur." In *Authentizität, Varietät oder Verballhornung. Germanistische Streifzüge durch Literatur, Kultur und Sprache im globalisierten Raum*, ed. Carmen Elisabeth Puchianu (Passau: Verlag Karl Stutz, 2014), 95–106.

Kirschner, Carola. *Hermen Bote. Städtische Literatur um 1500 zwischen Tradition und Innovation* (Essen: Item-Verlag, 1996).

Lindow, Wolfgang. "Nachwort." In Hermann Bote. *Ein kurtzweilig Lesen von Dil Ulenspiegel*, ed. Wolfgang Lindow (Stuttgart: Reclam, 2001), 273–304.

Luther, Martin. "Vorwort." In Stefan Klingebeil. *Von Priester Ehe des wirdigen herrn Licentiaten Steffan Klingebeyl* (Wittenberg: Nickel Schirlentz, 1528).

Pauli, Johannes. *Schimpf und Ernst*, ed. Hermann Österley (Stuttgart: Litterarischer Verein, 1866).

Rusterholz, Peter. "Till Eulenspiegel als Sprachkritiker." *Wirkendes Wort* 27 (1977), 18–26.

Scheidt, Kaspar. *Grobianus/ von groben sitten/ und vnhöflichen geberden* (Worms: Gregor Hoffman, 1551).

Schwarz, Alexander. "Wer sagt das? Zum Kampf um die Sprecherrolle im Eulenspiegelbuch." *Chloe. Beihefte zum Daphnis* 42 (2010), 493–507.

Schwarz, Alexander. "Leere statt Lehre im Eulenspiegel." *Daphnis* 40 (1–2) (2011), 89–113.

Solbach, Andreas. "*malevolentia* und *malignitas*: Moralisches Dilemma und biographische Integration im Ulenspiegel." In *Lose Leute. Figuren, Schauplätze und Künste des Vaganten in der Frühen Neuzeit*, ed. Julia Amslinger, Franz Fromholzer, and Jörg Wesche (München: Wilhelm Fink, 2019), 119–31.

Tenberg, Reinhard. *Die deutsche Till-Eulenspiegel-Rezeption bis zum Ende des 16. Jahrhunderts* (Würzburg: Königshausen & Neumann, 1996).

Wailes, Stephen L. "The Childishness of Till: Hermen Bote's Ulenspiegel." *The German Quarterly* 64 (2) (1991), 127–37.

Wunderlich, Werner. *Till Eulenspiegel* (Munich: Wilhelm Fink, 1984).

CHAPTER 2

The Year 1663: Exploring Ambiguities in a Pamphlet about the Turk (Erasmus Francisci, 1627–1694)

Gerhild Scholz Williams

The polyhistor Erasmus Francisci (1627–1694), "eine ein-Mann-Schreibfabrik" [a one-man writing factory],[1] wrote extensively about many things, including, at a time when the Turkish advance on Europe seemed all but unstoppable, the Ottoman state.[2] His Turkish-themed writings discuss the empire's political and military organizations and its actions during the sixteenth and seventeenth centuries.[3] Using historical, topographic, and generally contemporary reports, most of his *Turcica* aims both to entertain and to educate his audience.

Of Francisci's vast corpus of publications for entertainment and instruction—Dünnhaupt, citing Goedecke, mentions 125 volumes, covering most areas of contemporary knowledge (318)—I will examine one essay that specifically addresses the Turkish theme. Subsumed under the variety of *Buntschriftstellerei*, which Flemming Schock characterizes as "barockes Unterhaltungswissen" [baroque knowledge entertainment],[4] the text under discussion here is dedicated to Christoph Pellern, "Beider Rechten Doctori" of the Imperial City of Nürnberg and Francisci's patron. This text, like much of Francisci's writing, explores the role of print media in the reporting on and discussion of the Turk. This is especially true for the *Adlerblitz* (1684), which Francisci calls a "historical narrative."[5] In this tract, he repeatedly reminds his

---

1 Flemming Schock, "Gespräch und Zerstreuung. Mechanismen barocken Unterhaltungswissens am Beispiel Erasmus Francisci (1624–1697)," *DAPHNIS* 44 (2016): 320–39.

2 Gerhard Dünnhaupt, "Das Oevre des Erasmus Francisci (1627–1694) und sein Einfluß auf die deutsche Literatur," *Argenis* 2 (1978): 317–22; 17. Born and baptized as Erasmus von Finx in Lübeck, he gave up the "von" in his name (indicating nobility) and took the name of his grandfather and father, Francisci, in order to be able to earn a living.

3 Dünnhaupt, 1975, 317–22.; see also Gerhard Dünnhaupt, "Erasmus Francisci: Ein Nürnberger Polyhistor des siebzehnten Jahrhunderts. Biographie und Bibliographie," *Philobiblon: Eine Vierteljahsschrift für Buch- und Graphiksammler* 19 (1975): 272–303.

4 Schock, "Gespräch und Zerstreuung. Mechanismen barocken Unterhaltungswissens am Beispiel Erasmus Franciscis (1624–1697)," 320–39, here 20.

5 "Historische Erzählung": Erasmus Francisci, *Der blutig-lang=gereitzte/ endlich Sieghafft= entzündte/ Adler=Blitz/ Wider den Glantz dess barbarischen Sebels/ und Mord=Brandes* (Nuremberg: Johann Andreas Endters Seel. Söhne, 1684).

readers that news reporting is often biased, delivering either distorted news or downright falsehoods. This means, as we will see, that Francisci seemed to aim either to set the record straight or to alert his readers to the possibility that what had been reported was not supported by facts, and was often simply copied without any critical assessment of the information.[6]

The short tract reviewed here, entitled *Die Herandringende Türcken=Gefahr: Das ist; Wohlgemeinte/ doch unvorgreiffliche Erinnerung*,[7] recounts a conversation between two men exchanging views on different aspects of their experience with and knowledge of the Ottoman—his power and influence, history, present reality, and future plans. The back-and-forth of the conversation follows the model of the literary dialogue, which became immensely popular during the seventeenth century. Francisci frequently employs this amusing and instructive form of entertainment, as Flemming Schock notes in the case of the *Stats-Garten*.[8]

The conversation at hand explores in detail Turkish-German contacts and communications, carefully outlining the German understanding of the finer points of the military, political, and cultural differences between the Ottoman and the Christian powers. In addition, it demonstrates significant historical and cultural knowledge about the Eurasian past shared by the peoples of Eastern Europe and the Eastern Mediterranean. The publishing date of 1663 is also noteworthy. While the retreat of Suleiman's army after the first siege of Vienna (Sep 27, 1529–Oct 14, 1529) had receded from memory, the renewed Ottoman forays into Hungary were at this time cause for much concern, even anguish, especially in the imperial borderlands.

Although often critical of the Ottoman's vaunted cruelty, this conversation, like others published by Francisci about this time, tries to refrain from the unrelenting Ottoman-bashing characteristic of some contemporary newspapers and broadsheets. Twenty years later, after the unsuccessful Ottoman

---

6 Francisci is one of the few *Buntschriftsteller* who informs the reader in detail about his sources and his method of quoting these sources. I thank Flemming Schock for confirming my findings.

7 Erasmus Francisci, *Die herandringende Türcken=Gefahr: Das ist; Wohlgemeinte/ doch invorgreiffliche Erinnerung/ in was hochbesorgtem und gefährlichem Zustande/ unser liebes Vatterland Deutscher Nation/ und das gantze Heil. Römische Reich jetziger Zeit stecke* (Nuremberg 1663). Copy used here Herzog August Bibliothek, Wolfenbüttel: http//diglib.hab.de/drucke/wa-3759/start.htm?image=00005. All pagination in this text refers to this digital copy. Gerhild Scholz Williams, *Ottoman Eurasia in Early Modern German Literature: Cultural Translations (Francisci, Happel, Speer)* (Ann Arbor Michigan University Press, 2021).

8 Schock, 2016: 30.

siege of Vienna in 1683,[9] the tone of the writings became less restrained and at times slightly ironic, even a bit disrespectful and dismissive. After 1683, the widely shared *Türkenangst* of the mid-century clearly had receded into the background, finding its administrative and ideological conclusion in the Peace of Karlowitz, in 1699.[10]

The conversation reviewed here introduces us to two German friends—Frischmuth and Wolrath—who have come together in an unnamed German town for a visit. The conversation ranges widely across the complicated power plays occurring between Eastern and Central Europe and the Ottoman Empire, highlighting different hegemonic ambitions intertwined with the rivalry between Europe and its challenger from across the Mediterranean. Moving from West to East and North to South across the Bosporus, the reader begins to understand the geopolitical implications of this conflict, which involved so many European nations and peoples.[11]

But before getting to the main topic—namely, the *Türcken=Gefahr*—the conversation's introductory remarks elaborate on the benefit of acquiring knowledge through travel, especially for young people. Why is travel so important to a true education? Because, Francisci contends, when science and experience are joined, the resulting "Vermählung" [marriage] predicts happy outcomes—that is, young people learn from lived experience as much as they do from books: "dannenher junge Leute/ bevorab die jenige/ so das Gemeine Beste dermaleins zubedienen gesonnen/ klüglich thun/ wann sie nicht allein sich daheim aus den Büchern / besonder auch in die Ferne / durch Reisen/ unterrichten lassen/ und an den Sitten und Exempeln fremder Nationen ihre selbsteigene Qualitäten Spiegel" [Therefore, young people, especially those who are planning to serve the common good, would be smart if they not only stay at home and learn from books but also travel to distant places and in this way learn the customs and examples of foreign countries reflected in their own].[12]

---

9   Of the many works on the siege of Vienna, Wheatcroft, 2008, is comprehensive as well as readable.

10   Martin Wrede, "Die ausgezeichnete Nation: Identitätsstiftung im Reich Leopolds I. in Zeiten von Türkenkrieg und Türkensieg, 1663–1699.," in *Das Bild des Feindes: Konstruktion von Antagonismen und Kulturtransfer im Zeitalter der Türkenkriege (Ostmitteleuropa, Italien und Osmanisches Reich)*, ed. Eckhard Leuschner and Thomas Wünsch (Berlin: Mann Verlag, 2013), 21.

11   Jane Burbank, Fredrick Cooper, *Empires in World History: Power and the Politics of Difference* (Princeton/Oxford: Princeton UP, 2010).

12   He continues that "durch Besuchung fremder Länder ... die Geschicklichkeit deß Menschen ihre vollkommene Kraft erreichen/ und zum gemeinen Nutzen / oder guter Conversation bequem werden" (7) [by visiting foreign lands ... people accomplish great

Keeping this advice in mind, Frischmuth, having just completed his university studies, embarks on a journey to France for the "Vermehrung seiner Geschicklichkeit" [improvement of his talents], resolving to combat ignorance with "Raison und Vernunfft." Had news from his family ("den Seinigen") not reached him while underway that the Turk had renewed his military activities, his plan would no doubt have borne fruit. But with the Turk moving into Hungary, Frischmuth's beloved home country has come under threat.[13]

Forced to retrace his steps, Frischmuth stops for a visit with his best friend, Wolrath,[14] who makes every effort to extend his friend's stay (8). During their time together, they are "lustig und guter Dinge" [happy and in good spirits]. Their conversations are inspired by good wine and much intelligent discourse: "die Zunge mit den starcken Weinrancken nicht gebunden noch gelähmet/ sondern vielmehr geflügelt/ zu allerhand wollautenden verständigen Discursen behurtiget" [The tongue from strong vines neither bound nor paralyzed but rather taking on wings, was employed in much intelligent discourse] (9).

Under the conditions of present danger and well-oiled tongues, the friends explore the Turkish threat ("beschrienen Türcken=Gefahr") in great detail. The lengthy disquisitions confirm what we know from Francisci's other publications—namely, that he knew his sources well, and that, already in 1663, he had a firm grasp of the intricacies of the Ottoman government and military, and of its future plans.[15] For the most part, the dialogue presents carefully reasoned explorations of strengths and weaknesses on both sides of the conflict, Ottoman and Christian European, alongside a sober assessment of the cruel reality of war.[16]

Herr Wolrath inquires first about his friend's experience during his brief sojourn in France, and after Frischmuth has satisfied his friend's curiosity, he bemoans having to return home at the high point of his travels ("mitten in dem besten Lauff seiner Peregrination") because of the loud rumors of war ("beschrienen Türcken=Gefahr").

The danger of war seems heightened by the fact that, based on experience, Turks prefer to start their wars in August (the conversations appear to be taking

---

things for themselves and for the common good and find it good or helpful for good conversation].

13   "liebes Vatterland Teutscher Nation."

14   "Seiner besten Kleinodien/ als sein Kern=Freund."

15   Edward Seymour Forster, Foreword Karl A. Roider, ed. *The Turkish Letters of Ogier Ghiselin de Busbecq* (Baton Rouge: Louisiana State University Press, 1927/2005). Konrad Gessner (1516–1565) was a Swiss physician, naturalist, bibliographer, and philologist.

16   Wrede, "Die ausgezeichnete Nation: Identitätsstiftung im Reich Leopolds I. in Zeiten von Türkenkrieg und Türkensieg, 1663–1699," 21.

place in early or mid-summer). Wolrath mentions many historical examples of such seasonal consideration for warfare (16), and does not limit himself to the Turk alone. That said, he does maintain that Turks find it hard to fight in winter "wegen der Kälte/ zu Herbst und Frühlingszeiten / deß Regens und großen Gewässers halber" [In winter they cannot move because of the cold/ in Spring and Fall because of the rain and rising rivers] (15).[17]

Through the ebb and flow of the conversation, the two interlocutors reveal no shortage of personality and contour. Wolrath generally comes across as strident and opinionated, while Frischmuth seems more deliberate, prone to asking clarifying questions and commenting on the occasional incongruity in his friend's expositions. They both comment on the "elende Gestalt und Gelegenheit jetziger Zeiten," with Herr Frischmuth trying to calm his friend by reassuring him that "ihm nicht wohl einbilden könnte/ daß es so schlecht stünde/ wie man ausgäbe. Herr Wolrath hingegen die Gefahr mit lebhafften Farben abzumahlen sich bemühete."[18] Wolrath remains unconvinced, reminding Frischmuth of low points in the past, most adamantly of the defeat of Constantinople and East Rome in 1453 and the ensuing destruction and occupation of Christian lands (41). With Hungary, the bulwark of the German Empire ("Vormaur deß Reichs"), now again in danger, who would be safe? Germany, as a "Land ohne Mauern," seems defenseless against the approaching Turk. Wolrath finds the situation especially frightening since merchant spies keep the Turk well informed about the disunity tearing the Christian world apart.[19]

In a present-day context, where severe criticism of news reporting has entered the mainstream, the era of "fake news," we might find amusing Frischmuth's reminder to his friend that on his travels he saw many news reports ("Zeitungen und Spargementen") talking up the Turkish danger ("fliegendes Gerücht aufsattelt"), only later to find that they contained error and falsehoods ("die meisten den Irrthumen und falschen Berichten leihen würden" [41]). In fact, expressing his reservations about the truth value of any news reports, Frischmuth prefaces several of his remarks with "denn dafern

---

17   In fact, Suleiman had to lift the siege of Vienna (1529) because of bad weather, which plagued his army with illness and made troop movements very difficult.

18   "Herr Frischmuth could not imagine that things were quite as bad as people said. Herr Wolrath on the other hand painted the danger in vivid colors" (41).

19   "Die Kauffleute auff dem Meer/ ... so aus den Türckischen Ländern nach Venedig und anderen Christlichen Orten handeln/ und dem Türcken vor Spionen dienen/ ihm den verwirrten Zustand und Uneinigkeit der Christlichen Potentaten zu entdecken/ und ihn der guten Gelegenheit zu erinnern/ daß man sie überfallen könne" (76).

der Relation/ die ich neulichst erst gesehen/ zu trauen. ...." (41). Clearly, the two friends agree that not everything printed as news can or should be believed.[20]

At the same time, Wolrath wonders whether the frequent and widely expressed doubts about the veracity of news reports might lead to an underestimation of the Turkish menace. While some dismiss it as a small fire, he suggests that, in reality, the Turkish threat may burn dangerously hot: "Ich weiss nicht/ ob uns Teutschen der Geruch vergangen/ daß wir keine Brand riechen können/ eh und bevor die allgemeine Wolfart in Aschen liegt" [I don't know if we Germans lost our sense of smell such that we cannot discern any burning until everything is turned to ashes] (10).

Wolrath also points repeatedly to the still-virulent confessional strife among Christians, suggesting that they would do better to unite against the common enemy rather than wasting time and resources on the enmity between Lutheran, Reformed, and Catholic. In addition, Wolrath reminds his friend that some Christians (he singles out among them the Lutheran theologian Matthias Höe von Höenegg [1580–1645]) had even insinuated that the Turk was not as cruel an enemy as generally believed, based on the fact that Christians were tolerated in Turkish lands as long as they paid tribute.[21] It seems clear that, to avoid religious persecution, some Christians would in fact rather live under Turkish rule, under the rule of, in his words, the "Mahometischem Bluthund," than be subjects of a repressive Christian government.[22]

Wolrath rejects such attitudes as wrong-headed, suggesting that the Turk promises pleasant treatment ("annehmliche Bedingungen") to Christians under his rule, only to conquer and oppress once any resistance has been overcome. He compares them to the mythical sirens, whose sweet songs lured many a sailor to his death (18). Frischmuth, in turn, points to the fact that the Turk had generally kept his word concerning people of different religions living under his purview: "steiff und unverbrüchlich halten; bevorab in Religions Sachen" [Keeping (their word) strictly and unbroken, especially in matters of religion] (18).[23] He cites the "Herrn Ungarn," who tended to be more interested

---

20 "For if one can believe the newspaper I only recently saw ...."

21 "Es sei gleichwol der Türck nicht so ein grausamer Feind ... er könte doch die Christen / um gebührlichen Tribut unter seinem Regiment wol dulden" (43).

22 The Protestant uprising led by Imre Thököly would be an example of such liaison with the Turk; Gerhild Scholz Williams, *Mediating Culture in the Seventeenth-Century German Novel: Eberhard Werner Happel, 1647–1690*. (Ann Arbor: Michigan University Press, 2014), 50–84.

23 The Ottoman state "never considered the official religion as a belief that was to be imposed on its non-Muslim subjects": Tobias Graf, *The Sultan's Renegades: Christian-European Converts to Islam and the Making of the Ottoman Elite, 1575–1610* (Oxford: Oxford University Press, 2015), 10.

in the freedom of the Protestant religion and in retaining their privileges (43) than concerned with the religion of Hungary's government.[24]

Still, Wolrath does not want to let go of his negative assessment of the Turk and of the Muslim religion. Citing the Porte's multipronged efforts to convert Christians by various means, such as "Furcht/ Gefahr/ Geschenck und Anerbietung zum Abfall" [Fear, danger, presents, and respect to tempt (Christians) to abandon their faith], he points to the Ottoman practice of the "boy levy" (*devşirme*). He says that to this day ("noch biß auf den heutigen Tag") the Ottoman tears children from their mothers' breasts to be raised Turkish: "Erstgeborene anstatt Zinses/ mit Gewalt den armen Müttern von den Brüsten reissen/ beschneiden und in ihrem verfluchten Irr- und Scheusal unterrichten" [Instead of a tax they take the first born, with force from their mothers' breast, circumcise them, and instruct them in their horrible false teachings] (19). As if such cruelty did not suffice, the tributary states of Wallachia, Moldavia, and Transylvania are also forced to supply soldiers for Ottoman wars against the Christians.[25] He continues by noting one of the most recent altercations along the border, where the Turks had sent Christian peasants ahead of their army to serve as human shields (20). In response, Frischmuth poses the question of whether, in the face of great danger and fear of destruction, it would not be better to submit to a tyrant than to suffer death and destruction (20). This pacifist notion is clearly not acceptable to Wolrath, who counters that it would be better to die than to live in servitude ("lieber ehrlich gestorben/ als knechtisch und unchristlich gelebt" [ibid]).

Changing the direction of the conversation, Wolrath suggests that it is time for Christians to consider liberating Jerusalem and the Holy Places. To this Frischmuth responds with uncharacteristic irony by pointing out that no one is willing to protect the Holy Sepulcher without being paid ("deß Heiligen Grabs will niemand umsonst hüten"). Additionally, he notes little readiness or willingness to render support to such a campaign, not in France nor anywhere else in Europe (21). He continues that, with a nod to *Realpolitik*, few would dare to break the peace with the Turk, as doing so rarely ends well (21).

Again injecting positive information about the enemy into the conversation, Frischmuth interrupts Wolrath's harangue by saying that Muslims generally do not tolerate insulting or brutalizing Christians under their purview. But

---

24   He actually means Transylvania and Imre Töcköly, who rebelled against Vienna's oppression of Protestants and support for the Catholic Church—specifically, Jesuits. The Porte generally did not distinguish between various Christian groups, as long as they remained supportive. Graf, *The Sultan's Renegades: Christian-European Converts to Islam and the Making of the Ottoman Elite, 1575–1610*, Chapter 1.

25   "Gezwungen/ es sey ihnen lieb oder leid/ zu Felde zu gehen/ wider andere Christen" (19).

Wolrath will have none of it. He continues his diatribe and, predictably, arrives at the supposed predilection of the Turk for sodomy. He quotes Olearius,[26] who describes the Persians as also given to this type of sex, even openly and publicly writing about it: "daß viel derselben in öffentlichen Schriften solche ihre schändliche Passion zu erkennen geben/ und auf schöne Knaben allerhand verliebt Lieder componiren" [That many among them acknowledge their shameful passion in public writings and compose many love songs in praise of beautiful boys].

Wolrath then circles back to itemize what he describes as the Turk's exceptional cruelty, only occasionally interrupted by Frischmuth's brief and moderating comments (31–32). Among other things, he mentions the infamous prison of the Seven Towers, in Galata, a suburb of Constantinople, which is mentioned by almost every travel writer who visited the Porte. His exhaustive review of the life of captives in the Seven Towers is only occasionally interrupted by Frischmuth's questions. Wolrath names as one of his sources a report by Melchior von Seidlitz, a Protestant Silesian nobleman who had been imprisoned in the Seven Towers for several years and who had written about the experience after his safe return (32).[27]

Von Seidlitz's report was later confirmed by Walter Leslie, an ambassador to the Porte.[28] According to von Seidlitz and Leslie, the inmates of the Towers, all Christian captives, were conscripted as galley slaves, chained summer and winter half-naked to their benches, and forced to perform the cruelest of labor (36). Those prisoners not serving on ships were sent to the quarries to cut and carry stones for the many imperial construction projects in Constantinople (36).

---

26 *Beschreibung der muscowitischen und persischen Reise*, Schleswig, 1647.

27 *Pilgerbericht Melchior von Seydlitz, Wolff von Opffersdorff, Nicolaus von Reidburg und Moritz von Altmannshausen. Folgt ein Reise Jn das Heilige Land, Jerusalem. Anno 1556. Vierer vom Adel, mitt Namen, Melchior von Seidlitz Wolff von Opffersdorff Nicolaus von Reidburg vnd Moritz von Altmarshausen. Wie Sie vom Türcken gefangen vnd Jn schwehre gefengniß gelegt, vnd wider ledig worden, auch wider Jn Jr VatterLande kommen. 03. Mai 1556–Juli 1559.* Görlitz: Ambrosius Fritsch, 1580. A brief summary of Seidlitz's life and travel experiences appear in *Des Schlesischen Adels anderer Theil/ oder Fortsetzung Schlesischer Curiositäten. ...* Leipzig: Michael Rohrbach, 1728.

28 Paul P. Taverner, *Keiserliche Botschafft/ An die Ottomannische Pforte. Welche auff Befehl Ihrer Röm. Keis. Maj. Leopoldus des I. Der hochgebohrene Herr/ Herr Walter Leßlie/ ... Anfangs in Lateinischer Sprache von P. Paul Tavernern/ Jesuitern ... aus eigener Erfahrung beschrieben/ nunmehro aber/ Dem Teutschliebenden Leser zum besten verteuschet. durch B. Z. v. W.* (Breslau: Joh. Ad. Kästner, 1680). Walter Leslie (1607–1667) was the Austrian ambassador to the Porte. He was invested with the Order of the Golden Fleece in 1666. As ambassador he concluded the Peace Treaty of Vasvar with Sultan Mehmet IV. See Williams, *Mediating Culture in the Seventeenth-Century German Novel: Eberhard Werner Happel, 1647–1690*, 166–67.

Von Seidlitz tells of captives who, despite all abuse and cruelty, had gained the good will of the overseers (often themselves renegade Christians), who then removed their chains, allowing these fortunate prisoners to move about more freely. They typically worked at breaking stones, making bricks, and carrying wood. On the way to their assigned work, these men stole whatever they could find along the way. Once back in the prison they sold their loot to their fellow inmates. There was even a corner of the prison where the guard ("der Schreiber über die Gefangenen/ welcher gleichfalls ein Christ war" [A sentry assigned to the prisoners who was also a Christian][29] distributed wine and allowed for food to be sold. At night, the prisoners would set up long tables and, in the light of candles, play cards and dice for their stolen goods. Testifying to the diversity of those held in the Seven Towers, the dances accompanying these games were international ("auf Spanisch/ Welsch/ Ungarisch und Teutsche Manier" [in the Spanish, Italian, Hungarian, and German manner], and allowed the men, most of whom were in chains, to forget for a moment their misery (34).

At Mardi Gras (*Faßnacht*) they played at *Mummerey*, putting on costumes made of old sheep skins. In spite of their hard work, or maybe because of it, they flung themselves into crazy diversions ("Kurtzweil und Affenspiel"), knowing there was no escape from this prison other than a huge ransom. It was not uncommon for prisoners to die of hunger and thirst or from severe beatings. In the case of such deaths, there was a small chapel where prisoners were allowed to hold services for the dead (34). Frischmuth singles out this gesture of mercy, commenting that "das ist dennoch viel/ daß man ihnen solches zuläst; denn dadurch wird mancher/ in seinem Jammer getröstet" [Still, that is much because it comforts the afflicted in their misery] (35).

And then Frischmuth returns to the main topic of the conversation, to the question about what the Turk wanted in and with Hungary (39). Easy, replies Wolrath–Suleyman clearly was driven by three ambitions, one of which required invading and conquering much of Hungary: the first was to build a large temple, the second to build viaducts in the tradition of the Roman waterways, and the third to conquer Vienna. To accomplish the last ambition, he had to go through Hungary. Resistance to such an invasion would need many soldiers, at least fifty to ninety thousand men (41). Wolrath doubts these figures and returns to his critique of reporting: "darum vermeine ich/ es werde

---

29   "Fast aus allen Nationen der Christenheit allerley Volck und Zungen gefunden werden; weßwegen vielerley Kunst/ und wunderliche Abentheuer/ ungeachtet aller Angst und Noth/ da anzutreffen" [From almost all nations of Christendom many peoples and languages could be found there. For that reason one could meet there much art and strange adventures in spite of all the fear and suffering] (34).

irgenein Druckfehler in den Relationen/ die solches vor diesem ausgesprengt haben. Wie leicht ist es geschehen/ daß man eine Null zuviel schreibt" (41). Journalists often employ this hyperbole when talking about the arithmetic of war.[30]

In response, Frischmuth suggests that it may have been a Frenchman, a *Welscher*, who put a bunch of women into beds and pretended they were sick soldiers, thus suggesting to his superiors that there were enough soldiers but that they were simply not well enough for service. Meanwhile, according to Wolrath, land and people stand naked and defenseless in the path of the advancing army (41). It is a great worry that the "Donnerkeile dieses Türckischen Kriegsgewitters dürfften plötzlich das hochlöbliche Oesterreich/ und ferner andere anstossenden Reichs=Länder durchdringen" [For it is truly worrisome that the lightning bolts of the Turkish thunderstorm should suddenly pierce Austria and adjacent countries] (41). Frischmuth reassures him that God will not allow it.

At this point, Wolrath revisits his more immediate anxiety—namely, the tensions between the Empire and the German estates, as well as among "Stands= als Privat=Personen" (People of the nobility and high standing) within Germany (50). He fears that these internal and internecine strains are blinding the "liebe Vatterland" to the clear and present danger of war, causing many people do disregard or ignore the threat: "daß man auch die gröste Kriegs=gefarn / und endlich unsere daraus besorglich=erfolgende Ruin nicht beobachten oder sehen möchte/ noch wolte" [That people did not want to observe or to see the most dire threat of war, nor the resulting ruin] (50).

At this point the two friends return to the danger implicit in Germany's religious and political disunity. They liken the threat posed by Turks and Tartars to that emanating from "Ketzer und unchristlichen Christen" [from heretics and unchristian Christians] (73). In other words, the approaching danger is twofold: There is, first, the "external Turk," the obvious enemy. He must be distinguished from the "internal Turk," the estates and neighboring countries that refused to support the Empire against the Ottoman, "deren einer ist der Unterschied in Religions=Sachen; der andre rührt her aus politischen Dingen" [The one is the difference in matters of religion, the other is a matter of politics] (50).

In line with the deliberate, even thoughtful tone of this conversation, the two men agree that before addressing the approaching catastrophe and strategizing about how to defeat the Turk, his strengths had first to be identified. First and foremost, Wolrath emphasizes the Turkish superiority in "Land und

---

30   "This is exactly what I mean, there must be a mistake in reporting, ... how easy it is for the copier to add a zero or two."

Leuthen," which surpasses the troop numbers of Spain, France, England, Italy, and Germany combined (51). Second, Wolrath contends that the Turks surpass most European nations in bravery, a statement Frischmuth disputes. He insists to his friend that superior numbers of troops had propelled the Turks to victory in the past, not true manly virtue ("rechtschaffende Mannheit"). In fact, he continues, a brave German will defeat a "fool" every time (53).

Not true, responds Wolrath, maintaining that Germans trust a bit too much in their courage, which is barely a shadow of past courage and prowess. Those warriors who earned this reputation have long since carried the virtue to their "sleep"—that is, to their graves. In the intervening years it would seem that German "Damen und Frauen" have assumed "Cavalliers=Sitten" while their male counterparts have adopted "Jungfern=Hertzen und Zartheit."[31]

It is known, opines Wolrath, that every time Germans have been victorious over the Turk, the Turk has come back stronger, ready to annihilate the enemy (55). Wolrath reminds Frischmuth that the most courageous among the Turks in the army are the *Janitscharen und Spahis*, foot soldiers and cavalry, respectively, who are not native born (54). These soldiers are products of the *Devşirme*, the child tribute extracted from tributary peoples in Eastern European and Balkan countries—they have been trained "zum Krieg" from childhood on (55).[32] With such well-prepared soldiers it is no wonder that in war the Ottoman was generally superior to the Christian European powers (56). And, as it turns out, the Turks had another mechanism in place to produce superior fighting forces: the positions of the fallen were given not to the next of kin but, rather, to the "muthigsten und streitbarsten" (the most courageous and most able to fight) (56) in order to further strengthen military spirit and devotion to the Emperor, while simultaneously avoiding the creation of powerful familial elites through martial success.[33]

A third reason advanced for Ottoman superiority in war—something that is mentioned in most writings on the topic—is the provisioning of food and clothing. It was said that the Turks spent nearly as much on these items as they did on weapons, for the simple reason that the troops did not tolerate cold and inclement weather very well.[34]

In addition to these virtues ascribed to the Ottoman, Wolrath draws attention to the way Ottoman soldiers keep themselves fed with very modest

---

31   Johannes Praetorius makes the same point, ridiculing the "alamode" men of his time. See
      Williams, 2006.
32   Pollard, 2015: 395.
33   "Die Stellen der Verstorbenen wurden nicht/ durch die nächsten Erben/ noch vornehme
      Personen/ sondern durch die muthingsten und streitbarsten ersetzet."
34   "Sonderbare Vorsorge in Verpflegung der Völcker/so wol an Proviant/ als Kleidung ..."

sustenance. Equally praiseworthy, according to many European observers, was the fact that Turks did not drink alcohol and that women were forbidden to follow the army. The Turks, so the saying went, were already in the saddle when the Germans were still debating their combat pay.[35] And, unlike their Christian counterparts (to the dismay of the European military leaders, particularly in the Protestant ranks), Turkish soldiers were not prone to cursing: "Flüche und Gotteslästerungen/ wird man bey ihnen nicht hören/ keinen Ehebruch spüren" [Curses and blaspheming God will not be heard among them/ nor is there any breaking of marriage vows] (65).

As the conversation continues, we are confronted with a remarkably informed review of the differences in soldiers' responses to challenges on the field. Ottoman soldiers were taught great discipline early in life. Accordingly, and in spite of the fact that the Turkish army was composed of many diverse nations and peoples, it moved as one ("viel zusammen geloffenes Gesindel mit in den Streit führen/ ist doch die rechte Forze oder Stärcke von ihrer Armee ein solches Volck/ das von Kind auf in den Waffen geübt und dazu erzogen worden" [Even though leading many disparate folk into battle, it is the strength and force of their army that such troops were trained and educated from an early age in the use of weapons] (56). By contrast, German military superiority came less from training or manly strength than from their superior weapons—specifically, their heavy armaments, against which "Säbel/ Bogen/ Spiesse, und Büchse" were quite ineffectual (59). Over the years, however, the Turk had taken quite a bit of heavy armament as loot from the Christians and become quite proficient in its use ("mit unseren eigenen Inventionen und Waffen uns um die Ohren schiessen; weiß man leider zuviel" [Having taken from the Christian many heavy weapons, they target us after a while with our own inventions and weapons] (59). When Suleiman inquired about the defeat at Vienna (1529), the Grand Vizier responded that the enemy had sprayed them with canon fire "über und über" [over and over], whose fury (and not any lack of manly courage) had beaten them into flight: "die Christen hatten zu ihrem Beystand lauter Feuer; dasselbige hat uns überwunden" (60).

A further advantage in the race for better arms, Wolrath points out, was the Portuguese expulsion of the Jews, who fled to the Turkish lands, bringing with them many of their discoveries in weaponry and instruments of war.[36]

---

35   From a 1664 Lutheran Southern German pamphlet, quoted in Wrede, "Die ausgezeichnete Nation: Identitätsstiftung im Reich Leopolds I. in Zeiten von Türkenkrieg und Türkensieg, 1663–1699," 19–31, here 20.

36   "So hat der Christenheit nicht wenig geschadet/ daß Portugal die Juden ausgestossen; welche sich hernach bey den Türcken mit Entdeckung unsrer Griff und Vortheil mit Schiessen beliebt gemacht." [thus it brought much damage to Christendom when

In the text, the occasional Christian defeat of the Ottoman is ascribed to the fervent prayers of the besieged. In fact, it would be commendable, Wolrath goes on, if Catholic and Protestant communities would pray together against the enemy, who, rather than first asking, "are you Lutheran, Reformed, or Catholic, will strike with his sword" (84). The conviction that "das Gebet die Waffen wider den Feind am besten schärffte und schwinge" [Prayer was a potent weapon against the enemy] (83) confirms Wolrath's dictum that the ingredients needed for victory are "Gebet, Geld und Kriegsvolck" (81). Frischmuth responds, with audible irony, that prayer is the easiest to come by (81).

Wolrath then returns to his combative tone, suggesting that in the past the enemy often withdrew, allowing the Christians in the borderlands to wrongly assume that the danger had passed. While relishing this fleeting comfort, the Christian forces either became careless or preoccupied with the pleasures of the senses or, once again, with fighting each other. Thus, even if the Christians were to go to war against the Ottomans, their newly conscripted and untrained soldiers would be nowhere near ready for battle (68). Again, Wolrath blames the *Reichsfürsten* (electors) for not sufficiently supporting the imperial cause, either with troops or with money. "Geldfressende Pracht/ verschwenderische Uberfluß" [money-devouring luxury and wasteful spending] have weakened any effort and resolve to resist the enemy, leaving the estates too impoverished ("depauperirt") to contribute financially to any war effort (87). If as much money as had been spent ("verschlungen") on the "dreissig=jährigen Teutsche(n) Krieg" [Thirty Years War] (60) and as many soldiers who had died ("ins Grass gebissen") were still available, there would be no contest in the war against the Turk ("wir wolten die Hunde von Land und Leuten jagen" [we would easily to chase these dogs from their land and people] (61).

And this is not the only complication: after the war with Sweden ("Nordische Unruhe") had concluded, soldiers were paid and released. If any troops were to be needed now, they would have to be hired from foreign powers. But Portugal, Holland, and Spain were fighting against each other, and England lived in fear of internal unrest, leaving just France and Sweden to provide soldiers—which they were clearly loathe to do. Wolrath agrees that without the support of allies, the burden of war against the Turk would be too heavy. Should such support continue to prove elusive, the Holy Roman Empire would be wide open to the invading enemy, as would be France and the allies. In other words, their shared safety and security demanded shared action (93).

Portugal evicted its Jews who then went over to the Türck assisting thm with important discoveries in weaponary].

Frischmuth returns to the martial virtue of German soldiers as the Christians' greatest hope, an assessment rejected by Wolrath, who reminds his friend that "Disciplin ist die Seele des Krieges" [discipline is the soul of war], and exactly what is missing among the Germans. As long as the *Landsknecht*, the ordinary soldier, did not submit to military discipline, fighting would not be his major priority. Recalling the decline of Rome, he enumerates the many vices that impacted military readiness, such as "Wollust/ Fressen/ Sauffen/ Huren/ Buben/ Rauben/ Plündern" [Vice, sensuality, gluttony, drinking, whoring, adultery, robbing, plunder]. This, he continues, made the Romans of old, just like the present-day Germans, ineffectual fighters (97). Ever the optimist, Frischmuth objects, suggesting that discipline could surely be reintroduced among the "soldatesca." It was the task of the "hohen und niedern Officirern" to make good soldiers out of bad men by imposing harsh discipline.[37]

In addition, if he is to fight well, the "Landsknecht" must be fairly paid, and supplied with decent food, "sein richtigen monatlichen Sold und Proviant" [His monthly pay and supplies] (99). He should not have to secure his sustenance by stealing horses, sheep, or oxen from poor peasants. (Francisci cites Levenclavius's account[38] of soldiers rebelling against officers who had reduced the soldiers' pay. As a result, the soldiers refused to fight until they were paid fairly again.[39]) If soldiers were disciplined and well paid, they would put their lives and hearts into their craft; they would fear neither their superiors nor the Turk (101). Wolrath suggests that if the Germans were as close to Constantinople as the Turk was to the German borders, the Turk would beat the drums across all lands under his rule, calling the troops to arms, and not be as lax as the Germans seem to be.

---

37 "welche aus Schelmen redliche/ aus Bösen Fromme machen konnten/ durch harten Zwang … (durch) Belohnung und Straffe" (who would be able to transform bad soldiers to good ones under the hard pressure of reward and punishment) (99).

38 Johannes Leunclavius (1541–1594) was a German historian and orientalist and expert on Turkish history. He published "Historiae Musulmanae Turcorum, de monumentis ipsorum exscriptae, libri XVIII." Speer reports on similar marauding on both sides of the Ottoman-German border in the Hungarian borderlands.

39 Francisci, 1684. In the *Schau= und Ehrenplatz*, we actually hear of such soldiers who refused to serve and even started a riot against the officer: "Sie suchten … den Knechten ihren Sturm-Sold abzuziehen: sassen auch fast den halben Tag im Kriegs=Rath/ ehe man die Knechte bezahlte … sie begehrten aber den Sold auf die Hand/ und alle Viktualien. Sie smachten ein so wüstes Geschrey … liessen die Spiesse niderfallen … Also gab man ihnen die drey Sold/ und alle Victualien quit" [They tried to deprive the soldiers of their pay: sat around all day in their war council before paying the soldiers who demanded money in hand and food supplies. They created a great commotion and dropped their weapons … thus they were given their pay as well as all the supplies promised] (SE 183).

Wolrath closes with the rhetorical question "Und ihr Teutschen/ die ihr solches wissest/ zweiffelt ihr noch/ schlaftt ihr noch/ empfindet ihr noch dieses alles nicht?" [And you Germans who know all about this, are you still doubting, still sleeping, are you still not aware of any of this?]. Frischmuth responds, with audible resignation, "Mit solchen Klagen werden wir heute nichts ändern; sondern unsers Theils/ Gott anbefehlen müssen" [With such complaints we will not change anything, all we can do is recommend ourselves to God]. Still, one should not lose one's courage; God will provide.[40]

On this note, the two friends end their wide-ranging conversation, one that began with an unexpected reunion in the face of a threatening Turkish invasion and meandered widely across German and European politics in response to this threat. Over the course of this extensive dialogue, the reader is forced to weigh the friends' divergent opinions on topical matters, such as the reliability of the media and the nature of the Turkish threat, but never presented with a one-sided argument alone, nor simply confirmed in his or her prejudices. In this way, Francisci employs ambiguity to produce what, under the circumstances, one might be tempted to call a (relatively) fair and balanced portrayal of controversial subjects.

Bibliography

Burbank, Jane, Fredrick Cooper. *Empires in World History: Power and the Politics of Difference*. Princeton/Oxford: Princeton UP, 2010.

Dünnhaupt, Gerhard. "Das Oevre des Erasmus Francisci (1627–1694) und sein Einfluß auf die deutsche Literatur." *Argenis* 2 (1978): 317–22.

Dünnhaupt, Gerhard. "Erasmus Francisci: Ein Nürnberger Polyhistor des siebzehnten Jahrhunderts. Biographie und Bibliographie." *Philobiblon: Eine Vierteljahsschrift für Buch- und Graphiksammler* 19 (1975): 275–303.

Forster, Edward Seymour. "Foreword." Karl A. Roider, ed. *The Turkish Letters of Ogier Ghiselin de Busbecq*. Baton Rouge: Louisiana State University Press, 1927/2005.

Francisci, Erasmus. *Der blutig-lang=gereitzte/ endlich Sieghafft=entzündte/ Adler=Blitz/ Wider den Glantz dess barbarischen Sebels/ und Mord=Brandes*. Nuremberg: Johann Andreas Endters Seel. Söhne, 1684.

---

40   "Man muß den Muth nicht verloren geben: Gott wird uns beystehen/ und die Wenigkeit unserer Anzahl durch das Heerlager seiner H. Engel ersetzen" [One must not abandon courage: God will stand by us filling the dearth or our numbers with the multitude of his angels] (103).

Francisci, Erasmus. *Die herandringende Türcken=Gefahr: Das ist; Wohlgemeinte/ doch invorgreiffliche Erinnerung/ in was hochbesorgtem und gefährlichem Zustande/ unser liebes Vatterland Deutscher Nation/ und das gantze Heil. Römische Reich jetziger Zeit stecke.* Nuremberg, 1663.

Graf, Tobias. *The Sultan's Renegades: Christian-European Converts to Islam and the Making of the Ottoman Elite, 1575–1610.* Oxford: Oxford University Press, 2015.

Schock, Flemming. "Gespräch und Zerstreuung. Mechanismen barocken Unterhaltungswissens am Beispiel Erasmus Franciscis (1624–1697)." *DAPHNIS* 44 (2016): 320–39.

Taverner, Paul P. *Keiserliche Botschafft/ An die Ottomannische Pforte. Welche auff Befehl Ihrer Röm. Keis. Maj. Leopoldus des I. Der hochgebohrene Herr/ Herr Walter Leßlie/ ... Anfangs in Lateinischer Sprache von P. Paul Tavernern/ Jesuitern ... aus eigener Erfahrung beschrieben/ nunmehro aber/ Dem Teutschliebenden Leser zum besten verteuschet. durch B. Z. v. W.* Breslau: Joh. Ad. Kästner, 1680.

Williams, Gerhild Scholz. *Mediating Culture in the Seventeenth-Century German Novel: Eberhard Werner Happel, 1647–1690.* Ann Arbor: Michigan University Press, 2014.

Williams, Gerhild Scholz. *Ottoman Eurasia in Early Modern German Literature: Cultural Translations (Francisci, Happel, Speer).* Ann Arbor Michigan University Press, 2021.

Wrede, Martin. "Die ausgezeichnete Nation: Identitätsstiftung im Reich Leopolds I. in Zeiten von Türkenkrieg und Türkensieg, 1663–1699." In *Das Bild des Feindes: Konstruktion von Antagonismen und Kulturtransfer im Zeitalter der Türkenkriege (Ostmitteleuropa, Italien und Osmanisches Reich)*, edited by Eckhard Leuschner and Thomas Wünsch, 19–33. Berlin: Mann Verlag, 2013.

CHAPTER 3

The Translation of Horace's *Odes* by Andreas Heinrich Bucholtz

Victoria Gutsche

In 1639, Andreas Heinrich Bucholtz published the first German translation of the first book of Horace's *Odes*, with the title *Erstes Verdeutschtes/ und mit kurtzen Nothen erklärtes Odenbuch Des vortreflichen* [sic] *Römischen Poeten Q. Horatius Flaccus*.[1] Bucholtz, who was soon followed by other translators of Horace, such as Johann Bohemus (1643) or, a little later, Gotthilf Flamin Weidner (1690),[2] is thus at the beginning of an intensive discourse with Horace—which, however, did not really gain momentum until the eighteenth century.[3] This first translation of the *Odes* into the German vernacular has so far only been insufficiently recognized by literary scholars. Only Ingeborg Springer-Strand has examined Bucholtz's translation of Horace in more detail, in 1977, yielding important conclusions. Unfortunately, however, her efforts did not initiate an in-depth discussion.[4] In response to this lack of wider attention, the present study analyzes Bucholtz's translation of the *Odes* in more detail—inspired by and based on Springer-Strand's study. The aim of this paper is therefore not only to shed light on a work by Bucholtz that is largely unknown today but also to supplement the broader discussion of the German translation of classical texts at the beginning of the seventeenth century.

Horace's influence on Western literature should not be underestimated. Three aspects are important for understanding Bucholtz's book of odes: (1) his poems provided fundamental ethical insights into both Christian and non-Christian moral doctrine; (2) he was also recognized as a school author at a very early point, and the *Odes* were a mainstay of the early school curriculum; and (3) he created essential paradigms for the emergence of poetic self-confidence and for the definition of the role of poetry in society.[5] Propertius

---

1   Bucholtz, 1639a.
2   Bohemus, 1643; Weidner, 1690. For other translations, see Leonhardt, 2003: 333.
3   Pietsch, 1988: 7; Leonhardt, 2003: 323.
4   Springer-Strand, 1977: 458–68. Also worth mentioning is the study by Joseph, 1930, who is mainly interested in the style and poetic form of the translations. However, due to his obvious value judgements, this study is to be approached with caution. Joseph, 1930.
5   Baldo, 2010: 374.

and Ovid, for example, used Horace to express their high self-esteem as poets. For the seventeenth century, the ode "Exegi monumentum aere perennius" at the end of the third book of *Carmina*, which Martin Opitz integrated into his *Weltliche Poemata* (1644) in an equally prominent position—namely, at the end of the first book of the second part—is particularly noteworthy.[6] In this ode, which functions as a sphragis, Horace sets himself a monument as a poet, proclaiming the eternal fame of his work:

> Exegi monumentum aere perennius
> regalique situ pyramidum altius,
> quod non imber edax, non aquilo impotens
> possit diruere aut innumerabilis
> annorum series et fuga temporum.[7]

> [I have erected a monument more durable than bronze,
> Loftier than the regal pile of pyramids,
> that cannot be destroyed either by
> corroding rains or the tempestuous North wind,
> or the endless passage of the years,
> or the flight of centuries.][8]

Opitz's inclusion of Horace's self-confident statement in his collection also articulates the self-confident positioning of the modern poet in competition with classical literature. Like Horace, whose prediction was to prove true—he was an undisputed authority for centuries, especially for European poets—the modern poet like Opitz also proclaims eternity for his work. Thus, when Bucholtz translates the *Odes* of the vates Horatius, he implicitly claims eternal fame and, at the same time, through his translation, follows in the footsteps of Martin Opitz, whom he admired. Furthermore, the choice of the object of translation no longer has to be justified in view of Horace's authority.

Horace's texts in general, and the *Odes* in particular, have been read continuously—although not always with the same intensity—since ancient times, and European lyric poetry has referred in many ways to the form and content of the Horatian odes and epodes. Furthermore, Horace has been consistently represented in the European school curricula.[9] As Anja Stadeler

---

6 For Opitz's translation of the ode, see Ammon, 2008.
7 Horace, 2004: 216–17.
8 Alexander, 1999: 150.
9 Baldo, 2010: 375.

states that this is certainly also due to the fact that Horace's texts themselves already contain a didactic moment, as he often turns to young readers and presents himself as "praeceptor artis poeticae, philosophiae, armoris" and so on, making the text very useful for teaching.[10] The first known commentary on Horace, by Porphyrio, from the third century, served not only as a scholarly explanation of the texts but, above all, as an aid for reading Horace at school,[11] and later commentaries, such as those by Cristoforo Landin (1482) and Denis Lambin (1561), followed this example.[12] Especially in the Middle Ages, primarily in the tenth and eleventh centuries, Horace was an obligatory subject at school,[13] where his texts were interpreted in Christian terms. This is, of course, not surprising: students of Horace during this and later periods were Christians. According to Karsten Friis-Jensen, this attitude was "most likely a conscious pedagogical strategy."[14] Friis-Jensen points out that in the Middle Ages the *Odes* in particular gained prominence by virtue of their inclusion in a large number of commentaries and manuscripts, as well as the fact that they often stood at the beginning of the manuscripts.[15] Another "sign of Horace's popularity is a large number of quotations from all his works found in almost every genre of medieval Latin literature" and "the numerous imitations of his poems found in quantitative Latin poetry."[16] Even later, Horace does not lose his popularity: During the fourteenth century and the Renaissance, Petrarch was—besides Angelo Poliziano, Ludovico Ariosto, and Dante Alighieri—particularly noteworthy in this regard: "Petrarch loved Horace, not least his *Odes*; he wrote a letter to Horace in the form of a Horatian ode, and he imitated Horace's Epistles in his own Latin verse letters. There are also clear borrowings from Horace in [...] the Canzoniere."[17]

For the entire sixteenth century, the *Odes* were the model of a poetry book and were discussed widely throughout Spain and France—facilitated in large part by La Pléiade. In this context, Horace was no longer simply translated but imitated.[18] The same is true for Germany: *Libri Odarum quattuor, cum Epodo, et Saeculari Carmine*, by Conrad Celtis, who called himself the German

---

10   Stadeler, 2015: 52.
11   Tischer, 2006: 125.
12   Stadeler, 2015.
13   "In western Europe Horace was among the most widely read Roman poets throughout the Middle Ages," Friis-Jensen, 2007: 293.
14   Friis-Jensen, 2007: 294.
15   Friis-Jensen, 2007: 293–94.
16   Friis-Jensen, 2007: 296.
17   Friis-Jensen, 2007: 299. See also McGann, 2007: 305–17; Baldo, 2010: 378–79.
18   Baldo, 2010: 380–81; McGann, 2007: 306.

Horace, were published, posthumously, in 1513 and initiated a long tradition of neo-Latin Horace reception.[19] Celtis, however, like Georg Fabricius and Paul (Schede) Melissus, wrote in Latin, which means that reception of Horace in Germany was primarily neo-Latin one. Although there were a few authors—for example, Martin Opitz and Georg Rodolf Weckherlin—who published odes in German and who, based on and oriented to translations by Ronsard and the poets of La Plèiade, followed Horace and Pindar. However, there were no German translations of Horace, as there were into Italian, Spanish, English, and French.

Consequently, Andreas Heinrich Bucholtz, who published the first German translation of the first book of *Odes*, in 1639, was not able to refer to any vernacular models. Bucholtz does not translate Horace literally at all; he uses far more verses than Horace, adds commentaries to the odes to make them useful for students, and clarifies supposedly unclear passages in the original; in other words, Bucholtz presents an interpretive Horace translation.[20] This puts him in good company at the beginning of the seventeenth century. Franz Josef Worstbrock assumed in 1999 that in the Middle Ages the concept of reproducing content was dominant (*sensus de sensu*), the only reference for the narrator were the themes and topics themselves and the classical, authoritative text should be surpassed by one's own artistic achievement (*aemulatio*).[21] Humanism was dominated by the practice of formal *imitatio*, a "methodological translation," ("methodische Übersetzung")[22]—that is, translation of the original as accurately as possible (*verbum e verbo*). This model soon came under criticism as reductionist, and recent research has shown that it does not apply to the sixteenth and seventeenth centuries, as it does not reflect the diversity of different types of translation in the Middle Ages and early modern times.[23] In fact, as Regina Töpfer, Johannes Klaus Kipf, and Jörg Robert have stated, different concepts of translation existed side by side, which made classical works available in multiple vernacular versions and thus played an essential part in establishing German as a literary and scholarly language. The act of translation produced an adaptation of the source text: translators reduced or expanded the classical versions and updated or transposed their sources into other current literary forms and genre contexts in order to meet the requirements of the occasion and the expectations of their audiences.[24] In addition—regardless

---

19   For Conrad Celtis see Auhagen, 2000.
20   Springer-Strand, 1977: 463.
21   Worstbrock, 1999: 128–42.
22   Worstbrock, 1999: 130.
23   Töpfer et al., 2017: 11–14.
24   Töpfer et al., 2017: 12–24.

of whether the translator followed the principle *verbum e verbo* or *sensus de sensu*—world knowledge of antiquity was conveyed,[25] for example through the commentaries and by adapting classical texts for the school. Consideration of the intended audience, adaptation of the source text according to the capabilities and requirements of the German language, and, thus, the proclamation of German as a literary language alongside the transmission of ancient world knowledge: these are the most important characteristics of Bucholtz's translation.[26]

In the preface to his translation of Horace, Bucholtz explains and justifies the most important principles of his translation and argues for a programmatic approach, as formulated by Martin Opitz. He counters the accusation that German is a barbaric language, which, unlike the Greek, Latin, Italian, Spanish and French language, is neither "[der] Zierligkeit fähig" [capable of gracefulness] nor "mit Liebligkeiten vnd prächtigen Worten außgeputzt vnd geschmückt" [decorated with loveliness and sumptuous words].[27] Worse still, according to Bucholtz, is that such false judgments are also transferred to the nature of the Germans themselves:

> Insonderheit hat man sie zur Poeterey gar zu vndüchtig geschätzet/ [...]. Dieses hat man so fest war zu seyn gegläubet/ daß man vns Teutschen auch eine grobe vngeschickte Seele/ einen dünstigen verstopfften Verstandt/ eine schwere vndeutliche Zunge/ ein vnhöffliches barbarisches Leben vnd Wesen hat zumessen/ und gleich auffdringen wollen [...].[28]

> [Above all, the German language was judged to be incapable of poetry [...]. It was believed so strongly/ that we Germans were also accused of a coarse and clumsy soul/ a damp clogged mind/ a heavy unclear tongue/ an impolite barbaric life and being.][29]

In contrast to this, Bucholtz wants to show with his translation that German is well suited as a literary language—indeed, that German is even an "[e]dle[...]/ mächtige[...] vnd vberaußreiche[...] Sprach/ welche billich vnter die Vollkommensten zurechnen" [noble / powerful and extremely rich language/ which can be counted among the most perfect"];[30] no other language is

---

25   Töpfer et al., 2017: 17.
26   See also Springer-Strand, 1977: 459–60.
27   Bucholtz, 1639a: 6.
28   Bucholtz, 1639a: 6.
29   Transl. V.G.
30   Bucholtz, 1639a: 6.

superior to German, with the sole exception of Hebrew, as the holy language.[31] Luther, Bucholtz argues, already demonstrated this with his Bible translation. Bucholtz is thus primarily concerned with German as a literary language, which he tries to defend against widespread accusations from humanist scholars that German is an inferior language from a grammatical, lexical, phonetic, literary-rhetorical, and historical point of view. To this end, he points out that there are now sufficient examples to prove that German is a literary language—however, he does not provide concrete evidence, making only vague mention of "such excellent speakers,"[32] whom he does not want to name out of modesty. This is, of course, a well-known topos. In addition to these unnamed authors, the chancellery language [Kanzleisprache] also shows that German is an excellent language.[33] Here Bucholtz directly follows the argumentation of Martin Opitz, who also regarded the chancellery language of Saxony as an example of the best German and tried to promote vernacular literary and linguistic traditions.[34] Bucholtz is also in complete agreement with Opitz when he criticizes the mixing of languages and pleads for a pure German—that is, a German without foreign words or words borrowed from Latin or French.[35] Although he states that there is a lot of bad poetry—again in agreement with Opitz, who also argues that there is too much inferior poetry that discredits the genre altogether[36]—a particular thorn in his side is the excessive use of auxiliary verbs. Nevertheless, this does not contradict the fact that German had already attained "Vollkommenheit" [perfection].[37] In fact, the focus of the preface is an apology of the German language. However, Bucholtz not only aligns himself with his great role model, Opitz, whom he names by name,[38] but he also represents the agenda of the early modern language societies in a broader sense. There is no evidence that Bucholtz hoped to be accepted into such a society on the basis of his Horace translation; as far as is known, Bucholtz was not a member of any language society.

Only at the very end of the preface does Bucholtz comment on Horace and his translation of the *Odes*; the majority is devoted to defending German as a literary language. The preface to Bucholtz's translation of the *Ars poetica* is very similar. Here, too, the emphasis is on an apology of German as a literary

---

31   Bucholtz, 1639a: 7.
32   Bucholtz, 1639a: 7.
33   Bucholtz, 1639a: 7.
34   Robert, 2012: 32.
35   Bucholtz, 1639a: 8.
36   Opitz, 1624: Biij^v.
37   Bucholtz, 1639a: 8.
38   Bucholtz, 1639a: 9.

language. For example, according to Bucholtz the cultivation and elevation of German is a "dem Vatterlande [...] schuldige Pflicht" [patriotic duty].[39] The fact that the apology of German takes up much more space than the explanation of the translation is important with regard to the form and structure of the translation of the *Odes*, since Horace's odes were used by him first of all to prove that German is a literary language. Bucholtz is not interested in presenting a literal translation of the *Odes* or in transferring the aesthetic form of the ode to vernacular poetry, especially since the complicated verses and strophic forms of the Horatian *Odes* could hardly be reproduced adequately in the German language. Rather, he uses a wide variety of forms in his rendering of the *Odes*.[40] A guiding principle cannot be recognized, and Bucholtz does not explain why he chooses a particular meter or rhyme scheme over others. Only twice in his commentary does he briefly touch on the iambic and the dactylic, and notes that one meter is more suitable for serious objects and the other for cheerful ones.[41] He rewrites the Alcaic, Sapphic, and Asclepiadean strophes of Horace in very different ways; alexandrines and *vers commun* and other rhyming schemes are used in their stead, and two odes even become sonnets. The term *ode*, therefore, refers simply to a singable poem in Bucholtz's work. The translated odes and sonnets are meant to prove that the German language is literary and not inferior to the French or Italian languages.

Bucholtz does not explain why he translates Horace and not another classical author. Of course, given Horace's authoritative status, there was little need to explain why he should be translated. As mentioned before, Horace is one of the undisputed authorities, especially since Opitz himself translates an ode of Horace. Nevertheless, the fact that Bucholtz refrains from an explanation also has the consequence that, to a certain extent, the translated classical text becomes arbitrary; a translation of, for example, Pindar would also have been possible. Against this background, Bucholtz is not explicitly concerned with the *Odes* of Horace but, rather, with proving German's capabilities as a literary and scholarly language.

Furthermore, the translation transmits an ancient knowledge system into the early modern era. Even if Bucholtz does not explicitly mention it, his belief in the alterity between antiquity—or, more precisely, the *Odes* of Horace—and the present is obvious. His renditions are embellished with numerous additions and adds explanations of countries, cities, or gods in the commentaries. Thus, he travels well-worn paths of Horace reception and uses procedures

---

39   Bucholtz, 1639b: 11.
40   See also Joseph, 1930: 27–35.
41   Bucholtz, 1639b: 72, 18.

already known from antiquity, explaining the texts through commentaries to teach those "die derennoch nicht sonderlich erfahren seyn/ damit sie den Unterricht zugleich haben mögen" [who have not yet experienced very much/ so that they may at the same time have a lesson].[42] He also updates the original text and adapts it to the present. For example, in the ode 12 he translates Horace with the following verses:

> [...] unde vocalem temere insecutae
>   Orphea silvae
> arte materna rapidos morantem
> fluminum lapsus celerisque ventos,
> blandum et auritas fidibus canoris
>   ducere quercus.[43]

> [...] da dem Orpheus, als er liblich sang
> gantze Wälder frisch sind nachgelauffen/
> da ihn hört der Winde Gunst
> singen nach der Mutter Kunst.
> Da die grossen Eichen ohne Sinn
> gleich den Menschen ihr Gehör empfingen/
> fleißig zu vernehmen gingen hin/
> wie er seine Laute liesse klingen/
> die er gleich auff die Mannier
> pflag zu spielen wie Gautier.[44]

> [(...) as Orpheus, when he sang sweetly
> entire forests followed him freshly
> as the favor of the wind hears him
> Singing in the way of his mother's art.
> As the great senseless oaks
> like men received their hearing/
> were going to hear diligently/
> how he let his lute sound/
> which he used to play
> in the same way as Gautier.][45]

---

42 Bucholtz, 1639a: 11.

43 Horace, 2004: 44–46.

44 Bucholtz, 1639a: 53–54.

45 Transl. V.G.

Bucholtz's inclusion in his translation of the comparison with Ennemond
Gaultier, a French lutenist and composer, who was one of the masters of the
seventeenth-century French lute school, is a contemporary allusion that is
absent from the original. He also adds a reference to "Mußqueten Knall" [boom
of a musket].[46]

Bucholtz therefore not only comments on and interprets the classical texts
within the comments; he also does so through his translation. His translation contains about 80% more verses than the original,[47] a discrepancy that
becomes especially clear when Bucholtz sometimes translates Horace literally
in the commentaries. Thus, it might be said that Bucholtz does not function as
a translator here but, rather, as an "interpreter":

> Es wolle aber der günstige Leser wissen/ daß ich nicht bloß die Wörter
> zu vbersetzen mich beflissen habe/ welches auch gar vnzierlich klingen
> würde/ sondern nach dem meine Neygungen sich gehäuffet/ habe ich in
> vnterschiedlichen/ ja fast allen Orten zugleich ein Außleger der tieffen
> verborgenen vnd kurtzen Reden vnsers Poeten seyn wollen/ zu welchem
> Ende ich öffters einem [sic] oder mehr Versse [sic] habe fliegen lassen/
> welche mehr zur Außlegung gemeinet seyn/ als daß sie im Lateinischen
> Text ausdrücklich solten können gezeiget werden.[48]

> [But the reader should know that since I have not only translated the
> words, which would not sound elegant at all, I have yielded to my inclina-
> tion. I wanted to be an interpreter of the deep, hidden and short speeches
> of our poet at almost any given passage. To this end I have often included
> one or more verses which are intended more for interpretation than that
> they can be explicitly shown in the Latin text.][49]

The following presents another example of how Bucholtz interprets the original and how his translation always follows the postulate of clarity, as Ingeborg
Springer-Strand has also stated.[50] To illustrate the extent to which Bucholtz
extends the classical text with verbose paraphrases, the original ode and the
translation are quoted in full length.

---

46   Bucholtz, 1639a: 18.
47   Springer-Strand, 1977: 461.
48   Bucholtz, 1639a: 11. Springer-Strand, 1977: 461, quotes the same passage from the preface.
49   Transl. V.G.
50   Springer-Strand, 1977: 458–68.

Parcus deorum cultor et infrequens,
insanientis dum sapientiae
consultus erro, nunc retrorsum
vela dare atque iterare cursus
cogor relictos. namque Diespiter
igni corusco nubila dividens
plerumque, per purum tonantis
egit equos volucremque currum,
quo bruta tellus et vaga flumina,
quo Styx et invisi horrida Taenari
sedes Atlanteusque finis
concutitur. valet ima summis
mutare et insignem attenuat deus
obscura promens: hinc apicem rapax
Fortuna cum stridore acuto
sustulit, hic posuisse gaudet.[51]

Die XXXIV. Ode.
Von Gottes Allmacht vnd des Glücks Verenderung.

1. Ich der ich sonst bißher mich habe bey der Schaar
die Gott zu Lob vnd Ehr zusamen kommen war
als ein verruchter Mensch mich selten lassen sehen
hab' in der Weißheit/ als im tollen Wahn geirrt/
darinnen ich doch kunt' als wolgelehrt bestehen/
befinde/ daß hiedurch ich gäntzlich bin verwirrt/
so/ daß ich auch mein Schiff zurücke lassen wehen/
vnd muß den ersten Weg auffs newe wider gehen.
2. Dann Gott der hohe Gott/ der sonst/ wann wolcken sein/
den Donner hören/ vnd des helle Blitzes Schein
vns Menschen sehen lest; hatt nechst bey klaren Tagen
den Wetterwagen vnd die Pferde hergeführt/
daß auch die Erde selbst sich fürchten must vnd zagen/
das Wasser vnd die Hell mit schrecken sein gerührt
es konts der Hellenschlund am Taenarus nicht tragen/
des Atlas letztes End' ist mit hiedurch zuschlagen.
3. Gott kan das hohe bald verkehren/ daß es felt/
vnd was zu vnterst ist/ den Oberplatz behelt/

---

51   Horace, 2004: 84–85.

was treflich wird geschätzt/ muß/ wenn er wil/ verstäuben/
was nichtig vnd gering vnd elendt ist geacht/
das hebet er empor; es pflegets so zu treiben
das Glück das alles rafft; dz von dem stolzen pracht
nach seinem starcken Schlag nur Koth muß vberbleiben
beym andern setzt es Grund/ da muß die Gunst bekleiben.[52]

[1. I, who up to now have rarely been seen
as a wicked person in the crowd
that had come together to praise and honor God
have erred in wisdom/ like in foolish madness/
in which I could pass as a scholarly man
I think/ that I am completely confused by this/
so/ that I also have to let my ship blow back/
and have to go the first way again.
2. For God, the high God/ who usually/ when it is cloudy
let thunder be heard and let us men see bright lightning;
has at last on clear days
brought the weather wagon and the horses/
that even the earth itself must fear and despair/
the water and the brightness are agitated by terror
the hell-mouth at Taenarus could not bear it/
the last end of Atlas is shattered by this.
3. God can turn the high quickly upside down/
and what is at the bottom/ comes to the top/
What is highly appreciated/ must/ if he wants/ be crushed/
what is trivial and low and miserable must be respected.
He lifts it up; the fortune which takes everything
does it this way; that from the proud splendor
nothing but excrement must remain after its powerful stroke
at the other it sets the ground/ where the favor must remain.][53]

It is obvious how much Bucholtz has expanded the original: To name just one example, he clearly amplifies the discourse on the radical overthrow of everything great (i.e., the *vanitas* theme). More important, however, is the translator's attempt to clarify any ambiguities. Horace's ode I, 34 deals with how the speaker converts to the old faith through the experience of a terrifying thunderstorm.

---

52   Bucholtz, 1639a: 108–9.
53   Transl. V.G.

The original is usually read as the confession of Horace, who turns away from Epicureanism and embraces the old belief in the gods. However, the original text is ambiguous and has provoked numerous interpretations. There is no need to discuss the ode in detail, but it should be noted—following Walter Pötscher[54]—that it remains unclear why and whether the conversion actually takes place. A true Epicurean would not undergo conversion on account of a mere thunderstorm. However, the thunderstorm as depicted is actually impossible, because it takes place in the clear sky. Though even this is not clear when it is stated that such a thunderstorm "plerumque" [usually] is impossible.[55] The ode by Horace is quite ambivalent. Bucholtz eradicates this ambivalence in his interpretive translation: Even the title, "Von Gottes Allmacht vnd des Glücks Verenderung" [Of the omnipotence of God and the change of fortune],[56] indicates that it is a conversion; the beginning of the ode, in which the speaker describes his confusion, is also more detailed in Bucholtz's version. The unexpected lightning becomes a fact in Bucholtz's ode, proving God's omnipotence, and the speaker speaks in Bucholtz's translation as a believer in God. The ode, in other words, becomes an invocation of God and an invitation to repent in the face of God's omnipotence.[57]

In conclusion, the following can be noted: Bucholtz does not translate the *Odes* of Horace literally or try to imitate the Latin source; he instead interprets and adapts the *Odes* to the cultural-historical context. Against the background of the accusation that German is a barbaric language, he tries, following Martin Opitz, to prove with his translation that German is a fully fledged literary language and that it is capable of poetic and oratorical style second to none. The translation of the *Odes* must be seen in the broader context of language education and discipline as well as cultural transfer, which was promoted by the early modern language societies. Bucholtz primarily addresses students. He claims to be a teacher of German, German literature, and Horace's texts and thus occupying a role similar to that of Celtis. However, Bucholtz offers neither instruction nor even rules; instead, he provides practical examples, showing the manifold possibilities of the shaping of the German language. They are strongly oriented toward contemporary poetics, reflecting discussions not only about translation practice but also about German as a literary language.[58] Against the background of the phase of transition at the beginning of the

---

54   Pötscher, 1991: 822–39.
55   Pötscher, 1991: 828–31.
56   Bucholtz, 1639a: 108.
57   See also Krasser, 1996.
58   Leonhardt, 2003: 332, makes a similar argument.

century, the translation functions as a proclamation of a new era in literary history.

Nevertheless, the impact of Buchholtz's translation of the *Odes* has not been very significant—there was not even a second edition.[59] The same is true for Johann Bohemus's *Deß Hochberühmten Lateinischen Poetens Q. Horatii Flacci Vier Bücher Odarum/ oder Gesänge*, in which translations by his students are collected and which only had one further edition. Until 1820—as Jürgen Leonhardt notes—no fewer than thirty authors tried to translate the *Odes*, which "never led to a real result."[60]

Bibliography

Alexander, Sidney. *The Complete Odes and Satires of Horace* (Princeton, New Jersey: Princeton University Press, 1999).

Ammon, Frieder von. "Bewegung auf den Tafeln der Weltpoesie: Horaz-Übertragungen von Martin Opitz und Christian Morgenstern." *Parapluie. Elektronische Zeitschrift für Kulturen, Künste, Literaturen* 25 (2008), https://parapluie.de/archiv/uebertragungen/resonanzen/.

Auhagen, Ulrike, Eckard Lefèvre, and Eckart Schäfer, eds. *Horaz und Celtis* (Tübingen: Gunter Narr, 2000).

Baldo, Gianluigi. "Horaz (Quintus Horatius Flaccus). Carmina." In *Die Rezeption der antiken Literatur. Kulturhistorisches Werklexikon*, ed. Christine Walde (Stuttgart: Metzler, 2010), 373–96.

Bohemus, Johann. *Deß Hochberühmten Lateinischen Poetens Q. Horatii Flacci Vier Bücher Odarum/ oder Gesänge/ in Teutsche Poesi übersetzet* (Dresden: Bergen, 1643).

Breuer, Dieter. "Der Streit ueber die Frage, 'wo das beste Teutsch zu finden.'" In *Konfession und Sprache in der Frühen Neuzeit. Interdisziplinäre Perspektiven*, eds. Jürgen Macha, Anna Maria Balbach, and Sarah Horstkamp (Münster: Waxmann, 2012), 31–44.

Bucholtz, Andreas Heinrich. *Erstes Verdeutschtes/ und mit kurtzen Nothen erklärtes Odenbuch Des vortreflichen Römischen Poeten Q. Horatius Flaccus* (Rinteln: Lucius, 1639a).

---

59   In older works sometimes a second edition of the first book of the *Odes* is given for the year 1659. See, for example, Degen, 1794: 193. However, this edition cannot be verified. Possibly, it is a confusion with the second edition of Lukian's translation, which was published in the same year. See Bucholtz, 1659.

60   Leonhardt, 2003: 332.

Bucholtz, Andreas Heinrich. *Verteutschte vnd mit kurtzen Noten erklärte Poetereykunst Des vortreflichen Römischen Poeten Q. Horatius Flaccus* (Rinteln: Lucius, 1639b).

Bucholtz, Andreas Heinrich. *Lucian von Samosata Warhafftige Geschichte* [...]/ *Auß dem Griechischen ins Teutsche ubersetzet/ und mit kurtzen Nohten erkläret* (Rinteln: Lucius, 1659).

Degen, Johann Friedrich. *Versuch einer vollständigen Litteratur der deutschen Uebersetzungen der Römer*. Vol. 1 (Altenburg: Richter, 1794).

Friis-Jensen, Karsten. "The Reception of Horace in the Middle Ages." In *The Cambridge Companion to Horace*, ed. Stephen Harrison (Cambridge: Cambridge University Press, 2007), 291–304.

Horace. *Odes and Epodes*. Ed. and trans. Niall Rudd. Loeb Classical Library 33 (Cambridge, MA: Harvard University Press, 2004).

Joseph, Albrecht. *Die Oden des Horaz in deutschen Übersetzungen aus dem 17. Jahrhundert. Ein Beitrag zur Analyse des barocken Sprachstils* (Rottach: L. Uhlschmid, 1930).

Krasser, Helmut. "Büßer, Spötter oder Künstler. Zur Interpretationsgeschichte der Horazode 1,34." In *Zeitgenosse Horaz. Der Dichter und seine Leser seit zwei Jahrtausenden*, eds. Helmut Krasser and Ernst A. Schmidt (Tübingen: Gunter Narr, 1996), 311–43.

Leonhardt, Jürgen. "Ramlers Übersetzungen antiker Texte." In *Urbanität als Aufklärung. Karl Wilhelm Ramler und die Kultur des 18. Jahrhunderts*, eds. Laurenz Lütteken, Ute Pott, and Carsten Zelle (Göttingen: Wallstein, 2003), 323–55.

McGann, Michael. "The Reception of Horace in the Renaissance." In *The Cambridge Companion to Horace*, ed. Stephen Harrison (Cambridge: Cambridge University Press, 2007), 305–17.

Opitz, Martin. *Buch von der Deutschen Poeterey. In welchem alle ihre Eigenschafft und zugehör gründtlich erzehlet/ vnd mit exempeln ausgeführet wird* (Brieg, Breslau: Gründer, Müller, 1624).

Pietsch, Wolfgang J. *Friedrich von Hagedorn und Horaz—Untersuchungen zur Horaz-Rezeption in der deutschen Literatur des 18. Jahrhunderts* (Hildesheim: Olms, 1988).

Pötscher, Walter. "Horaz, Carm. 1, 34 und die persönliche Religiosität des Autors." *Latomus* 50 (4) (1991), 822–39.

Robert, Jörg. "Vetus Poesis—nova ratio carminum. Martin Opitz und der Beginn der Deutschen Poeterey." In *Maske und Mosaik. Poetik, Sprache, Wissen im 16. Jahrhundert*, eds. Jan-Dirk Müller and Jörg Robert (Münster: Lit, 2007), 397–440.

Springer-Strand, Ingeborg. "Der Übersetzer als 'Außleger.' Zu Andreas Heinrich Bucholtz's Übertragung der Oden des Horaz." *MLN* 92 (3) (1977), 458–68.

Stadeler, Anja. *Horazrezeption in der Renaissance: Strategien der Horazkommentierung bei Cristoforo Landino und Denis Lambin* (Berlin: De Gruyter, 2015).

Tischer, Ute. *Die zeitgeschichtliche Anspielung in der antiken Literaturerklärung. Leipziger Studien zur klassischen Philologie* (Tübingen: Gunter Narr, 2006).

Töpfer, Regina, Johannes Klaus Kipf, and Jörg Robert. "Einleitung. Humanistische Antikenübersetzung und frühneuzeitliche Poetik in Deutschland (1450–1620)." In *Humanistische Antikenübersetzung und frühneuzeitliche Poetik in Deutschland (1450–1620)*, eds. Regina Töpfer, Johannes Klaus Kipf, and Jörg Robert (Berlin: De Gruyter, 2017), 1–24.

Weidner, Gotthilf Flamin. *Die Lieder Des berühmten Lateinischen Poeten Q. Horatius Flaccus/ in Hoch-Teutsche Reime übersetzet* (Leipzig: Meyer, 1690).

Worstbrock, Franz-Josef. "Wiedererzählen und Übersetzen." In *Mittelalter und frühe Neuzeit. Übergänge, Umbrüche und Neuansätze*, ed. Walter Haug (Tübingen: Max Niemeyer, 1999), 128–42.

CHAPTER 4

Cabeza de Vaca's (Mostly) Non-Iberian Offspring: Images of the "Other" in (Some of) the Other European Accounts

Dwight E. Raak TenHuisen

1 Introduction

Readers familiar with the now extensive bibliography on Alvar Núñez Cabeza de Vaca are aware of the widely differing interpretations regarding the descriptions of indigenous peoples in Cabeza de Vaca's *Relación*. The interpretations that scholars offer of Cabeza de Vaca himself vary even more greatly. As Carlos Jáuregui points out in his article "Cabeza de Vaca, Mala Cosa y las vicissitudes de la extrañeza," Cabeza de Vaca has been presented by a large percentage of the critics as the "conquered conqueror" or the "peaceful conqueror," who, transculturated and moved by alterity, is no longer able to differentiate himself from the Other.[1] He therefore does not represent the indigenous peoples as monsters, cannibals, sodomites, or savages in cahoots with the devil but, rather, as empathetic and humanitarian. Jáuregui posits that it is Cabeza de Vaca's empathy toward the indigenous that leads Rolena Adorno to describe him as Lascasista, but Jáuregui is not sympathetic to these readings, stating that the varying descriptions of the indigenous peoples in the *Relación* are actually not as empathetic as these critics state, and rather than disrupting classical distinctions between civilization and barbarism, Cabeza de Vaca's descriptions reiterate them. Along with other critics before him, Jáuregui points out that ultimately Cabeza de Vaca seeks to demonstrate in his text that he fulfilled the mission of the expedition and thereby facilitated the conquest, even if by peaceful means.[2]

As Jáuregui states, the descriptions of indigenous peoples that Cabeza de Vaca offers in his *Relación* are not always sympathetic. Several descriptions of the Other, in fact, could only have been read as classic examples of barbarism. As Dwight TenHuisen has argued, the descriptions of the indigenous peoples are directly related to the self that Cabeza de Vaca fashions throughout

---

1 Jáuregui, 2014.
2 Jáuregui, 2014: 422.

© KONINKLIJKE BRILL NV, LEIDEN, 2023 | DOI:10.1163/9789004682245_006

the text, a self that is depicted as going through the classic rites of passage described by Arnold van Gennep and Victor Turner.[3] As a captive on Malhado, Cabeza de Vaca separates himself from his culture (marked by his nakedness) and then enters a liminal state in which identity is in flux and opposites coexist; finally, he emerges with a new identity as a confessor saint. Early in the text, descriptions of the indigenous people are brief and limited to battle scenes. This paucity of description stands in contrast, however, to several lengthy passages describing in very positive terms the flora and fauna that the expedition encounters in Florida.

In the land betwixt and between that is the Island of Malhado, Cabeza de Vaca regularly juxtaposes opposites in the descriptions of the indigenous. In contrast to the earlier "Separation" section, the hagiographic "Transition" section contains many lengthy descriptions of native Americans, including their appearance, dress, dwellings, and eating habits, as well as rituals surrounding marriage, death, and treatment of the elderly. Critics seeking to discern a pattern in these descriptions have been puzzled, confused, and frustrated. Cabeza de Vaca does, in fact, make contradictory statements that can best be understood within the framework of the liminal state, which Alison Goddard Elliott argues in her book *Roads to Paradise: Reading the Lives of the Early Saints* is common to the ascetic saints.[4] The simultaneous presentation of opposites in the presentation of native Americans can be seen by juxtaposing excerpts showing solidarity (nurturing) with those showing division or desertion from each of three lengthy descriptive passages in the heart of the text. Within each of the passages, Cabeza de Vaca makes statements that appear to be completely positive and then follows them with questionable material related to something normally taboo, or, conversely, he makes extremely negative statements about something taboo, and then follows them with seemingly rational and positive explanations. In the first lengthy description of the indigenous people in the text, Cabeza de Vaca presents the Malhados as loving and nurturing, but he ends by explaining that their mourning customs result in starving their families to death.

> Es la gente del mundo que más aman a sus hijos y major tratamiento les hazen. Y quando acaesçe que a alguno se le muere el hijo, llóranle los padres y los parientes y todo el pueblo. Y el llanto dura un año cumplido, que cada día por la mañana antes que amanesca comiençan primero a llorar los padres, y tras esto todo el pueblo. Y esto mismo hazen

---

3   TenHuisen, 2005.
4   Goddard, 1987: 168–180, 204–209.

al mediodía y quando amaneçe. Y pasado un año que los han llorado, házenle las honrras del muerto y lávanse y límpianse del tizne que traen.

Otra costumbre ay, y es que quando algún hijo o hermano muere, en la casa donde muriere tres meses no buscan de comer, antes se dexan morir de hambre. Y los parientes y los vezinos les proven de lo que an de comer. Y como en el tiempo que aquí estuvimos murió tanta gente dellos, en las más casas avía muy gran hambre por guardar también su costumbre y çerimonia.[5]

[These people love their children more and treat them better than any other people in the world. And when it happens that one of their children dies, the parents and the relatives and all the rest of the people weep. And the weeping lasts a whole year, that is, each day in the morning before sunrise, first the parents begin to weep, and after this the entire community also weeps. And they do this at noon, and at daybreak. And after a year of mourning has passed, they perform the honors of the dead and wash and cleanse themselves of the ashes they wear. ... They have another custom, which is that when a child or a sibling dies, in the household in which the death occurs they cease to seek food for three months, but rather they allow themselves to starve. And their relatives and neighbors supply them with the food they are to eat. And because in the time we were there so many of them died, in most of the houses there was very great hunger in the effort to also keep their custom and ceremony.][6]

In the second extended description of the indigenous Other, Cabeza de Vaca begins with what seems to be scathingly negative details, and then provides a justification for murdering a child—to avoid incest or inbreeding.

Esto hazen éstos por una costumbre que tienen, y es, que matan sus mismos hijos por sueños, y a las hijas en nasçiendo las dexan comer a perros, y las echan por aí. La razón porque ellos lo hazen es, según ellos dizen, porque todos los de la tierra son sus enemigos y con ellos tienen continua guerra, y que si acaso casassen sus hijas, multiplicarían tanto sus enemigos que los subjetarían y tomarían, y por esta causa querían más matallas, que no que dellas mismas nasçiesse quien fuese su enemigo. Nosotros les diximos que porqué no las casavan con ellos mismos y también entre

5   Pautz and Adorno, 1999.
6   Pautz and Adorno, 1999: 109–11.

ellos. Dixeron que era cosa fea casarlas con sus parientes y que era muy mejor matarlas que darlas a su pariente ni a su enemigo.[7]

[These people do this because of a custom they have, and it is, that they kill their own children because of dreams, and when female children are born, they allow dogs to eat them, and cast them away from there. The reason they do this, according to what they say, is that all the people of the land are their enemies, and with them they have continual war, and that if by chance they should marry off their daughters, their enemies would multiply so much that they would be captured and enslaved by them, and for this reason they preferred rather to kill them, than that there be born of them those who would be their enemies. We asked them why they did not marry them themselves and also among one another. They said it was an ugly thing to marry them to their relatives, and that it was much better to kill them than to give them either to a relative or to an enemy.][8]

In the third and final detailed description of rites and customs, Cabeza de Vaca seems to present the most nurturing custom of all—nursing children for twelve years to ensure their survival. But this is quickly followed by the statement that they allow other people's children to die.

Desde la isla de Malhado todos los indios que hasta esta tierra vimos tienen por costumbre, desde el día que sus mugeres se sienten preñadas, no dormir juntos hasta que passen dos años que an criado los hijos, los quales maman hasta que son de edad de doze años, que ya entonçes están en edad que por sí saben buscar de comer. Preguntámosles que por qué los criavan assí, y dezían que por la mucha hambre que en la tierra avía que acontesçía muchas vezes, como nosotros veíamos, estar dos o tres días sin comer, y a las vezes quatro; y por esta causa los dexavan mamar porque en los tiempos de hambre no moriessen, y que ya que algunos escapassen, saldrían muy delicados y de pocas fuerças. Y si acaso acontesce caer enfermos algunos, déxanlos morir en aquellos campos si no es hijo, y todos los demás, si no pueden ir con ellos, se quedan, mas para llevar un hijo o hermano se cargan y lo llevan a cuestas.[9]

---

7   Pautz and Adorno, 1999: fol. 31ᵛ/136–fol. 32ʳ/138.
8   Pautz and Adorno, 1999: 137–39.
9   Pautz and Adorno, 1999: fol. 41ᵛ/176–fol. 42ʳ/178.

[From the island of Malhado to this land all the Indians whom we saw have as a custom, from the day their wives know they are pregnant, not to sleep with them until after two years of nurturing their children, who suckle until they are twelve years old, at which time they are of an age that by themselves they know how to search for food. We asked them why they raised them in this manner, and they said that because of the great hunger in the land it happened many times, as we had seen, that they went two or three days without eating, and sometimes four; and for this reason, they let their children suckle so that in times of hunger they would not die, since even if some should survive [without it], they would end up sickly and of little strength. And if by chance it happens that some fall ill, they leave them to die in those fields if it is not a child of their own, and all the rest, if they cannot go with them, remain, but in order to transport a child or a sibling, they carry them and bear them on their backs.][10]

After an interruption of some pages, Cabeza de Vaca adds that the same people who nurse their children for twelve years rape and beat women who happen to move after someone calls out "Who wants a drink?":

> Y quando las mugeres oyen estas bozes, luego se paran sin osarse mudar, y aunque estén mucho cargadas no osan hazer otra cosa. Y si acoaso alguna dellas se mueve, la deshonrran y la dan de palos, y con muy gran enojo derraman el agua que tienen (preparada) para bever.[11]

> [And when the women hear these shouts, they immediately stop without daring to move, and although they may be carrying heavy loads, they do not dare to do another thing. And if by chance one of them moves, they dishonor her and beat her with sticks and with very great rage they pour out the water that they have (prepared) for drinking.][12]

In all of these excerpts, we see not only some of the reiterations of classical barbarism that Jáuregui mentions but also the meeting of opposites characteristic of the liminal state.

---

10 Pautz and Adorno, 1999: 177–79.
11 Pautz and Adorno, 1999: fol. 44^{v}/188.
12 Pautz and Adorno, 1999: 189.

2   Hagiography

The internal "Transition" section of the *Relación* is also, as many have noted, imbued with hagiographic discourse, and, as Turner describes in his study of pilgrimages, throughout the *Relación* there is a general sacralization of the pilgrim route. From wandering in the wilderness to the burning bush to the feeding of the thousands, or from the many miracle healings to the resurrection of a dead man, readers cannot ignore it. In "Transition," the indigenous people move from barbaric threat at "Separation" to the roles of guide/food-provider/protector, roles that angels and animals fulfill in medieval hagiography.[13] As Cabeza de Vaca emerges with his new identity, near the end of the text, in the "Incorporation" section, the descriptions of the people and landscape that he encounters become increasingly positive.[14] The hermit saint emerges to evangelize and pacify the indigenous, and the principle means through which Cabeza de Vaca does this is his miraculous healings. Thus, the varying descriptions of the Other, empathetic and not, disruptive of classical representations of barbarism or not, are tied to Cabeza de Vaca's fashioning of his identity as a miracle-working saint.

Space does not allow for a review of the scholarly interpretations of those miraculous healings. Suffice it to say that there are almost as many explanations as readers, since the miracles, along with the mysterious figure of Mala Cosa, are among the most salient aspects of the text. As Jáuregui recounts, some critics interpret Mala Cosa as an indigenous shaman, others as trickster, and others as a representation of the psychological trauma induced by Castilian colonization of the area. While leaving aside recent interpretations of the miracles in the text, the reception of those miracles in the eighty years following the 1542 publication date presents an early and unique glimpse of the epistemological shift that Cañizares-Esguerra traces in *How to Write the History of the New World* and that Ralph Bauer sees in nascent form in Samuel Purchas: the moment when "European witnesses to the New World suddenly lost credibility" and editors of travel compilations read the narratives with a new art of reading.[15] We see, in fact, what Joan-Pau Rubiés asserts in his article "Travel Writing and Humanist Culture: A Blunted Impact"—that "the seeds for Enlightenment debates about the reliability of native sources" and European witnesses "can be traced back to the far from homogeneous reception of primary ethnographies and native records by sixteenth-century writers with a

---

13   Elliott, 1987: 172.
14   TenHuisen, 2005: 111–12.
15   Cañizares-Esguerra, 2001: 1.

humanist educational horizon."[16] Although he speaks of heterogeneous receptions, Rubiés speaks himself of "a general shift in the genre of travel writing, as the traditional control of the ethnographic discourses by practical explorers, missionaries and armchair cosmographers was challenged."[17] The reception of Cabeza de Vaca's *Relación* can therefore give us a glimpse of that general shift, and it is the description of the indigenous on and around Malhado, as well as the miraculous cures, that are most prominent in the reception of the text outside of the Iberian Peninsula.

In his oft-mentioned article "Los 'milagros' de Alvar Núñez Cabeza de Vaca," Jacques Lafaye outlines the history of the reception of these miracles in subsequent texts. Lafaye argues that the early contemporary references to Cabeza de Vaca do not mention the miraculous cures and that Cabeza de Vaca and his companions "did not feel themselves to be authors of miracles but just occasional recipients of wonders that God worked through them."[18] It is not until López de Gómara publishes his *Historia general* that the word *miracle* is introduced to describe Cabeza de Vaca, and Lafaye points out that the miracles take up about one fifth of the section dedicated to Cabeza de Vaca in Gómara. Thus, the miracles take on a more important presence in Gómara than in Cabeza de Vaca's *Relación*. The Inca Garcilaso abbreviates Gómara's summary even more. According to Lafaye, by the eighteenth century Cabeza de Vaca had become a saint who worked "infinite" miracles.[19] Lafaye's claim that Cabeza de Vaca did not believe himself to be a worker of miracles should be held lightly; although he does not state explicitly that he worked miracles or resurrected a dead man, Cabeza de Vaca very clearly and intentionally manipulated the hagiographic discourse to present himself as saint, even if he didn't claim to be one.

It is important to note, however, that all of Lafaye's sources on the reception of the Cabeza de Vaca miracles are Spanish. As Rubiés argues, "any analysis ... must be properly comparative" and "the existence of national paradigms, analyzed through their mutual interaction rather than in isolation, not only provides us with the basis for a geography of reception but, more interestingly, with the basis for a general chronology of intellectual transformation,"[20] intellectual transformations of the type that both Rubiés and Cañizares-Esguerra trace.

---

16   Rubiés, 2006: 152.
17   Rubiés, 2006: 151.
18   Lafaye, 1962: 140. (Translation mine).
19   Lafaye, 1962: 150.
20   Rubiés, 2006: 150.

3   *Prole* [Offspring]

The reception of Cabeza de Vaca's text outside of the Iberian context is important because Lafaye's portrayal of an intensification of the miracles in subsequent references to Cabeza de Vaca does not match the reception of similar
texts from the sixteenth century. Lafaye's reading at least does not suggest that
the eyewitness lost authority or that travel compilers were reading sources in
new ways.

In volume 3 of her exhaustive study of Cabeza de Vaca, Rolena Adorno dedicates fifty-six pages to the "Readers of Cabeza de Vaca's *Relación* (Sixteenth
through Eighteenth Centuries)," and she summarizes that reception in her
2004 study entitled "La prole de Cabeza de Vaca: El legado multicentenario de
una de la primeras jornadas europeas en América del Norte."[21] The title of the
present essay is a feeble allusion to those studies in general and to the article
more specifically. Most of the sixteenth- and early seventeenth-century editions that Adorno treats in her reception history are from the Iberian spheres
of interest—Biedma, Gentleman of Elvas, Oviedo, Inca Garcilaso, Santa Cruz,
Las Casas, Gómara, Castañeda, Jaramillo, López de Velasco, Acosta, etc. Adorno
does devote significant space to two Italian editions: Ramusio's translation of
1556 and Benzoni's "reading" in *La historia del Mondo Nuovo*, and she also dedicates several pages to the English "readings" of Hakluyt and Purchas.

3.1   *Ramusio & Purchas*
Even though they have been treated extensively elsewhere, it is worth pausing
here to briefly detail the case of Ramusio and Purchas before moving on to
other non-Iberian receptions of Cabeza de Vaca. Adorno explains that Ramusio
used Cabeza de Vaca's 1542 *Relación* as the basis for his Italian translation, and
she states that he "was an important source of geographic information pertaining to the Spanish province of *Florida*. This pragmatic and utilitarian interest, rather than any historic or belletristic one, explains the prompt effort to
translate the work."[22] And in "La prole de Cabeza de Vaca," she emphasizes
the "pragmatic and utilitarian interest in the knowledge of geography" as
the impetus for the translation, over and against the historical and theoretic
motives of Oviedo and Las Casas. Her description of Ramusio as utilitarian
is similar to Rubiés's description of him as "practical." Rubiés adds that "[a]ll
the northern collections relied on Ramusio as a model. Notwithstanding some
important variations in editorial practice, these humanist collectors not only

---

21   Adorno, 2004.
22   Pautz and Adorno, 1999: 140.

made available a vast number of narratives in original or translation, but also came to define the scientific and ideological pretensions of the genre as central to the cosmographical culture of the Renaissance."[23]

Ralph Bauer dedicates half of his book *The Cultural Geography of Colonial American Literatures* to the study of Cabeza de Vaca and Samuel Purchas, and there is no need to repeat his arguments here. His synopsis of Purchas's treatment of the *Relación* is helpful, however:

> Purchas had excised most of the early historical sections, which had detailed the confrontation between the author and Pánfilo de Narváez. … With regards to the middle sections, consisting mainly of Cabeza de Vaca's spiritual autobiography, Purchas annotated heavily, invoking [diverse] writers … to discredit Cabeza de Vaca's accounts of miraculous healings as a Catholic "superstition" … Purchas' cuts were slightest in Cabeza de Vaca's ethnographic and naturalistic descriptions.[24]

Bauer summarizes by saying that Purchas "edited his materials with an eye to bare geographic and ethnographic information."[25] As Bauer notes, Purchas edits out almost all instances of self-fashioning, as well as any deed or action that Cabeza de Vaca relays as heroic, especially over and against the nefarious leader. It is a bit more difficult, however, to accept the claim that Purchas edited with an eye to geographic and ethnographic information, since he does leave intact the miracles and the resurrection of the dead man that Cabeza de Vaca details. Granted, Purchas does mock them, declaring the account completely unbelievable, but their presence and his derision do bear witness to the fact that elements beyond the ethnographic are left in, which is decidedly not the case in other earlier receptions of the text.

3.2 *Boemus Aubanus*

Despite her very lengthy list, there are a few non-Iberian readers from the sixteenth century that Adorno does not treat or mention, and they reveal a similar yet more extensive process occurring a full fifty to seventy years before Purchas published his paraphrase/translation of Cabeza de Vaca's *Relación*.

Rubiés suggests that "Germany in the first half of the sixteenth century is not the best point from which to assess the impact (of discovery and conquest of America)," and he uses as his example the popular ethnographic synthesis

---

23 Rubiés, 2006: 163.
24 Bauer, 2003.
25 Bauer, 2003: 79.

that Johannes Boemus published in Augsburg in 1520, *Omnium gentes mores, ritus et leges*.[26] This extremely popular text is often trotted out as an example of a reactionary work that completely ignores the Portuguese and Spanish discoveries almost thirty years after Columbus set sail for Castile. Despite some forty-seven editions in many European languages (French, Spanish, Italian, English, and German, in addition to the original Latin) over the next 100 years, subsequent editions were slow to add material that reflected European travel and expansion in the sixteenth century. Three editions, however, reveal that these editors and compilers, too, were readers of Cabeza de Vaca, and they certainly do not leave the *Relación* intact.

As Adorno points out, López de Gómara was a careful reader of Cabeza de Vaca's *Relación*, and Gómara took delight in heckling Narváez, noting that, unlike Cabeza de Vaca, Narváez had failed to carry out the mission. We see this very clearly when Gómara inserts, "Quien no poblare, no hará buena conquista, y no conquistando la tierra, no se convertirá la gente; así que la máxima del conquistar ha de ser poblar [Whoever does not settle will not make a good conquest, and by not conquering the land, the people will not be converted; so the maxim of conquering must be to settle]." Adorno agrees with Lafaye, pointing out that "Gómara highlighted the men's curing episodes ... declaring the resuscitation of the dead man a miracle."[27] In chapter XIII of the third book in the Spanish translation of Boemus's *Omnium gentium, El livro de las costumbres de todas las gentes del mundo, y de las Indias*, published in 1556 in Antwerp, Francisco de Thámara lifts the Cabeza de Vaca section almost word for word from Gómara, but he reduces it considerably, from around 4000 words to 950. Although the declaration of the resurrection as a miracle is gone, Thámara's reduction leaves the description of the miraculous cures and the resurrection of the dead man interlaced with the ethnographic descriptions of the indigenous peoples they encounter:

> entierranse todos, saluo los médicos, que por honrra los queman, y entretanto baylan y cantan, y guardan la ceniza para beuerla al cabo del año los parientes y mujeres. Estos medicos curan con botones de fuego, y soplando el cauterio o llaga, jasan adonde ay dolor, chupã la sajadura. Aquí los Christianos sanaron a muchos enfermos, rezando, soplando, y santiguando. De Malhado atraueiando muchas tierras, llegaron a vna que llamã de los Yaguases, los quales son grandes mentirosos, ladrones, borrachos de su vino, y agoreros, y muy ligeros de sus personas. Traen la tetilla

---

26   Rubiés, 2006: 135.
27   Pautz and Adorno, 1999: 137.

y beço horadado, vsan contra natura, mudanse como Alarabes, los viejos y mugeres se visten y calçan de cuero de venado, y de vacas que a cierto tiempo del año vienen de azia el Norte. Comen mil suziedades, compran las mujeres, andan desnudos y tan picados de mosquitos, que parence de sant Lazaro. Por toda esta tierra que es muy larga anduuo Albar Nuñez Cabeça de Vaca, con otros quatro compañeros, que solos escaparon de trezientos que salieron a teirra con Naruaez, los quales anduuieron perdidos desnudos y hambrientos nueue años y mas, donde sanarõ muchos enfermos, y resuscitados vn muerto, según ellos dixeron. Entre las Abardaos estuuieron algún tiempo: estos son astutos guerreros.[28]

[They bury everyone, except the physicians, whom they burn out of honor, and meanwhile they dance and sing, and they keep the ashes in order for the relatives and wives to drink them at the end of the year. These physicians cure with fire buttons, and blowing the cautery or wound, they cut where there is pain and suck the cut. Here the Christians cured many sick people, praying, blowing and making the sign of the cross. Crossing many lands from Malhado, they arrived at one which they call the Yaguases, who were great liars, thieves, practiced [the sin] against nature, move like the Alarabes, the old people and the women dress and wear shoes made from the leather of deer and cows which come north at a certain time of the year. They eat thousands of filthy things, they buy women, they walk naked and [are] bitten by mosquitos, such that they look like Saint Lazarus. Alvar Núñez Cabeza de Vaca walked through all of this land, which is very long, with four other companions, the only ones to escape from the 300 who left with Narvaez, who walked around lost, naked and hungry for nine years or more, where they healed many sick and resurrected a dead man, as they said. They were among the Abardaos some time: these are astute warriors.]

Thus, with the reference to the miraculous cures and resurrection, we have, perhaps, a general continuation of the Iberian reception described by Lafaye.

The Italian version of *Omnium gentium, Gli costumi, le leggi, et lusanze di tutte le genti*, translated by Lucio Fauno and printed by Geronimo Giglio in Venice in 1558, also contains a description that clearly comes from Gómara.[29] It is unlikely, however, that chapter VII, "Dell'Isola Florida; & dell'Isola Malhado, & del paese detto Panuco, e suoi habitatori," was based on the Thamara edition,

---

28 Boemus and Tamara, 1556: fol. 317^r–317^v.
29 Boemus and Giglio, 1558.

since there are a few sentences in the Italian that are very faithful to Gómara but are not in the Thámara reduction. More importantly, however, the Italian translation removes Cabeza de Vaca and his Spanish companions completely. The same section quoted above is rendered as follows in the Italian version:

> Tutti si sepeliscono, dalli Medici in poi, i quali ardono, per honorarli, & mentre che ardeno, gli altri ballano, saltano, e cantanno. Fanno gli ossi in poluere, & conseruano la cenere per beuerla dopo fornito l'anno tra i parenti, et le donne, iquali allhora si cauano del sangue. In queste contradi ui è un terra detta Languazi, gli habitatori della quale sono buggiardi, ladri, imbriachi, & grandi indouini, & sognandosi cosa trista uccidono i proprii figliuoli; sono sodomiti, et mutansi di luoco à luoco, come sogliono far gli Alarbi, & portano seco le store, con lequale fanno le loro case. I uecchi & le donne si uestono con pelli di Cerui, & di Vacche. Mangiano ragni, formiche, uermi, salamandre, lucerte, serpi, legna, terra, et sterco di pecore; e essendo tanto affamati, tutta uia se ne uanno lietamente ballando, & cantando. Comprano le donne da i loro nemici per un'arco, et due saette, ouero per una rete da pescare, & poi le uccidono. Vanno nudi, & sono molto morduti dalle zenzale, de maniera, che paiono leprosi, et sono in perpetua guerra con questi animaletti, et portano facelle de legno accese per cacciarle. Gli Albardi son astuti guerrieri.[30]

> [Everyone is buried, except for the physicians, whom they burn, to honor them, & while they burn, the others dance, leap, and sing. They make the bones into powder, & keep the ashes to drink supplying them after a year among the relatives, and the women, who then bleed themselves. In these districts there is a land called Languazi, whose inhabitants are liars, thieves, drunkards, & great soothsayers, & dreaming of a sad thing, they kill their own children; they are sodomites, and they change from place to place, as the Alarbi usually do, & they bring with them their stores with which they build their houses. The men & the women wear the skins of deer & cows. They eat spiders, ants, worms, salamanders, lizards, snakes, wood, earth, and sheep dung; and being so hungry, all of them go away happily dancing and singing. They buy women from their enemies for a bow and two arrows, or for a fishing net, & then kill them. They go naked, and are badly bitten by mosquitos, in the way that they look like lepers, and they are in perpetual war with these little animals, and they carry lit wooden torches to chase them away. The Albardis are cunning warriors.]

---

30   Boemus and Giglio, 1558: fols. 197ᵛ–198ʳ.

There are no miraculous cures, no resurrection; Cabeza de Vaca and his companions are not even named. Giglio's version concerns itself only with the description of the indigenous in this very section—particularly, the negative or "barbaric" descriptions. Also completely excised from the Italian is the reception that the miracle-working Spaniards received near the end of their pilgrimage, when they began to encounter dressed women along their route, the end of "Transition" and the beginning of "Incorporation," the point at which the more-civilized tropes begin to reappear. Gone, for example, is this section from the Thamara volume:

> No comían sin que primero lo santiguasen los Christianos, y lo assoplassen. Llegaron a tierra que por costumbre o por acatamiento dellos ni llorauan ni reyan, ni se hablauan. Recebian a los Españoles las caras a la pared, las cabeças baxas, y los cabellos sobre los ojos. En el valle que llamaron de los Coraçones, por seiscientos que les dieron de venados, vuieron algunas saetas con puntas de esmeraldas harto buenas, y algunas turquesas y plumajes. Alli traen las mujeres camisas de algodón fino, mangas de lo mismo y faldillas hasta el suelo de venado adobado sin pelo, y abiertas por delante.[31]

> [They did not eat without first having the Christians bless it and blow on it. They arrived to the land where, either because of custom or reverence for them, they neither cried nor laughed nor spoke amongst themselves. They received the Spaniards with their faces to the wall, their heads held low and their hair over their eyes. In the valley that they named Hearts, due to the six hundred deer hearts that they gave to them, they saw arrows with very good emerald points and some turquoise and feathers. There the women wear dresses of fine cotton, sleeves of the same and skirts to the ground made of tanned deer without hair, and open in front.]

The personal narrative of Cabeza de Vaca's deeds and transformation from the original, still present in Gómara and Thamara, has been removed completely in the Italian version, leaving only ethnographic descriptions of the inhabitants in and around the island of Malhado as found in Cabeza de Vaca's *Relación*, descriptions that notably focus more on the details that European readers would have found "barbaric," including the homosexuals and the women who breastfeed their children for twelve years:

---

31   Boemus and Tamara, 1556: fols. 317ᵛ–318ʳ.

Si maritano con altri huomini, che siano impotenti, ouero Eunuchi, liquali vanno vestiti come donne, ne possono portare, ne tirare di arco. Le donne lattano i figliuoli dieci, e dodici anni, et fino che si sanno procurare il uiuere da loro istessi. Non mangiano di quello, che la moglie cuocina, quando ha is suoi mesi. Il paese detto Pauco è 500 leghe di costa, et è molto rico, et gli habitatori sono huomini crudeli, et sodomiti: tengono públicamente in un luoco appartato molti giouani doue ui uanno la notte à ssogare le sue sfrenate uoglie. Si cauano la barba, foransi le nari, et l' orecchie, per portarui qualche cosa, et per ornamento si limano i denti di forte, che gli fanno come una sega. Non si maritano fin che non hanno quarant' anni.[32]

[They get married to other men who are impotent, or eunuchs, who dressed like women can neither carry nor shoot a bow. The women nurse their children ten, and twelve years, and until they know how to live on their own. They do not eat what the wife cooks when she has her monthlies. The town called Pauco is 500 leagues from the coast, and is very rich, and the inhabitants are cruel men and sodomites: they publicly keep many young boys in a secluded place where they spend the night to quench their unbridled lusts. They pierce their chin, nostrils and ears to wear something, and for decoration they file their teeth sharply, which makes them like a saw. They do not get married until they are forty.]

3.3 Belleforest

There is a third edition of Boemus, an extensive French version, which reveals a unique and more careful reading of Cabeza de Vaca: The 1570 edition of *Histoire Universelle du monde* by Françoys de Belleforest published in Paris.[33] Although the French translation of Gómara came out very quickly and was available to Belleforest, it is clear that he based his description of the people of Florida and the Ilhe de Malhado on a more complete version of Cabeza de Vaca's *Relación*. There are considerably more details in Belleforest than in Gómara. The most likely source, given Belleforest's command of Italian, is Ramusio's translation from 1556. Belleforest mentions Cabeza de Vaca's name and account several times: "Or les peuples plus par Nunnez remarques sont ceux de l'isle de Malhado" [Now the people most commented on by Núñez are those from the Island of Malhado];[34] "comme racompte Aluaro Nunez en

---

32 Boemus and Giglio, 1558: fol. 198[r].
33 Belleforest, 1570.
34 Belleforest, 1572: fol. 271[r].

ses raports" [as Alvar Núñez says in his reports];[35] etc. The descriptions of the inhabitants of Malhado are lengthier and more detailed than those found in Gómara and the Spanish and Italian Boemus editions. The Cabeza de Vaca material in the *Histoire* is unique, however, for two additional reasons: The inhabitants of Malhado are described as cannibals, a label famously lacking in Cabeza de Vaca's *Relación*, and there is significant space in Belleforest's *Histoire* dedicated to Mala Cosa, the "malin esprit," "ceste mauuaise chose," that enigmatic figure that appears in the center of Cabeza de Vaca's *Relación*. Other than the references to Cabeza de Vaca's account and the fact that the Christians make fun of the physicians and their way of practicing medicine ("se moquassent de ceste façon"),[36] however, the personal narrative found in Cabeza de Vaca is absent. There is no account of the miraculous cures and the resurrection of the dead man in Belleforest. Like the Spanish and Italian editions of Boemus, the Belleforest *Histoire Universelle* removes the self-fashioning and personal *historia* of Cabeza de Vaca, limiting itself to "ethnographic description" of the inhabitants of Malhado and the neighboring peoples.

Belleforest followed his *Histoire* five years later with his *Cosmographie universelle de tout le monde*.[37] There are remarkable differences between the *Histoire* and the *Cosmographie* in how they present the material taken from Cabeza de Vaca's *Relación*. In chapter XXI of the seventh book (*Des Terres Descovuertes des nostre temps, ausquelles on a donné le nom de nouueau monde, & d'Indes Occidentales, ou Amerique*) of volume II, Belleforest references Cabeza de Vaca's *Relación* explicity and directly: "De ceste Isle, & habitans d'celle le susdit Aluaro parle en ceste sorte: Nous mismes nom Malchado à ceste Isle, le peuple que nous y trouuasmes est grãd, & bien disposts, & ne portre pour toute armes que des arcs, & des flesches, mais ils en tirent fort dextrement" [Of this Island, and of its inhabitants, the above-mentioned Alvar Núñez speaks in this manner: We called this island Malhado, the people whom we found there are tall and well disposed, and for arms they carry only bows and fleches, but they draw them dextrously].[38] Belleforest limits his summary of Cabeza de Vaca's entire *Relación* to the section on Malhado and the neighboring peoples, focusing exclusively on familial relations, mourning customs, marriage, and dress. While Belleforest's *Cosmographie* continues to reference Cabeza de Vaca and is still a lengthier description than what we find in the Spanish and Italian Boemus volumes, the references to the cannibalism of the

35   Belleforest, 1572: fol. 272[v].
36   Belleforest, 1572: fol. 271[v].
37   Belleforest, 1575.
38   Münster and Belleforest, 1575: fol. 2231[r].

inhabitants of Malhado, as well as their practices of divination, sorcery and "sin against nature," are removed. The description of Mala Cosa, so prominent in the *Histoire*, is also absent. All references to miraculous cures are removed, and nowhere is any of the self-fashioning of Cabeza de Vaca presented. While the indigenous physicians are still described briefly in the *Cosmographie*—"Ils enterrent (comme dit est) leurs morts trestous, sauf ceux que sont mede-cins entre eux, (de la medicine desquels auons parlé cy dessus, qui se fait en sucçant la partie malade) lesquels ils bruslent" [They quickly bury (as was said) their dead, except those who are physicians among them (about whose medicine we speak above, which is done by sucking the sick part), whom they burn][39]—gone is the reference in the *Histoire* to how the Christians laughed at the indigenous physicians, and there is no mention of the miraculous cures performed by the Spaniards. In short, the *Cosmographie* removed all of the personal narrative found in the *Relación,* as well as almost all of the negative descriptions of the indigenous inhabitants of Malhado, including the descrip-tion of Mala Cosa found in the *Histoire*.

4   Similar Reception of Staden's *Wahrhaftige Historia*

In all three of the Boemus editions and in both Belleforest texts, we see how the narrative *historia* and the self-fashioning of the *Relación* are separated from the "ethnographic details." As in the Purchas translation forty-five years later, the cuts made to the original text accentuate the ethnographic descriptions, fully in keeping with what readers would expect with a collection of the mores and customs of other peoples. A similar reception history of Hans Staden's *Wahrhaftige Historia* demonstrates that this is part of a larger phenomenon.

Published in 1557 in Lutheran Marburg, Germany, Staden's *Wahrhaftige Historia* describes his captivity among the cannibalistic Tupinamba in colonial Brazil, and it is generally described in German-language criticism as Protestant propaganda. Staden and his text exude Lutheranism, yet, like Cabeza de Vaca, Staden relies heavily on the discourse of hagiography, and martyrdom in par-ticular. Throughout his text he presents himself as the pious saint chosen by God: due to his steadfastness and his miracles, he is delivered from his trial among the cannibals.

Wahrhaftige Historia was a best seller in German-speaking lands, and in the sixteenth century alone it was reprinted four times in German, as well as

---

39   Münster and Belleforest, 1575: fol. 2231^r–2231^v.

being translated into Dutch and Latin. Along with Jean de Léry's account of his sojourn in Brazil, Staden's *Wahrhaftige Historia* was reprinted by the Flemish Calvinist Theodor de Bry in the third volume of his series *India Occidentalis* (commonly known as the *Grands Voyages*). Not surprisingly for scholars familiar with the de Bry images, it is the engravings of the reprint that are most important. Even though many critics argue that de Bry wildly and imaginatively reinterprets the original woodcuts and invents new engravings with fantastic details, a careful comparison of the original woodcuts to the de Bry engravings reveals that de Bry is actually quite faithful to the originals.

What is most surprising, and most relevant to the study of the non-Iberian versions of Cabeza de Vaca's *Relación*, however, is the fact that de Bry actually leaves out several woodcuts in the narrative account of Staden's text. The four that are missing are precisely those that demonstrate Staden's piety and exemplarity. Neither the prayer scenes nor the miracle scenes are reproduced. Although de Bry holds Staden up as an example to be emulated in his prologue, his visual representation of the text greatly diminishes this aspect. Staden is not an offensive Roman Catholic saint but, rather, an exemplary Lutheran, yet his prayers and piety are removed from visual representation.

The title of de Bry's reprint reveals the new interpretation he puts on Staden's text. The original title, *Warhaftig* historia und *beschreibung* einer Landtschafft *der Wilden/ Nacketen/* Grimmigen *Menschfressen* Leuthen/ *in der Newenwelt America gelegen* ... [my emphasis], becomes in de Bry Wunderbarliche und *warhafftige Beschreibung der wilden nacketen Menschenfresser* ... [my emphasis]. De Bry drops the words *Landschaft, Grimmigen, Leuthen,* and *Historia* from the title and adds *Wunderbarliche*. Thus, the interest in landscape is gone, the Tupinamba are no longer "man-eating people" but merely "man eaters," and Staden's personal narrative is no longer of interest. What de Bry presents his readers with is the "wonderful and true description of wild, naked man eaters," and Staden's text is a vehicle for bringing this knowledge to de Bry's readers. The changes in the title reflect precisely what occurs with the engravings. While de Bry maintains the original division of the text into personal narrative and ethnographic description, the dropping of the *historia* from the title shifts the interest toward the description of the natives, thus matching the omission of engravings reflecting the pious woodcuts.

De Bry in a very real sense reduces the personal narrative of Staden. In a similar vein, Wolfgang Neuber demonstrates in his article "Der geschlachtete Kannibale" that in the sixteenth- and seventeenth-century Dutch reprints of Staden, there is also a clear and marked reduction in the importance and centrality of Staden's narrative, despite that being the essential and quintessentially

Lutheran aspect of the text.[40] In the seventeenth century, the personal narrative is separated from the ethnographic descriptions.

5 Conclusions

As Mary Campbell has shown in her analysis of the first volume of de Bry's *India Occidentalis*, the castaway narrative (or captivity narrative, and pilgrimage in Cabeza de Vaca's case) is "the anti-ethnographic genre of voyage literature."[41] Campbell notes how de Bry eliminates flora and fauna, focusing specifically on the ethnographic, reducing experience to fact and creating an "ethnographic present." Although Campbell cautiously warns that "to speak about ... de Bry in [his] relationship to ethnography is an anachronism," her focus on the "abandonment of narrative," "reliance on ... the visually oriented schemata of classification," "the reduction of experience to facts," and the creation of an "ethnographic-present" leads her to describe de Bry's first volume as "proto-ethnographic."[42] We see a very similar move at play in de Bry's third volume of *India Occidentales*, which reprints Hans Staden's *Wahrhaftige Historia* and Jean de Léry's *Histoire d'un voyage*.

This same phenomenon can be seen twenty years earlier, in the reception of Cabeza de Vaca's hagiographic pilgrimage. As "the anti-ethnographic genre of voyage literature," it must be removed in the Boemus, Belleforest, and Purchas texts. Subsequent readers of Cabeza de Vaca outside of the Iberian peninsula show little interest in his personal narrative, and in their volumes we can already see in the sixteenth century the transformations in the reading of these narratives that Cañizares-Esguerra finds in the eighteenth century and that Bauer sees in Purchas fifty years later. Descriptions of flora and fauna are also excised from these texts. The result of the creation of this "ethnographic present" in the subsequent non-Iberian readings of Cabeza de Vaca, however, is a notable alteration in the presentation of the indigenous Other. The descriptions of the indigenous Other in Cabeza de Vaca are tied directly to the self-fashioning of the author, and the removal of that *historia* gives us a simpler and flatter Other, whether domesticated or barbarized, than what is in the original *Relación*.

---

40 Neuber, 2005.
41 Campbell, 1999: 37.
42 Campbell, 1999: 51–67.

Bibliography

Adorno, Rolena. "La prole de Cabeza de Vaca: El legado multicentenario de una de las primeras jornadas europeas en América del Norte." *Revista de Crítica Literaria Latinoamericana* 30 (60) (2004), 251–68.

Bauer, Ralph. *The Cultural Geography of Colonial American Literatures: Empire, Travel, Modernity.* Cambridge Studies in American Literature and Culture (Cambridge: Cambridge University Press, 2003).

de Belleforest, François. *La cosmographie vniuerselle de tout le monde. En laquelle, suiuant les auteurs plus dignes de foy, sont au vray descriptes toutes les parties habitables, & non habitables de la terre, & de la mer, leurs assiettes & choses qu'elles produisent ... auec plusieurs autres choses, le sommaire desquelles se void en la page suiuante.* (Paris: Nicolas Chesneau, 1575).

de Belleforest, François. *L'histoire vniuerselle du monde, contenant l'entiere description & situation des quatre parties de la terre, la diuisio[n] & estenduë d'vne chacune region & prouince d'icelles. Ensemble l'origine & particulieres mœurs, loix, coustumes, religion, & ceremonies, de toutes les nations, & peuples par qui elles sont habitées. Diuisee en quatre liures* (Paris: G. Mallot, 1572).

Boemus, Joannes, and Francisco Tamara. *El libro de las costumbres de todas las gentes del mundo, y de las Indias* (Antwerp: Martin Nucio, 1556).

Boemus, Joannes, and Girolamo Giglio. *Gli costumi, le leggi, et l'usanze di tutte le genti : raccolte qui' insieme da molti illustri scrittori* (Venice: G. Giglio, 1558).

Campbell, Mary Baine. *Wonder and Science: Imagining Worlds in Early Modern Europe* (Ithaca, NY: Cornell University Press, 1999).

Cañizares-Esguerra, Jorge. *How to Write the History of the New World: Histories, Epistemologies & Identities in the Eighteenth-Century Atlantic World* (Stanford: Stanford University Press, 2001).

Elliott, Alison Goddard. *Roads to Paradise: Reading the Lives of the Early* Saints (Hanover, NH: University Press of New England, 1987).

Jáuregui, Carlos A. "Cabeza de Vaca, Mala Cosa y las vicisitudes de la extrañeza." *Revista de Estudios Hispánicos* 48 (2014), 421–47.

Lafaye, Jacques. "Les Miracles d'Alvar Nunez Cabeza de Vaca (1527–1536)." *Bulletin Hispanique* 64 (1962), 136–53.

Münster, Sebastian, and François de Belleforest. *La cosmographie vniuerselle de tout le monde. : En laquelle, suiuant les auteurs plus dignes de foy, sont au vray descriptes toutes les parties habitables, & non habitables de la terre, & de la mer, leurs assiettes & choses qu'elles produisent ... auec plusieurs autres choses, le sommaire desquelles se void en la page suiuante* (Paris: Nicolas Chesneau, 1575).

Neuber, Wolfgang. "Der geschlachtete Kannibale. Zu einigen niederländischen Ausgaben von Hans Stadens Reisebericht." In *Cognition and the Book: Typologies of*

Formal Organisation of Knowledge in the Printed Book of the Early Modern Period, eds. Karl A. E. Enenkel and Wolfgang Neuber. Leiden (Leiden: Brill, 2005), 333–66.

Pautz, Patrick Charles, and Rolena Adorno. *Alvar Nunez Cabeza de Vaca: His Account, His Life, and the Expedition of Panfilo de Narvaez* (Lincoln: University of Nebraska Press, 1999).

Rubiés, Joan-Pau. "Travel Writing and Humanistic Culture: A Blunted Impact?" *Journal of Early Modern History* 10 (1/2) (February 2006), 131–68.

TenHuisen, Dwight E. R. *Alterity and Hagiography in the Early Modern Captivity Narrative: Naufragios, Wahrhaftige Historia and Peregrinção*. PhD Dissertation (University of Illinois at Urbana-Champaign, 2005).

PART 2

At Court and in Town: Text, Sound, and Image

∴

Toward a Definition of Royalty: Images of Sophie Charlotte, First Queen in Prussia

Sara Smart

In 1684, the Welph princess Sophie Charlotte of Braunschweig-Lüneburg (1668–1705) arrived in Berlin as a sixteen-year-old bride, the second wife of Friedrich III (1657–1713), then the twenty-seven-year-old electoral prince and heir to the Hohenzollern Elector Friedrich Wilhelm of Brandenburg (1620–1688). Friedrich's first wife, Elisabeth Henriette of Hessen-Kassel (1661–1683), had died only the previous year, and the sheer speed with which this second marriage was arranged indicates its importance to the two dynasties. The relationship between the Welphs and the Hohenzollerns, the two burgeoning powers in the north of the Empire, was based on an admixture of solidarity and rivalry (Göse, 2012: 173, 190–92; Hahn, 1999: 31–33). For both sides, the marital alliance was the product of political calculation and self-interest, providing a valuable source of prestige in their tenacious pursuit of influence and authority. Their success in this pursuit is illustrated by two major events of the following decades: the bestowal on Sophie Charlotte's father, Duke Ernst August of Braunschweig-Lüneburg (1629–1698), of the new, ninth electoral dignity in 1692 and Friedrich's establishment of the Hohenzollern kingship in Prussia in 1701. In an elaborate ceremony in Königsberg, Friedrich crowned himself king and then crowned Sophie Charlotte queen, signaling a momentous shift upward for the Hohenzollerns in the hierarchy of princes, in the Empire and beyond.

Of all the Hohenzollern consorts of the early modern period, the first Prussian queen has a profile that has endured over the centuries. This rests in no small measure on her architectural legacy, the palace of Lietzenburg, renamed Charlottenburg on her death, built on ground gifted to her by Friedrich in 1695. Equally, her association with Gottfried Wilhelm Leibniz (1646–1716) is well known, not least because it was idealized by her grandson Friedrich the Great (1712–1786), who enhanced her image as the philosopher queen (Heuvel, 1999: 90). This portrayal continued to capture the imagination of later generations, as attested in Adolph Menzel's famous pencil sketch from the mid-nineteenth century, which depicts Sophie Charlotte and Leibniz strolling in the grounds of Lietzenburg, engaged in earnest conversation. The origins of this profile of Sophie Charlotte as queen are the focus of the present study, which engages

© KONINKLIJKE BRILL NV, LEIDEN, 2023 | DOI:10.1163/9789004682245_007

with the very earliest depictions of her in the years immediately surrounding the coronation. Based on the copious print culture characteristic of the court at this time, the article assesses the qualities attributed to her, the way in which these are articulated, and the interplay between tradition and innovation in the styling of her image. The aim is to determine how her role as queen is defined.

1   The Early Portrayals of the Electress and Queen

One of the earliest depictions of Sophie Charlotte as electress in the court's print culture is firmly rooted in Hohenzollern iconography. To commemorate Friedrich's succession in 1688, a series of poems was written by his court poet Johann von Besser (1654–1729). Drawing on Friedrich's successes as military commander at the start of the Nine Years' War—notably the siege of Kaiserswerth in June 1689 and the liberation of Bonn the following October—Besser projected an image of the new elector as heir to his father, whose famous victory over the Swedes at the battle of Fehrbellin in 1675 had established his reputation as the victorious Great Elector (Göse, 2012: 179–80).[1] To complement his elaboration of Friedrich's martial hereditary, Besser draws attention to Sophie Charlotte's presence at the soldiers' camp: she is styled as the second Pallas, whose mere glance rouses the troops to greater glory (Besser, 1720: 126). This depiction echoes the treatment of both wives of Friedrich Wilhelm. In the case of his first wife, Luise Henriette of Orange (1627–1667), the vita contained in her funeral volume records her supportive presence on his campaign in Jutland during the first Northern War,[2] while his second wife, Dorothea of Holstein-Sonderburg-Glücksburg (1636–1689), is memorialized in the visual arts and in Besser's poetry as the elector's companion in arms (Börsch-Supan, 1990: 162; Besser, 1720: 12). In each instance, the portrayal of the consort as military helpmeet contributes to the cultivation of the image of the Hohenzollerns as martial dynasty, an image that underlined the strength on which the kingship was based.

With the creation of the monarchy, a new mode of representation consonant with the glory of the moment was required. It fell to Besser to produce this manner of portrayal. In his role as Friedrich's master of ceremonies, Besser had

---

1   These poems are included in Besser's complete works. See Besser 1720: 17–24, 124–29.
2   The vita is contained in *Sieben Leichpredigten Nebst Unterschiedlichen Anderen Traur- und Trost-Schrifften* [...] (no date). For references to Luise Henriette's presence on campaign, see 79–80.

been closely involved in planning the events in Königsberg and wrote the official record of the coronation. The resulting *Krönungs-Geschichte*, a text of fifty-seven pages, fulfils a variety of functions. As its illustrated accompaniment, which contained magnificent engravings of the ceremonies, was not published until 1712, Besser was tasked with capturing the sublime nature of Hohenzollern royalty. He achieved this by interweaving explanation and description. For instance, Friedrich's self-coronation, his coronation of Sophie Charlotte, and their subsequent anointment are interpreted in terms of Friedrich's absolute authority in Prussia. An impression of this authority is evoked in a detailed account of the appearance of the newly crowned king and queen: Friedrich was dressed in scarlet, with a royal mantle of purple velvet embroidered with eagles and crowns and lined with ermine; a costly clasp consisting of three diamonds held the mantle in place; and his gold scepter was worked with diamonds and rubies while the crown, too, was covered in diamonds. As regards the queen, "Die Kleidung [...] bestand aus einem güldenen Brocat mit Ponso-Bluhmen / und aus einem Demant-Schmucke / [...] Ihr Mantel und Krone waren wie des Königes; [...] Auf der rechten Seite der Brust hatte Sie noch einen Strauß oder Aigrette von lauter Birn-Perlen; unter denen fürnehmlich die Eine wol unvergleichlich seyn muß" [the dress [...] was of golden brocade with red poppies and diamond ornaments / [...] Her mantle and crown were like the King's; [...] On the right side of her bodice she also had a spray or aigrette of drop pearls, among which one in particular is probably without peer] (Besser, 1702: 24).[3] The function of such display, so Besser informs the reader, is to act as a measure of the dignity of the newly created monarchy, the rhetoric of opulence reflecting what he presents as the traditional equivalence between rank and the display of magnificence. As if to confirm this association, he concentrates on the impact on the assembled courtiers when they first encounter this demonstration of majesty. They are appropriately overwhelmed—"von einer rechten Bestürtzung gerühret" [immediately abashed] (Besser, 1702: 25). In other words, the image of Sophie Charlotte complements that of Friedrich: together they incorporate the exalted, awe-inspiring character of their elevation.

Besser is quick to add that such an appearance is merely a manifestation of the characteristics that already define the couple. Yet while the *Krönungs-Geschichte* dwells in depth on Friedrich's inherent royalty—his qualities and achievements, his reputation and dynastic heritage—it treats Sophie Charlotte in comparatively bland terms. Besser's letter of dedication is illustrative of this. He styles her as Friedrich's "Kronwürdige Gemahlin" [spouse worthy of

---

3 For the English translation by Pamela Selwyn of major extracts from the *Krönungs-Geschichte*, see Friedrich and Smart, 2010: 227–60.

a crown] (Besser, 1702: B2ᵛ), but justifies this claim with reference to just two factors: first, the royal genealogy of her mother, Sophie of Hanover (1630–1714), the daughter of the Winter King and Queen, Friedrich V of the Palatinate (1596–1632) and Elizabeth Stuart (1596–1662), and second, her physical beauty, which makes her a queen among women. It is the second factor, the concern with the external, to which Besser returns in his substantial poem prefacing the report in which he evokes the experiences of a stranger traveling across Friedrich's lands. When this stranger arrives in Berlin and encounters Sophie Charlotte among her ladies-in-waiting, he has no hesitation in recognizing the queen: her regal deportment, her manner, and her radiance identify her as a queen among women. Sophie Charlotte may be an essential figure in Besser's account, his preoccupation with her queenly appearance contributing to the projection of an image of royalty. Nonetheless, the striking absence of engagement with the queen's interior life as reflected in these instances is evidence of her secondary, or support, role in a production in which the king stars.

2 The Commemoration of Sophie Charlotte's Death

A shift from the concentration on the external to the internal, to the qualities and virtues that define the queen, occurs four years later in the court publications following Sophie Charlotte's unexpected death aged thirty-six. On a visit to Hanover she fell ill, contracting a form of pneumonia, and died on 1 February 1705. The lengthy report in the *Theatrum Europæum* of the mourning procedure in Hanover and Berlin suggests a high level of interest in the events surrounding her death: the embalmed body was laid in state from 26 to 28 February, the return of the coffin to Berlin on a carriage drawn by eight horses began on 9 March in a precisely orchestrated procession of court officials and soldiers, the tolling of bells and firing of salvos announced the arrival of the entourage at the towns and villages en route, and on 22 March the procession reached its destination. The funeral took place three months later, on 28 June.[4] For Friedrich this was an occasion when mourning went hand in hand with the demonstration of the new monarchy's dignity. In order to commemorate the first queen, dynastic burial traditions were brought to a hitherto unknown peak of grandeur and spectacle. To achieve this, Friedrich drew on the considerable artistic talent that he had already gathered in Berlin to transform

---

4 For a report of the death and an account of the mourning procedure and funeral, see "Beschreibung der Geschichten Europæ und anderer Welt-Theile vor das Jahr 1705," in *Theatri Europæ Siebzehender Teil* (1718: Teil 2: 1705, 126–33).

the city into a royal residence: Andreas Schlüter (c.1659–1714) designed an elaborate sarcophagus;[5] the architect Johann Friedrich Eosander von Göthe (1669–1728) transformed the interior of the cathedral in Berlin, erecting what is referred to in the primary sources as a mausoleum, the first to be dedicated to a Hohenzollern consort; and Samuel Theodor Gericke (1665–1729), professor of perspective at Friedrich's recently established Academy of Arts, produced a cycle of ten paintings that decorated the mausoleum. Representing different stages of Sophie Charlotte's life, the cycle served as homage to her perfections.

Four extant sources illuminate the character of the funeral. The first, the massive funeral volume *Christ-Königliches Trauer- Und Ehren-Gedächtnüs*, outstrips in its lavishness the funeral works of other Hohenzollern consorts. At its core are the standard elements of such a publication: the funeral sermon and the vita, the official biography of the deceased read out after the sermon. In addition, the volume contains Besser's epicedium of seventy stanzas, as well as a text entitled *Leichen-Procession*, which describes the ceremonial procedures surrounding the return of the body to Berlin and details the elaborate procession to the funeral in the cathedral. This procession is illustrated in a series of eighty-two engravings. Other engravings provide detailed views of the mausoleum. The second source is an anonymous work. Entitled *Kurtze Beschreibung*, it is in fact a lengthy account of forty pages that records the decoration of the mausoleum and provides the official interpretation of its iconography. The description of the cathedral given in *Theatrum Europæum* leans closely on this source. In the third, *Erklärung Derer In dem [...] Mausoleo [...] befindlichen Gemählde*, Gericke describes the works in his cycle and illuminates their often complex symbolism. The final source is another vita. Although similar to the vita contained in the funeral volume, this publication is in places less hyperbolic in tone, suggesting that it was directed at a non-noble audience.[6]

Together these sources reflect the cumulative effort dedicated to the burial and commemoration of the first Hohenzollern queen. To the sound of trumpets and drums, Sophie Charlotte's body was borne on a carriage beneath an elaborate baldachin. At the head of the coffin, which was draped in a cloth decorated with crowns and eagles, were three cushions on which a crown was prominently positioned. Around the coffin the massive funeral procession was arranged according to the dictates of ceremonial procedure.[7] While Friedrich,

---

5 For details of this sarcophagus, see Brüggemann, 2015: 160–61.
6 The two biographies have the same title differentiated by a minor difference in spelling. Quotations from the vita in the funeral volume will be referenced by the title *Ehren-Gedächtniß* followed by the page number. Those from the separate publication will be referenced by the title *Ehren-Gedächtnüß* followed by the abbreviation *s.p.*, followed by the signature.
7 For analysis of the ceremonial procedure, see Steiner, 2001.

surrounded by Swiss guards, and other members of the royal family were in close proximity, the many other mourners—including Friedrich's ministers, courtiers, and clergy, representatives of his territories and institutions of learning—were grouped with attention paid to rank and precedence. When the procession arrived at the cathedral for the funeral service, it encountered a display that was at once "*magnifique* und *suprenant*" [magnificent and surprising] (*Kurtze Beschreibung*, 6). Together the *Kurtze Beschreibung* and the engravings contained in the funeral volume provide an impression of monumental scale. At the entrance, a portal had been constructed around fifty-foot ionic columns. Two winged figures each measuring fourteen feet gave the impression of supporting the portal. Described as dried Arabian mummies, they symbolized immortal fame. At the portal's apex, a ten-foot skeleton appeared to spread a black velvet cloth that formed a type of pavilion. Underneath, two winged figures carried a cartouche decorated with the arms of Prussia and Lüneburg. The transformation of the interior of the cathedral into a mausoleum required massive refashioning and extensive decoration.[8] For example, the gothic pillars were restyled into elaborate architectural columns decorated with winged skulls, and statues and emblems testified to the virtues of the queen. Fixed above the columns were two huge wax figures, complete with human hair and wings made of swans' feathers, representing eternity and good reputation. Gericke's cycle contributed to the spectacle, each work measuring ten feet in length and over six feet in height. Referred to as both paintings and illuminations, these works comprised white taffeta canvas painted with blue symbolic figures and were lit from behind. The magnificence crescendoed in the decoration of the chancel, where the coffin rested. This was positioned beneath a form of pavilion created from black velvet and was surrounded by further symbolic statuary. In the folds of the velvet two flying figures held cypress branches and coats of arms, while the whole structure was surmounted by two further flying figures blowing the trumpets of fame and holding a golden cloth with an inscription summarizing the meaning that informed the entire structure: Sophie Charlotte's incomparable virtue leads to her immortality.

3   **The Representation of the Queen in Death—Piety, Wisdom, and Reason**

In recording minutely the overwhelming grandeur of the mausoleum, the *Kurtze Beschreibung* projects a detailed image of the queen and her virtues.

---

8   An engraving of the mausoleum published in the funeral volume is included in the *Theatrum Europæum*.

The striking level of complementarity between this image and the treatment of Sophie Charlotte in the other funeral sources points to the official fashioning—indeed, control—of Sophie Charlotte's image in death. Whether articulated in prose or verse, painting, statuary, or emblem, the portrayal of the queen and her defining qualities displays a remarkable congruency. The following analysis focuses primarily on the presentation of the virtue of piety, but also includes the treatment of her wisdom and reason. It demonstrates the way in which the coherence of message is articulated in diverse media, revealing how dynastic tradition and new accents are blended to create a distinctive profile in the characterization of the queen.

The centrality of piety in the canon of virtues ascribed to the early modern consort is reflected in the design of the chancel. Four bronze statues representing Friedrich's principal territories and dedicated to Sophie Charlotte's key virtues were positioned on columns in each corner, with the queen's piety aligned with the new kingdom of Prussia. An accompanying inscription on the column, that the piety of the consort has transformed the court into an altar, articulates a fundamental principle of the dynastic state—namely, that the piety of the ruling family is informed by the exemplary faith of the consort (Bepler, 2010: 134–38). Within Hohenzollern tradition this exemplary piety had been styled so as to respond to the confessional division that had pertained in Brandenburg and Prussia since Elector Johann Sigismund's (1572–1619) public embrace of the Reformed faith, in 1613. From this point the court represented a Reformed enclave, divorced from the majority Lutheranism of the Hohenzollerns' subjects. Throughout the century this schism was a source of tension that the dynasty sought to negotiate. One means of appeasing Lutheran hostility was to emphasize the consort's position as *Landesmutter* to all her subjects, independent of their confession, by endowing her with a non-doctrinaire faith. The public character of the consorts' funeral volume was exploited to convey this message, as illustrated in the case of the first Reformed electress, Elisabeth Charlotte of the Palatinate (1597–1660), the mother of the Great Elector. In her funeral sermon the court chaplain Bartholomäus Stosch downplays her adherence to Reformed doctrine, emphasizing instead that her faith is based on beliefs shared by Lutherans and the Reformed.[9] Similarly, Sophie Charlotte's piety is characterized by its generic Protestantism, unencumbered by Lutheran or Calvinist doctrine. For example, her chosen funeral text, John 11:25–26, is interpreted by Benjamin Ursin von Bär, the Hohenzollerns' Reformed court chaplain, so as to underline her certain faith in the redemptive

---

9 On the career of Stosch (1604–1686), see Thadden, 1959: 179–84. For further details of the presentation of Elisabeth Charlotte's faith, see Smart, 2017.

power of Christ's blood to achieve the forgiveness of sin, the fundamental Protestant tenet around which both confessions could unite.[10]

This representation of her faith is echoed in visual form in the ninth painting of Gericke's cycle. Sophie Charlotte is shown sitting on a rock, indicative of the steadfastness of her faith. To one side of her are the tablets with the Ten Commandments and the bread and wine of communion, and to the other, the Lamb of God bears the sins of the world. The uncluttered symbolism is redolent of Lucas Cranach the Elder's illustration of Luther's teaching in his iconic work *Law and Gospel*: the Decalogue represents the law of the Old Testament, which the fallen human being is unable to keep, forcing them to remain a prisoner of sin; the gospel of the New Testament with its message of grace is represented by the paschal lamb, the symbol of Christ's Crucifixion through which sin is overcome and humankind saved; the host and wine signify Christ's redeeming blood.[11] In other words, in his depiction of the queen's piety, Gericke has assembled the iconography of Protestantism as developed by Luther and Cranach during the Reformation. With one hand pointing to the lamb and the other to her heart, she is styled as an embodiment of a core Protestant faith, unshakable in her confidence in the power of the Crucifixion to bring grace and release from sin.

Another traditional hallmark of the piety of the Hohenzollern consort is endurance in suffering. This quality also defines Sophie Charlotte. Such is the strength of her exemplary faith that she is able to bear the troubles that befall her in life with calm, a theme addressed in the vitae. The analogy between lightning striking the tallest spires and misfortune befalling the highest in the land prompts praise of the queen's heroic constancy in adversity. Such an attitude is predicated on her calm acceptance of God's will, as illustrated in her approach to death. The vitae dwell at length on her deathbed suffering: the queen has severe difficulty breathing, she has headaches and pains in her abdomen, she sweats unevenly; when she is bled, she does not respond, and when she expectorates, the phlegm is flecked with blood. Yet as the suffering intensifies she remains tranquil, displaying in her prayers a "Demuths-Reu-und Glaubensvolle[s] Hertz ... [a humble, remorseful, and faithful heart] (*Ehren-Gedächtnüß*, s.p., M2ʳ). All those in attendance testify that when her end was imminent, the queen "[liess] die geringste Kleinmüthigkeit nicht vermercken [...] / sondern von solcher Zeit an / ihrem Tod unerschrocken entgegen gesehen" [did not display the slightest want of courage, ... but from that time

---

10   On the career of Ursin von Bär (1646–1720), see Thadden, 1959: 188–91.
11   For analysis of the visual articulation of the Protestant theology of justification in the work of Lucas Cranach the Elder, see Koerner, 1996: 363–79.

on faced her death without fear] (*Ehren-Gedächtniß*, 85). While the emphasis on the deceased's preparedness for death is a distinctive feature of the early modern funeral volume in general, in the case of the consort her faithful fearlessness speaks the character of the dynasty. The representation of Sophie Charlotte as the "Großmüthige Fürstin" [valiant princess] (*Ehren-Gedächtnüß*, s.p., N2ᵛ) situates her within a specifically Reformed tradition. For example, in Elisabeth Charlotte's vita attention is drawn to her heroic endurance of the manifold suffering that she and her natal and marital dynasties endured in the Thirty Years' War precisely because of their Reformed faith. Heroism in adversity, patient acceptance of God's will, endurance in trial—these qualities are, of course, an expression of the deep religiosity of the age, but within the Reformed dynasty they are an iteration of an identity that stretches back to the confessional persecution of the late-sixteenth and seventeenth centuries (Smart, 2017: 378). Within this context, Sophie Charlotte is simply the latest embodiment of this heritage.

In her case, however, this message extends beyond the funeral volume and is repeated in the various media of the mausoleum. In addition to the four statues in the chancel, eight statues of female figures representing virtues that characterize the queen are positioned on columns in the nave. Included among them is calmness of mind that enables her to withstand adversity. The statue tramples underfoot a skeleton, wrapped in a shroud, so symbolizing the victory of this virtue over death. The theme finds emphatic expression in the final painting in Gericke's cycle, in which the queen's death is depicted as a sublime moment. Her mortality is represented by two images, a broken hourglass borne by a grieving *putto* and a lamp wrested from the arms of a personification of health by a figure representing time. The queen's "unvergleichliche Großmühtigkeit" [incomparable bravery] (Gericke, C2ʳ) is rendered by a crowned female figure seated on a lion, who supports the dying queen as her corporality, symbolized by an outer garment, literally falls from her. At this moment of death, the queen looks upward with a radiant expression, her eyes fixed on a figure representing eternity, its head covered by a cloth and its feet hidden behind clouds in order to convey eternity's unknown nature. The visual symbolism may be new in Hohenzollern funeral tradition, but Gericke's emphatic contrast between body and spirit, transience and eternity, and the queen's triumph as she passes from one sphere to the next is simply a visual manifestation of a time-honored representation of the consort.

An unusual feature of Sophie Charlotte's funeral publications is the focus on the sincerity and privacy of her faith and her abhorrence of Pharisaism. The contrast between the consort's personal piety and the religious hypocrisy of others is not a new topos; it appears in Luise Henriette's funeral volume (*Sieben*

Leichpredigten, 46–48). What is novel, however, is the emphatic application of this topos. The inscription beneath the statue dedicated to her piety in the chancel draws a distinction between the joyous expression characteristic of the queen when in communion with God and the hypocritical expression and the contrived gestures of those who do not share her "wahre Andacht" [true devotion] and "Auffrichtigkeit des Hertzens" [sincerity of heart] (*Kurtze Beschreibung,* 19). The antithesis reappears in the funeral volume. The description of her given in Ursinus von Bär's sermon as "eine Verborgene des Herrn / die Ihr Leben in Christo auch vor der Welt wolt verborgen haben" [one whose relationship with God was kept close, who also sought to conceal her life in Christ from the world], to whom "der blosse Schein der Gottseeligkeit" [the mere feigning of godliness] was anathema (*Christ-Königliches Trauer- Und Ehren-Gedächtüs,* 30), is complemented in the vita, in which her "standhafte [...] Gottesfurcht" [steadfast fear of the Lord] is defined in contradistinction to those who are irreligious and, above all, to those whose behavior is distinguished by "angemaßte Frömmigkeit" [assumed piety] and "die Maßke der Scheinheiligkeit" [the mask of hypocrisy], behind which the greatest sins tend to hide (*Ehren-Gedächtniß,* 64). In his epicedium Besser, too, remarks on this distinguishing characteristic:

> Sich stellen, scheinlich thun, das hat Sie nicht gekönnet,
> Und weniger vor GOtt, der alles sehen kan.
> Wofern man Christenthum, die Hände falten, nennet,
> Die Augen stets verdrehn, so geht es Sie nicht an;
> Sie sprach: was ist es noth, dem Heuchler nachzuaffen?
> Wir haben es mit GOtt, ders Hertze sieht, zu schaffen.[12]

> [To strike a pose, to feign, this she was never able to do,
> and much less so before God, who sees everything.
> What's called Christian faith and comprises folding one's hands in prayer
> and constantly lifting one's eyes to heaven, that was of no interest to her.
> She said: why is it necessary to ape the hypocrite?
> Our concern is with God, who sees into our hearts.]

The frequency with which this contrast occurs indicates its importance in the portrayal of the queen's piety, yet there is no one reason for its significance. Rather, there are three possible, though not necessarily contradictory, explanations: the first is Sophie Charlotte's upbringing, the second and most complex

---

12   The epicedium is included in Besser, 1720: 145–58. For the quotation, see 149.

links to Friedrich's religious policy, and the third relates to Sophie Charlotte's philosophical interests.

As regards her upbringing, her mother Sophie of Hanover was undogmatic in matters pertaining to religion, as exemplified by her support of Leibniz's efforts to bring about a union of the Catholic and Protestant churches (Zedler, 1989: 46). With regard to the confession of her daughter's future bridegroom, she admitted to an indifference as to whether he was Catholic, Lutheran, or Calvinist (Ghayegh-Pisheh, 2000: 22). From the perspective of Hanoverian marriage diplomacy, Sophie Charlotte was a valuable tool in forging new alliances. In this context, confessional orthodoxy was wholly subordinate to political ambition, as demonstrated by plans to marry her to prominent Catholics; after the prospect of a marriage with the Dauphin proved illusory, the Hanoverians began negotiations to engineer a match with the son of the Catholic elector, Maximilian of Bavaria (Bepler, 2015: 126; Ghayegh-Pisheh, 2000: 21–22). The recognition that a young princess needed to embrace confessional plurality in order to fulfil her future role as consort was not untypical in this period (Wade, 2015: 507–8). Indeed, before her marriage Sophie Charlotte took communion in the Reformed manner to mark her switch from the official Lutheranism of her father's dynasty to the Reformed faith of her husband's (Schönpflug, 2013: 117). In her case, it seems likely that the confessional cosmopolitanism that characterized her parents' attitude toward her marriage engendered a religious practice that, in eschewing purity of catechism, was characterized by its individual and private character.

Seen within the wider context of the religious character of the Empire at the turn of the century, the stylization of Sophie Charlotte's piety takes on further significance. The rejection of Pharisaism and the endorsement of individual piety are immediately identifiable as tenets that distinguish the Pietist movement. Informed by the call for a renewal of an internal faith, the movement condemned the self-satisfied observance of religious practice that was devoid of spiritual meaning. Rather than keeping the letter of the law, the individual should engage in the active practice of Christian charity (Kruse, 1990: 81). The primary significance of the contrast between empty exteriority and vital inner faith can be gauged by the importance that Philipp Jakob Spener (1635–1705), the father of Lutheran Pietism in Germany (Wallmann, 1990: 37), attached to the controversial sermon he delivered in July 1669 in Frankfurt am Main, where he was serving as superintendent of the Lutheran Church. Based on Matthew 5:20 and entitled "Von der Pharisäer ungültiger und frommer Kinder Gottes wahren Gerechtigkeit," [On the vain righteousness of the Pharisees and the true righteousness of the pious children of God], the sermon caused outrage among some, but prompted soul-searching among others, thus initiating, in Spener's assessment, the Pietist movement in Frankfurt (Wallmann, 1990: 42; Brecht, 1993: 296; Kruse, 1990: 80).

Spener came to Berlin in 1691 after serving six years in Dresden as chief court chaplain to the elector of Saxony, Johann Georg III (1647–1691), and his family. As the Saxon elector was at this time the leader of the Corpus Evangelicorum, the body comprising the Protestant estates in the imperial diet, Spener's position enjoyed particular esteem (Brecht, 1993: 329). Yet he accepted Friedrich's call to serve as provost of the St. Nikolaikirche and as a consistorial councilor. For Spener the appeal of these posts lay in the greater degree of religious tolerance that, in contrast to Lutheran Saxony, pertained in Brandenburg-Prussia as a consequence of bi-confessionalism (Wallmann, 1990: 58; Kruse, 1990: 77). For Friedrich, ever focused on raising the profile of his residence, Spener's attraction was based in part on his reputation as a prominent churchman (Brecht, 1993: 352). Another factor was Spener's challenge to doctrinaire groups within the Lutheran church. His criticism of rigid orthodoxy, which he regarded as uninspired by the strength of personal faith and thus inimical to the Pietist movement, only enhanced his appeal to Friedrich and his advisors (Kruse, 1990: 83). Hohenzollern religious policy, in its efforts to establish a peaceful coexistence between the Lutheran and the Reformed, had repeatedly encountered the intransigent opposition of Lutheran orthodoxy. In this respect, Spener and Friedrich shared a common adversary. In Berlin, Spener profited from the Hohenzollern concern with fostering confessional tolerance, which enabled the Pietist movement to gather momentum. As a consequence of his close association with some of Friedrich's key advisors, he secured positions for others who were in sympathy with his view—most famously, August Hermann Francke (1663–1727), appointed professor of Greek and Oriental languages at Friedrich's newly established university in Halle, where he founded his famous orphanage (Wallmann, 1990: 58; Brecht, 1993: 353–54).

Yet Spener does not appear to have cultivated close relations to the ruling family, in marked contrast to the situation in Dresden. For all that his relationship with Johann Georg III was strained, he enjoyed the confidence of the electress Anna Sophie of Denmark (1647–1717), whom he continued to visit after he left Dresden and who brought him into contact with her sisters, Wilhelmine Ernestine (1650–1706), the widowed electress of the Palatinate, and Ulrike Eleonore (1656–1693), the wife of Karl XI of Sweden (Brecht, 1993: 333–34). While Sophie Charlotte may be renowned for her conversations and correspondence with Leibniz, which embraced the discussion of religion and spiritual matters, she is not associated with the attendance of conventicles, the small group meetings designed to foster personal piety that were so characteristic of Pietism. Moreover, her cultivation of theater, which had already provoked the criticism of the Reformed court chaplain Christian Cochius (1632–1699) in 1695, may possibly have been an alienating factor in her relations with the Pietist community: while she enthusiastically supported ballet and Italian opera and instigated the construction of a theater within the grounds of Lietzenburg, Pietist opposition to the performance of theater in Berlin was particularly strident (Frenzel, 1959: 24–27; Brecht, 1993: 353; Göse, 2012: 321–22, 332).

If Sophie Charlotte's ties to the Pietist movement were merely loose, the question arises about why the portrayal of her piety is given an overtly Pietist shading. The answer lies in Friedrich's religious policy, both within and beyond his own borders. Friedrich valued Pietism as a force to bring about reconciliation between Lutherans and the Reformed in his own territories. With his emphasis on renewal and inner faith, Spener was not exercised by confessional polemics, attaching greater importance to the promotion of the non-doctrinaire, inclusively Protestant ideal of the priesthood of all believers. By focusing on common belief, Spener and his followers sought to bridge inner-Protestant division. These conciliatory principles inform the image of the queen: her studiedly non-confessional faith as well as the contrast between personal piety and the preoccupation with hollow formality echo Spener's values and condemnation of the orthodox preoccupation with the law rather than the spirit. In other words, the stylization of Sophie Charlotte's piety harnesses the cross-confessional, propitiatory Pietist impulse with the result that she is portrayed as uninterested in—and remote from—confessional division. The impact is the same as that of Gericke's painting: Sophie Charlotte is represented as the queen of all her subjects, independent of their allegiance to the Lutheran or Reformed churches.

In this respect, the manner of portrayal is, if not a matching pendant, very similar to Friedrich's depiction in his public Statement of Faith, formulated between 1697 and 1700. In this he presents himself as a committed but dispassionate Protestant. He professes disagreement with aspects of the teaching of Luther, Zwingli, and Calvin, before he ultimately aligns himself with the Reformed tradition, arguing that this most closely matches his own beliefs. This adherence to a core Protestantism was designed to placate the hostility of the Lutheran majority of his subjects that believed he was biased toward his co-religionists (Luh, 2001: 160; Göse, 2012: 315). In downplaying Protestant division by displaying critical distance to both Luther and Calvin, the statement positions Friedrich as the Protestant *Landesvater* of all subjects of his bi-confessional territories. The level of complementarity between the styling of the queen's personal, studiedly non-doctrinaire piety and the Statement of Faith suggests a consistent, long-term policy to promote an image of dynastic tolerance and impartiality to a domestic audience.

The Statement of Faith was also directed at a second, non-domestic audience. Following the conversion of Johann Georg III's successor, Elector Friedrich August I (1670–1733) to Catholicism in June 1697, and his subsequent coronation as King August II of Poland, Friedrich regarded himself as the premier Protestant prince of the Empire and believed that he should assume the leadership of the Corpus Evangelicorum. However, he met with the resistance of the Lutheran estates of the Empire; for them, his Reformed faith and the suspicion that he might favor his co-religionists were problematic. The Statement of Faith was aimed at those uncooperative Lutherans and sought to persuade them of Friedrich's suitability based on the Hohenzollern brand of supraconfessional Protestantism. Moreover, Friedrich was convinced of the need for Protestant unity to counter the threat posed by hostile Catholic powers, most clearly represented by Louis XIV and his policy of re-Catholicization (Luh, 2001: 157–58). In 1697 he had instigated discussions between his Reformed court chaplain, the famous irenicist Daniel Jablonski (1660–1741), and representatives of the Lutheran Hanoverian court, including Leibniz.[13] The aim was to create a union between the Lutheran and Reformed churches of the Empire. Although this initiative failed, Friedrich established a Collegium Irenicum Stabilitum in 1703 to continue his efforts—in this instance to work toward the union of the two churches in Brandenburg-Prussia (Meyer, 2003: 159; Luh, 2001: 162–63). Seen against this backdrop, the lavish commemoration of the queen's piety in the mausoleum and the wide dissemination of its description in the funeral publications underpin the Hohenzollern claim to preeminence among the Protestant powers. It is also feasible that the emphasis on the personal sincerity of her faith in opposition to religious hypocrisy is informed by an irenicism that seeks to unite believers around fundamental truths.

The third and final explanation of the significance attached to the contrast between the integrity of Sophie Charlotte's faith and the dissembling of others lies in her love of learning. In both vitae her intellectuality is underlined. Listed among her greatest pleasures is "der Umgang mit wenigen aber ausgesonderten Personen" [her contact with a small but select group of people]; in this

---

13   For discussion of Jablonski's irenicist activities and networks, see Braun, 1990; Meyer, 2003; and Schunka, 2014. Since I completed research for this article Alexander Schunka's major study of relations based on a shared Protestantism between Brandenburg-Prussia and Great Britain in the late-seventeenth and early-eighteenth centuries has appeared. This provides close analysis of the political, theological, and confessional complexion of Brandenburg-Prussia. See Schunka, 2019.

circle "[wurden] die wichtigsten Wahrheiten in Ihrer Gegenwart untersucht und die schweresten Fragen erortert / ... Die lehrreichsten Anmerckungen der Geschicht-Schreiber / die edlesten Gedancken der Staats und Tugend-Lehrer wurden wiederholet" [the most important truths were explored in her presence and the most difficult questions discussed ... the most learned observations of historians and the noblest thoughts of educators in statecraft and virtue were recalled] (*Ehren-Gedächtniß*, 74–75). There is no question about the purpose of such intellectual activity: "Der Zweck Ihrer Wissenschaft war / GOTT und sich selbst zu erkennen" [the aim of her scholarship was to know God and herself] (*Ehren-Gedächtniß*, 72). The identities of those who made up her special circle are not revealed, but Leibniz was of pivotal importance. His association with the Welph dynasty reached back to 1676, when he was initially appointed as court librarian in Hanover, and he remained in Welph service for the rest of his life. His close relationship with Sophie Charlotte's mother, Sophie of Hanover, is recorded in the three hundred letters they exchanged over a period of thirty years.[14] Her engagement in his theory of monads and his wider philosophy provided a model for her daughter. Sophie Charlotte's developing curiosity in Leibniz's philosophical ideas probably dates to a summer visit to Hanover in 1698, when she and her mother spent time together with him. This resulted in an invitation to Lietzenburg, where he became a welcome guest.

Leibniz fulfilled the role of mentor to Sophie Charlotte, encouraging her innate interest in current philosophical and religious debates and enabling her, through answers to her questions, to grasp detail and nuance. Topics discussed included John Locke's "Essay Concerning Human Understanding" (1690), Pierre Bayle's *Dictionnaire historique et critique* (1697), with its challenge to religious orthodoxy, and the views of the Irish freethinker and deist John Toland, who spent time at Lietzenburg, where he could air freely his highly controversial views.[15] Her encouragement of debate, be it between Toland and Isaac Beausobre, her Huguenot court chaplain, or between Beausobre and the Jesuit Carlo Mauritius Vota, former confessor to the king of Poland, further sharpens the impression of her non-orthodox, intellectual curiosity. For Sophie Charlotte, Leibniz opened up a world of cosmopolitan, non-doctrinaire thought, where plurality of religious viewpoints was the norm. The aim of her enquiry may have been to know God better, but her knowledge of him was the product of ideas that would presumably have unsettled the guardians of orthodoxy. The

---

14   For analysis of the relationship and correspondence between Leibniz and Sophie, see Zedler, 1989: 45–51.

15   For discussion of Sophie Charlotte's relationship with Leibniz, see Ross, 1999; and Zedler, 1989: 53–59. On her knowledge of other philosophers, see Heuvel, 1999.

significance of the emphasis on the privacy of Sophie Charlotte's own relationship with God in the funeral publications may thus extend beyond the context of Hohenzollern religious policy and hint at a hitherto unknown level of complexity and subtlety in the Hohenzollern consort's understanding of piety. That such understanding is, however, untainted by dangerously heterodox views is implied by its unambiguously positive juxtaposition with the sanctimony and cant of the Pharisee.

The analysis of the representation of Sophie Charlotte's piety has shown the multifaceted nature of this definitive virtue. Its different facets are interwoven and expanded on in the various commemorative media. It is a composite virtue, comprising, on the one hand, dynastic traditions, and on the other, a unique accent in the treatment of the personal piety specific to the queen, which defies neat, one-dimensional categorization. Whether this may be explained with reference to non-doctrinaire attitudes brought from her natal court, or to Hohenzollern confessional policies, or to the fruits of the debates in Lietzenburg, or whether it encompasses all three readings, the defining abhorrence of religious hypocrisy distinguishes the queen's piety from that of other consorts. Nonetheless there is complementarity between the old and the new. Sophie Charlotte's depiction in accordance with Hohenzollern tradition as an embodiment of core Protestantism harmonizes with the emphatically non-doctrinaire characterization her personal faith. Both testify to the nonpartisan portrayal of the Hohenzollern consort as a means of seeking reconciliation between the Reformed and Lutheran communities.

The link between spiritual edification and the consort as intellectual scholar, an entirely new departure in the portrayal of the Hohenzollern consort, remains a constant in the funeral publications. Sophie Charlotte's love of learning is much vaunted, which suggests that the image of the philosopher queen was regarded as an enhancement of monarchical dignity. The vitae highlight her precocity as a child, evident in her "sinnreich[er] Verstand" [profound reason] (*Ehren-Gedächtniß*, 47). As an adult, she honed her powers of argument through reading from her extensive library. In the sermon's laudation, Ursinus von Bär commends her reason and strength of judgement. The statues surrounding the coffin dedicated to her virtues include her love of wisdom and the perfection of her reason. The uniqueness of a female scholar can be inferred from the inscription accompanying the statue dedicated to wisdom: "Sophia Charlotta / Verachtete den Weiblichen Putz / Und begab sich auff eine Männliche Weise / Denen höhern Wissenschafften zu dienen" [... despised female adornment and set out in the manner of man to serve the higher arts and sciences] (*Kurtze Beschreibung*, 21). The male gendering underlines the extent to which her intellectual pursuits do not fit within the traditional mould of female panegyric. Nonetheless this innovative celebration of female intellectual prowess is uniformly sited within the traditional framework of piety. The firm association between Sophie Charlotte's learning and her knowledge of God is reiterated in the inscriptions beneath both statues, a pairing that finds symbolic visual expression in Gericke's treatment of her intellect. The second painting in his cycle focuses on Sophie Charlotte's education, depicting her as a child, on her head a garland of mustard leaves, symbolizing the powers of memory and reason. She stands before a seated figure representing wisdom styled as Minerva, complete with armor and a highly polished shield. Gericke's interpretation of Minerva's armor is central to the moral thrust of this work: just as the armor protects against evil, so the shining shield represents "die hellpollirte und auserlesene kluge Sitten-Lehren / welche die himmlische Weißheit in der Schrifft uns zeiget" [the brightly polished, excellent, and clever lessons on morality, which heavenly wisdom reveals to us in the Bible] (Gericke, A2^r). A direct counterpart is provided by the eighth painting, a celebration of the time the adult Sophie Charlotte dedicates to study. She is now depicted as Minerva. Among the figures that surround her is a child carrying a staff around which is wound a snake, a common image of cleverness, and which, as interpreted by Gericke, connotes the striving of the spirit upward towards the divine. In short, the depictions of Sophie Charlotte as scholarly princess or philosopher queen are both characterized by their spiritual charge. Arguably, the novelty of the image of a queen with insights into hitherto unrevealed truths mirrors the dynamics at the beginning of the eighteenth century, when new directions were being followed to find solutions to the perennial problem of confessional rigidity. In this respect, the image of the queen invests the new monarchy not just with a supraconfessional authority but also a forward-looking openness in matters of faith.

One aspect of Sophie Charlotte's intellectual endeavour that is omitted in the vitae is her close involvement in the establishment of the Royal Prussian Society of Sciences. In 1697 she expressed interest in the construction of an observatory in Berlin, which sparked the idea in Leibniz to combine the observatory with the establishment of a society of sciences to parallel the Royal Society and the Académie Royale des Sciences, founded in 1660 and 1666 respectively. Together with Jablonski, Leibniz worked on a proposal that in March 1700 was submitted to Friedrich, who went on to sign the society's deed of foundation the following July. In the same year the foundation stone for the observatory was laid, although the building was not completed until 1708. Sophie Charlotte's active engagement in the project and her role in encouraging Friedrich to support it were crucial to the realization of Leibniz's plans.[16]

---

16   On the establishment of the Prussian Society of Sciences, see Brather, 1993.

While there may be no explicit reference to these events in the funeral publications, this background informs a group of emblems sited on cartouches attached to pillars in the nave of the cathedral. Described as heroic emblems and positioned beneath crowned eagles, these emblems employ astronomical reference to celebrate the queen. An instance is supplied by the tenth emblem, in which her death is likened to an eclipse of the sun. Together, the motto "Er [der Tod] stehet ihr nicht im Wege" [He [death] does not stand in her way], the depiction of an eclipse in the *pictura*, and the *inscriptio* "SIE hat wieder Willen des Todes sich wieder nach ihrem Ursprung gewandt" [Against the will of death, she has returned to her origins once more] (*Kurze Beschreibung*, 35) underline that in the same way as the sun reappears after an eclipse, so her soul will ascend to heaven. At one level the emblem simply echoes the traditional interpretation of the queen's life and death, but at another it alludes, if only obliquely, to her interest in a scientific view of the universe that went far beyond the confines of tradition.

Bibliography

Bepler, Jill. "Enduring Loss and Memorializing Women. The Cultural Roles of Dynastic Widows in Early Modern Germany." In *Enduring Loss in Early Modern Germany. Cross Disciplinary Perspectives*, ed. Lynn Tatlock, Studies in Central European Histories 1 (Leiden: Brill, 2010), 133–60.

Bepler, Jill. "Welfen und Hohenzollern vom 16. bis zum 18. Jahrhundert." In *Frauensache. Wie Brandenburg Preußen wurde*, ed. Generaldirektion der Stiftung Preußische Schlösser und Gärten Berlin-Brandenburg (Dresden: Sandstein, 2005), 122–31.

Besser, Johann von. *Preußische Krönungs-Geschichte / Oder Verlauf der Ceremonien / Mit welchen Der Allerdurchlauchtigste / Großmächtigste Fürst und Herr / Herr Friderich der Dritte / Marggraf und Churfürst zu Brandenburg / Die Königliche Würde Des von Ihm gestiffteten Königreichs Preussen angenommen / [...]* (Cölln an der Spree: Ulrich Liebpert, 1702).

Besser, Johann von. *Des Herrn von B. Schrifften, Beydes in gebundener und ungebundener Rede; So viel man derer, Theils aus ihrem ehemahligen Drucke, theils auch aus guter Freunde schrifftlichen Communication, zusammen bringen können*, 2nd ed. (Leipzig: Gleditisch, 1720).

Börsch-Supan, Helmut. "Zeitgenössische Bildnisse des Großen Kurfürsten." In *Ein sonderbares Licht in Teutschland. Beiträge zur Geschichte des Großen Kurfürsten von Brandenburg (1640–1688)*, ed. Gerd Heinrich (Berlin: Duncker & Humblot, 1990), 151–66.

Brather, Hans-Stephan. *Leibniz und seine Akademie. Ausgewählte Quellen zur Geschichte der Berliner Sozietät der Wissenschaften 1697–1716* (Berlin: Akademie Verlag, 1993).

Braun, Dietrich. "Daniel Ernst Jablonski." In *Berlinische Lebensbilder. Theologen*, ed. Gerd Heinrich (Berlin: Colloquium Verlag, 1990), 89–109.

Brecht, Martin. "Philipp Jakob Spener, sein Programm und dessen Auswirkungen." In *Der Pietismus vom siebzehnten bis zum frühen achtzehnten Jahrhundert*, ed. Martin Brecht, Geschichte des Pietismus 1 (Göttingen: Vandenhoeck & Ruprecht, 1993), 278–389.

Brüggemann, Linda. *Herrschaft und Tod in der Frühen Neuzeit. Das Sterbe- und Begräbniszeremoniell preußischer Herrscher vom Großen Kurfürsten bis zu Friedrich Wilhelm II. (1688–1797)*, Geschichtswissenschaften 33 (Munich: Herbert Utz Verlag, 2015).

Christ-Königliches Trauer- Und Ehren-Gedächtnüs / Der Weyland Allerdurchlauchtigsten Großmächtigsten Fürstin und Frauen / Frauen Sophien Charlotten / Königin in Preussen / Marggräffin und Churfürstin zu Brandenburg/ [...] Als dieselbe am I. Febr. 1705. zu Hannover höchstseeligst in dem Herrn entschlaffen. Und Darauf den 28. Junii, mit Königl. Solennitäten in die Königl. und Chur-fürstliche Grufft der Dohm-Kirche in Berlin beygesetzet worden [...] (Cölln an der Spree: Ulrich Liebpert, no date).

Ehren-Gedächtnüß / Der Allerdurchlauchtigsten Großmächtigsten Fürstin und Frauen / Frauen Sophien Charlotten / Königin in Preussen / [...] Unser weiland allergnädigsten Königin / Frauen und Landes-Mutter Höchstseliger Gedächtnüß (Cölln an der Spree: Ulrich Liebpert, no date).

Friedrich, Karin, and Sara Smart, eds. *The Cultivation of Monarchy and the Rise of Berlin: Brandenburg-Prussia 1700* (Farnham: Ashgate, 2010).

Ghayegh-Pisheh, K. *Sophie Charlotte von Preußen. Eine Königin und Ihre Zeit* (Stuttgart: *ibidem*-Verlag, 2000).

Gericke, Samuel Theodor. *Erklärung Derer In dem Königl. höchst-prächtig erbauten Mausoleo Allhier zu Berlin befindlichen Gemählde / Worinnen Der Allerdurchlauchtigsten Höchstseligsten Fürstin und Frauen / Fn. Sophia Charlotten / Ersten Königin in Preussen [...] Glorwürdigster Gedächtniß / Höchstrühmliches Vollbrachtes Leben / Durch Hieroglyphische Figuren vorgestellet und abgebildet worden* (Berlin: Gotthard Schlechtiger, no date).

Göse, Frank. *Friedrich I. (1657–1713). Ein König in Preußen* (Regensburg: Verlag Friedrich Pustet, 2012).

Hahn, Peter-Michael. "Hofkultur und Hohe Politik. Sophie Charlotte von Braunschweig-Lüneburg, die erste Königin in Preußen aus dem Hause Hannover." In *Sophie Charlotte und ihr Schloß. Ein Musenhof des Barock in Brandenburg-Preußen*, ed. Die Generaldirektion der Stiftung Preußische Schlösser und Gärten Berlin-Brandenburg (Munich: Prestel, 1999), 31–42.

Heuvel, Gerd van den. "Die Philosophie in der Hofkultur." In *Sophie Charlotte und ihr Schloß. Ein Musenhof des Barock in Brandenburg-Preußen*, ed. Die Generaldirektion der Stiftung Preußische Schlösser und Gärten Berlin-Brandenburg (Munich: Prestel, 1999), 90–94.

Koerner, Joseph Leo. *The Moment of Self-Portraiture in German Renaissance Art* (Chicago: University of Chicago Press, 1996).

Komander, Gerhild. "Tod und Trauer am brandenburg-preußischen Hof." In *Sophie Charlotte und ihr Schloß. Ein Musenhof des Barock in Brandenburg-Preußen*, ed. Die Generaldirektion der Stiftung Preußische Schlösser und Gärten Berlin-Brandenburg (Munich: Prestel, 1999), 171–77.

Kurtze Beschreibung Des Prächtigen Mausolei, Welches Seine Königl. Majestät in Preussen / Zur Unsterblichen Ehre Des immerwährenden Andenckens vor Dero Glorwürdigste und Höchst-Seeligste Gemahlin Sophien Charlotten / Allhier im Duhm auffrichten lassen: [...] (Berlin: Johann Wessel, no date).

Kruse, Martin. "Philipp Jakob Spener." In *Berlinische Lebensbilder. Theologen*, ed. Gerd Heinrich (Berlin: Colloquium Verlag, 1990), 75–87.

Luh, Jürgen. "Die Religionspolitik Friedrichs III./I." In *Preußen 1701. Eine europäische Geschichte*. Volume 2. *Essays*, eds. Franziska Windt, Christoph Lind, and Sepp-Gustav Gröschel (Berlin: Henschel, 2001), 156–64.

Meyer, Dietrich. "Daniel Ernst Jablonksi und seine Unionspläne." In *Irenik und Antikonfessionalismus im 17. und 18. Jahrhundert*, ed. Harm Klueting, Hildesheimer Forschungen. Tagungs- und Forschungsberichte aus dem Dombibliothek Hildesheim 2, ed. Jochen Bepler (Hildesheim: Olms, 2003), 153–75.

Ross, George MacDonald. "Leibniz und Sophie Charlotte." In *Sophie Charlotte und ihr Schloß. Ein Musenhof des Barock in Brandenburg-Preußen*, ed. Die Generaldirektion der Stiftung Preußische Schlösser und Gärten Berlin-Brandenburg (Munich: Prestel, 1999), 95–105.

Schönpflug, Daniel. *Die Heiraten der Hohenzollern. Verwandtschaft, Politik und Ritual in Europa 1640–1918*, Kritische Studien zur Geschichtswissenschaft 207 (Göttingen: Vandenhoeck & Ruprecht, 2013).

Schunka, Alexander. "Im Dienst des internationalen Protestantismus. Der Berliner Hofprediger Daniel Ernst Jablonski (1660–1741)." In *Religion Macht Politik. Hofgeistlichkeit im Europa der Frühen Neuzeit (1500–1800)*, eds. Matthias Meinhardt, Ulrike Gleixner, Martin H. Jung, and Siegrid Westphal, Wolfenbütteler Forschungen 137 (Wiesbaden: Harrassowitz, 2014), 361–78.

Schunka, Alexander. *Ein neuer Blick nach Westen. Deutsche Protestanten und Großbritannien (1688–1740)* (Wiesbaden: Harrassowitz, 2019).

Sieben Leichpredigten Nebst Unterschiedlichen Anderen Traur-und Trost-Schrifften Auff Den frühzeitigen / doch höchstseligen Abscheid Der weyland Durchläuchtigsten

Fürstin und Frauen / Frauen Louysen, Marggräffinn und Churfüstinn zu Brandenburg [...] *Deren Churfürstlicher Cörper Am 8. Junij Anno 1667. von der Seelen abgesondert / Und am 26. Novembris desselbigen Jahres* [...] *in das Erb-Begräbnüß der Thum-Kirchen zu Cölln an der Spree ist beygesetzet worden* (Cölln an der Spree: Georg Schultze, no date).

Smart, Sara. "The Arrival of Sheba, the Suffering of Job, and the Triumph of the Calvinist Dowager. The Portrayal of the Dynastic Widow in Brandenburg-Prussia." In *Frauen—Bücher—Höfe: Wissen und Sammeln vor 1800. Women—Books—Courts: Knowledge and Collecting before 1800. Essays in Honor of Jill Bepler*, eds. Volker Bauer, Elizabeth Harding, Gerhild Scholz Williams, and Mara R. Wade (Wiesbaden: Harrassowitz, 2018), 371–82.

Steiner, Uwe. "Triumphale Trauer. Die Trauerfeierlichkeiten aus Anlaß des Tods der ersten preußischen Königin in Berlin im Jahre 1705." *Forschungen zur brandenburgischen und preußischen Geschichte Neue Folge* 11 (2001), 23–52.

Thadden, Rudolf von. *Die brandenburgisch-preußischen Hofprediger im 17. und 18. Jahrhundert. Ein Beitrag zur Geschichte der absolutistischen Staatsgesellschaft in Brandeburg-Preußen* (Berlin: Walter de Gruyter, 1959).

Theatri Europæi Siebenzehender Theil. Oder Außführlich fortgeführte Friedens-und Kriegs-Beschreibung. [...] *bey Reichs-und Crayß-Versammlungen: An Kayserl. auch Chur-und Fürstl. Höfen /* [...] *vom 1704ten Jahr, biß Ausgangs 1706ten vorgegangen / und sich begeben haben* [...] (Frankfurt am Main: Anton Heinscheit, 1718). The digitized edition is available at https://www.deutsche-digitale-bibliothek.de/item /OU3L5N6OCZRMHJ4A4S62GIVNEHGK5J7F.

Wallmann, Johannes. *Der Pietismus*, vol. 4 of *Die Kirche in ihrer Geschichte. Ein Handbuch*, ed. Berndt Moeller, (Göttingen: Vandenhoeck & Ruprecht, 1990).

Wade, Mara R. "Women's Networks of Knowledge. The Emblem Book as Stammbuch." In *Knowledge in Motion. Constructing Transcultural Experience in the Medieval and Early Modern Periods (1200–1750)*, eds. Gerhild Scholz Williams and Christian Schneider, *Daphnis* 45 (2017), 492–509.

Zedler, Beatrice H. "The Three Princesses." *Hypatia. The History of Women in Philosophy* 4 (1) (1989), 28–63.

CHAPTER 6

German Nuptial Music in the Seventeenth Century: Sound in Service of the Sacred

Janette Tilley

Weddings were an important public performance in early modern Germany that enacted, in the ritualized public spaces of civic life, certain understandings about the relationship between the sexes, domestic order, and, more generally, social order. Few other public performances could claim the degree of social saturation that weddings did. In Protestant Germany, every member of society had the potential to take part, and had likely participated in some way at one point or another. Weddings, ubiquitous and necessary from a variety of legal and religious standpoints, were inscribed with more information about social dynamics, changing ideas about relationships, and hierarchies than perhaps any other public ritual or performance.

Naturally, much scholarly attention has been paid to the social and civic implications of weddings, sumptuary laws, and, in a broader view, public ritual.[1] The policing of domestic and social order through wedding ordinances helped maintain historic hierarchies that were rooted in much older social systems. The Reformation changed very little about the wedded state itself. Like the pre-Reformation church, Lutheranism continued to regard marriage as having three key qualities: it was sacred, consensual, and indissoluble. What differed was ideological and regulatory. For Luther, of course, the wedded state was recommended to all, not as a weak alternative to sexual continence and the chaste monastic life. Luther's sexual realism led him to endorse social regulation rather than abstinence as a way of controlling and directing the sexual proclivities of the faithful, lest they lead to sin. Protestants removed marriage from the sacraments and placed enforcement of laws related to it in the hands of an ostensibly secular—that is, civic—body. The story of Protestant weddings and their performative aspects, whether regal or burgher, has tended, therefore,

---

1 The list of studies is extensive; a few worthy of note include Wiesner-Hanks, 2000; Harrington, 1995; Karant-Nunn, 1999; see also the collection of essays edited by Rüdiger Schnell, 1997; and Brauner, 1994. Wedding sermons have attracted significantly less scholarly attention than funeral sermons, as Susan C. Karant-Nunn points out, though the situation has rapidly changed in recent years. Such a reversal has not taken place in the study of wedding music.

© KONINKLIJKE BRILL NV, LEIDEN, 2023 | DOI:10.1163/9789004682245_008

to point to the civic function of the wedding performance—inscribing social hierarchies through choreography in the public sphere. From the public reading of banns to the processions in the street to the banquet, each element of the ritual carried markers of social meaning, orienting couples and their families within the immanent social framework.

Yet this focus on the secular or civic elements of the early modern wedding ignores the deep-seated enmeshment of worldly marriage and end times that had persisted from early Christianity. For more than two centuries after the Reformation, the *Kirchgang*, or public procession to church, stood as a metonym for the event itself.[2] And while the Protestant wedding ceremony lacked the sanctifying efficacy of the Catholic sacrament, it remained an institution with the same three key qualities of sanctity, consensuality, and permanence. These qualities, now no longer facts of its sacramental status, needed to be inscribed in other ways—most conspicuously, as we shall see, through musical choices.

1 The Last Wedding

Early seventeenth-century devotional literature is full of references to Christ as the bridegroom, to individual Christians as the faithful and beloved bride, and to their unity in death, imagined as a heavenly wedding. A parallel between marriage and death was widespread in the century after the Reformation. This imagery was so thoroughly a part of the early modern Protestant framing of human experience that references extend well beyond the expected genres of *Erbauungsliteratur*, even turning up in common idioms. Michael Praetorius (1571–1621), court composer in Wolfenbüttel, makes reference to his anticipated blissful eternal wedding in the third and final preface to his encyclopedic *Syntagma musicum*, added in 1619, when the author may have been ruminating on his own mortality. He closes this additional preface by remarking on the wedding of "vnsers himlischen Breutigams Jesu Christi/ mit den himlischen *Cantoribus* vnd *perfectissimis Musicis* allen H. Engeln vnd Erz Engeln für dem

---

2 Already in the seventeenth century, local ordinances needed to address a problem with couples foregoing the church altogether, and printed *Agenda* explicitly prohibited house weddings, except in cases of illness. Certainly, by the first decades of the eighteenth century, the civic function of the marriage ceremony was well rooted in the Protestant imagination, if not in its laws. It would take another 150 years before the Prussian Law on Registration of Civil Status and the Formation of Marriage codified mandatory civil marriages in Prussia and, finally, in 1875, the *Reichspersonenstandgesetz* expressly made church unions null and void, mandating union before a public register.

Stuel des Lambs stehen/ eine stätig immerwehrende *Cantorei* halten" [our bridegroom Jesus Christ with the heavenly *Cantor* and all the immaculate musicians, the heavenly angels and archangels who stand at the seat of the lamb and hold an eternal *Cantorei*].[3] It was not only in the florid language of published rhetoric or the performative space of the church where men understood themselves to be awaiting their final wedding. Even in as functional and quotidian a document as a court ledger, this imagery is real: in 1616, Duke Friedrich Ulrich made an extra payment to his long-serving lutenist, Gregorius Huwet, "zu gnediger Verehrung uf seine Letzte Hochzeit" [for merciful reverence on his final wedding]. Huwet had served the Wolfenbüttel court for many years, including the court of the duke's father, and must have died that year, as payments to the lutenist, which had been substantial, ceased.[4]

Similar use of the term appears in an account of Protestant persecutions in late sixteenth-century Amsterdam, recounted in the late nineteenth century by one C. P. Hofstede de Groot. De Groot writes of a preacher condemned to death at the stake:

> Freunde der Frau gingen sie aufzusuchen, um während der Vollstreckung des Urteils sie zu trösten. Aber die Frau war nich daheim und nirgends zu finden. Um den Mittag kam sie zu ihren Kinderchen zurück. Man fragte sie: wo sie gewesen sei.—"Auf dem Dam; was meint ihr, daß ich meinen Bräutigam in seiner Not verlassen sollte? Ich mußte sehen, wie er seine letzte Hochzeit hielt."[5]

> [Friends of his wife went looking to comfort her during the execution. But the wife was not at home and was nowhere to be found. Around midday she returned home to her children. Someone asked her where she had been. "At the civic square, what did you think, that I would abandon my bridegroom in his need? I had to see how he held up at his final wedding."]

As a means of coping with mortality, and even martyrdom, the last wedding was a potent imaginative tool. The topos of the mystical final marriage with Christ was not merely a comforting idea, however, but an ontic necessity, for it lent earthly marriage its required sanctity, confirmed its dissolubility, and, especially for Protestants, affirmed the faithful's act of free will. The usefulness

---

3 Praetorius, 1619: 11r–11v.
4 Court ledger quoted in Wirth, 2017: 225.
5 Hofstede de Groot, 1893: 132. Several times in this book, de Groot refers to those led to the gallows or the stake as having a disposition as if going to a wedding ("als ginge es zur Hochzeit").

of the imagery circled back on itself, as Protestants adopted the language of marriage to confirm their faith, sometimes in the face of persecution, and to define their hoped-for eternal relationship with Christ.

2   Wedding Ceremonies

Within the wedding service itself, this personal eschatological lesson was typically absent from the formal proceedings. The seventeenth-century wedding service was largely oriented toward what we might regard as civic matters. The published *Agenda* dictated the texts to be read during the ceremony and often advised preachers on their duties. On a few occasions, musical suggestions were made.

First and foremost, the preacher was instructed to determine the appropriateness of the match, confirm an acceptable familial distance, and, through the reading of the banns, establish that the couple was free of prior contracts. Next, the couple was asked for their intent and consent, answering with the familiar "ja," or "I do." Notably, the consensual text here was identical for the two, asking only that each, before God and the assembled congregation, agree to each other as spouse. A Leipzig *Agenda* from 1658 is exemplary of this rather plain statement of consent:

> Demnach ihr euch in den heiligen Ehestand mit einander geben wollet/ auch deßwegen öffentlich auffgeboten worden/ So frage ich euch N. wolt ihr gegenwertige N. zum ehelichen Weibe haben/ so gebt des euer Bekäntnüß/ und sprecht Ja. Deßgleichen frage ich euch N. wolt ihr gegenwertigen N zum ehelichen Mann haben/ so gebt des auch euer Bekäntnüß/ und sagt Ja.[6]

> [Since you wish to give yourselves to each other in holy matrimony, and are called to do so openly, thus I ask you N. do you wish to take this N. as your wedded wife, so give your agreement and say yes. Similarly, I ask you N. do you take this N. as your wedded husband, so give your agreement and say yes.]

A simple blessing was given, followed by readings from Genesis, Paul's letter to the Ephesians (Instructions for Christian Households 5:25–29), and Psalm 128. The readings all affirm the social function of marriage—that work be divided

---

6   *Agenda*, Leipzig, 1658: 34v.

between the couple in fulfillment of God's will at creation, that women submit household authority to men, and that men love and care for their wives. Psalm 128 confirms the sanctity of a model household, and Paul's advice likewise focuses on the behavior of the nuptial couple. Proverbs 18:22, "Wer eine Ehefrau findet, der findet was gutes" [He who finds a wife finds a good thing], typically rounded out the scriptural selections.

Missing from the *Agenda* and marriage vows before roughly 1680 is much mention of love and affection. Rather, the language employed by all Protestant jurisdictions was primarily concerned with consent, while scriptural selections outlined the roles each marriage partner would play. Vows were simple statements of affirmation, lacking any emotional orientation, specific moral responsibilities, or pledges that fell along gender lines familiar in modern marriage oaths. These would come by the end of the century. An *Agenda* from 1697, by way of example, offers this lengthy statement of vows that admits a much wider moral and emotional framework than most oaths of the seventeenth century:

> N. Herr Bräutigam ihr stehet alhier für GOttes Angesicht und seinen Engeln/ auch für dieser Christlichen Gemein/ und begehret mit dieser euer lieben Braut ehlichen *Copuliret* seyn/ demnach frage ich euch/ obs euer endlicher Wille und beständige Meinung auch sey/ diese euer gelibte Braut zu lieben und zu ehren/ bey ihr zu wohnen mit Vernunfft und Verstand/ mit ihr vorlieb zunehmen Glück und Unglück/ Reichthum und Armuth/ Creutz und Kranckheit/ wie es euch der liebe GOtt nach seinem väterlichen Willen und euer Seligkeit zuschicken wird/ und sie in keinem Wege verlassen/ euch auch nicht von ihr scheiden/ es scheide euch dann der allmächtige Gott durch den zeitlichen Tod wieder voneinander. So ihr das in eurem Hertze beschlossen/wolt ihrs mit einem Ja=Wort bekräfftigen. Ja.
>
> N. N. Tugendsame Braut/ ihr höret/ welcher massen sich euer Bräutigam gegen euch erklaret/ so wil euch nun hinwieder auch gebühren/ daß ihr ihn hertzlich liebet/ ehret/ ihm auch Unterthänig und Gehorsam seyd/ mit ihm vorlieb nehmet Glück und Unglück/ Reichthum und Armut/ Creutz und Kranckheit/ wie es euch der liebe Gott nach seinem väterlichen Willen zuschicken und geben wird/ ihr wolt ihn auch nich verlassen in Lieb und Leid/ Glück oder Unglück/ euch auch nicht von ihm abwenden und scheiden/ es scheide euch dann der allmächtige Gott durch den zeitlichen Tod wieder von ihm/ so ihr das auch in eurem Hertzen beschlossen/ wolt ihr es mit einem Ja-Wort bekräfftigen. Ja.[7]

---

7 *Agenda*, Frankfurt an der Oder, 1697: 112–14.

[Bridegroom N., you stand here before God and his angels and also before this Christian congregation and desire to be joined in matrimony with this your beloved bride, so I ask you if it is your final resolve and enduring intention to love and honor this, your beloved bride, to live with her in reason and sound mind, to endure with her in happiness and misfortune, in richness and poverty, suffering and sickness, as bestowed on you by loving God according to his fatherly will and your bliss, and never leave her in any way, nor be separated from her, for only the almighty God through death may separate you from each other. To seal this in your heart, will you affirm this with "I do".

I do.

N.N., virtuous bride, you hear how your bridegroom has declared his intentions toward you; thus, will you likewise give your due, that you will love him with your heart, honor him, be subservient and obedient to him, endure with him in happiness and misfortune, in richness and poverty, suffering and sickness, as bestowed on you by loving God according to his fatherly will, and that you will never leave him in love and pain, happiness or sorrow, and never turn away and leave him, for only the almighty God through death may separate you from him. To seal this in your heart, will you affirm this with "I do".

I do.]

The ceremony concluded with an invocation that almost all Lutheran jurisdictions adopted, gesturing to the tenet holding earthly marriage as a simulacrum of the holy and eternal marriage of Christ with his church, the body faithful.

Herr Gott/ der du Mann und Weib geschaffen/ und zum Ehestand verordnet hast/ dazu mit Früchten des Leibs gesegnet/ und das Sacrament deines lieben Sohns Jesu CHRisti/ und der Kirchen seiner Braut darinne bezeichnet/ Wir bitten deine grundlose Güte/ Du wollest doch dein Geschöpff/ Ordnung/ und Segen/ nicht lassen verrücken noch verderben/ sondern gnädiglich in uns bewahren/ durch JEsum CHRist unsern HERRN/ Amen.[8]

[Lord God, you who created man and woman, and prescribed that they should marry, and thereby be blessed with fruits of their bodies, and thereby show the sacrament of your beloved son, Jesus Christ, and the church, his bride. We ask of your unworthy goodness that you let your

---

8 *Agenda*, Leipzig, 1658: 39r.

creation, order, and blessing be neither displaced nor spoiled, but merci-
fully allow it to perpetuate in us, through Jesus Christ our Lord, Amen.]

While wedding services drew widely from the Old and New Testaments, piec-
ing together passages that provide scriptural justification for marriage, one
book of scripture that is most explicitly concerned with love, affection, and
desire is curiously missing from *Agenda* of the seventeenth century: the Song
of Songs.

3   Song of Songs

The Song of Songs was an important part of the imaginative structure that
supported the Protestant marriage ideal, since it, both explicitly and implicitly, through exegetical tradition, embodies the trio of marriage characteristics. The book's canonicity assured that it would be understood as a sacred
story, not a lurid tale of physical lust. Exegetes from at least the second century had asserted the book's holiness, but none took hold of the imagination
more than the mystical-eschatological reading of Bernard of Clairvaux, who
read the book as an intensely personal conversation with Christ.[9] The Song of
Songs was also understood to describe a consensual union: the content of the
book confirms this in the affirmative statements of the two interlocutors, who
assert their love for one another freely, without external compulsion. Finally,
the understanding that this book described not the love between shepherds
or real historical people but that of God for each Christian soul reinforced the
indissoluble nature of marriage. Clearly the final wedding would be eternal,
and if the book was meant to be read such that earthly marriage is seen as a
simulacrum of that eternal wedding, then that characteristic too must obtain.
Johann Gerhard (1582–1637), one of the seventeenth century's great Lutheran
dogmatists, writing in his tome on the Song of Songs, makes an explicit comparison. The union of Christ and the soul is a spiritual union that shares qualities with the personal and the essential unions of divine mystery: Christ is both
God and man, united in one person, and the trinity is one, united in essence.
Moreover, the personal and essential union of God and man in Christ can be
likened, according to Gerhard, to the final union of God and the soul. And
because this is an indissoluble and inseparable union, it can be compared to a

---

9 For an overview of historical exegesis, see Exum, 2005; and Murphy, 1990. On Lutheran reception of Bernard, see Koch, 1994: 333–51.

marriage.[10] Later, Gerhard points out that one of the purposes of this scriptural book is *conjugii commendationen*, or praise of the sacred state of marriage: "daß Ehegatten ihren Ehestand als ein Bilde und Spiegel der geistlichen Vermählung Christi und seiner Braut der christlichen Kirchen und aller wahren Gläubigen ansehen" [wedded partners should see mirrored in their union an image of the spiritual union of Christ and his bride, the church and all true faithful].[11]

The ecclesiastic reading of the Song of Songs—one that regarded the entire church as Christ's bride—would by the early seventeenth century be read with greater mystical and intensely personal feeling, thanks to the New Piety movement. As a result, each individual faithful soul became the bride of Christ in much devotional literature of the period. While this intensification of the mystical and personal relationship with Christ began to enter devotional literature, it remained outside the official language of the marriage ritual. Musical performance, though, gave it sonic expression.

4 Wedding Music

Agenda say little about music at wedding services except to suggest the *Te Deum* or the hymn "Wohl dem der in Gottes Furchten stehet," a popular hymn attributed to Martin Luther and based on Psalm 128, which is already enshrined in the wedding service. The text's reference to a pious family and household made it an obvious choice for weddings, and almost all *Agenda* from the seventeenth century name it explicitly.

Sumptuary laws, in contrast, fill in important details about how weddings reinforced social strata and permitted families a public visual and aural platform for articulating social difference. In most jurisdictions, *Ordnungen* regulated clothing along with the expenses and consumption associated with public ceremonies: engagements, weddings, baptisms, and funerals. Weddings were generally regulated in several ways, including time of day, number of guests, amount of and type of food and wine, and payment permitted to those employed by the event, such as cooks, servers, and musicians. Weddings were generally limited to two times of day—morning and late afternoon—in order not to interfere with the day's labors, and the wedding was not to last more than roughly an hour so that guests might get on with their day. Organists were cautioned not to prelude for too long, lest the proceedings exceed the allocated time, and public processions to church were carefully controlled to prevent

---

10   Gerhard, 1652: preface, unpaginated print.
11   Gerhard, 1652: chapter 8 item 5.

them from becoming distractions.[12] In some cities, processing to church with
musicians, usually the civically employed *Stadtpfeiffer*, was permitted for certain classes of citizen.[13] Nürnberg for example, laid out the fees to be paid to its
six *Stadtpfeiffern* for processions to church, as well as any performance within
the church and, later, at the banquet.[14] Schweinfurt permitted its first-class
citizens four trumpets or trombones for their wedding processions, its second-
class citizens three, and the third class only two musicians—violinists or harp-
ists only—creating clear aural markers of social strata.[15] Rostock, by contrast,
banned musicians from accompanying processions to church completely, as
they tended to distract the town.[16]

---

12   See, for example, the detailed *Ordnung* from Erfurt: *E. E. Rahts Der Stadt Erffuhrt Anno 1653*
     (item 9).
13   For a detailed study of civic musicians in the early eighteenth century, see Kevorkian, 2012.
14   Each musician would receive a half a Gulden for processing the couple to church and
     an additional half Gulden for any further performance in the church. Performance at
     the banquet or the newlywed's door would incur payment of one Gulden. *Verneuerte
     Hochzeit=Ordnung*, 1662: Biij.
15   "Es sollen auch/ Siebendens/ keinem/ als der zu der Ersten *Class* gehörig/ Vier *Musicanten*
     mit Zincken und Posaunen zu dem Kirchgang so wohl/ als bey der Mahlzeit/ erlaubt seyn;
     Denen von der Andern *Class* aber allein Drey; und denen in der Dritten *Class* nur Zwey
     Musicanten oder Spielleut/ doch allein mit Geigen oder Harpffen bey dem Kirchgang zu
     erscheinen/ auch sonsten des Blasens mit Zincken/ Posaunen oder Trommeten/ (aus-
     genommen der Shallmeyen oder Flöhten in einer Hochzeit der Andern *Class*, massen
     der Dritten *Class* allein die Geigen durchgehends zugelassen) bey der Mahlzeit sich zu
     enthalten/ alles bey Straff Zweyer Gulden/ und sollen solche/ wie auch andere auffwar-
     tende Personen sich ihres nachgesetzten Verdienstes und Belohnung halben begnügen
     lassen/ inmassen dann verordnet ist." "Seventh, none outside those belonging to the first
     class shall be permitted four musicians with cornets and trombones for the church pro-
     cession as well as the meal; those of the second class, three; and those of the third class,
     only two musicians or performers, and only violins or harps shall appear for the church
     procession, and no blowing of cornets, trombones, or trumpets (outside of shawms or
     flutes for weddings of the second class, the third class shall have only strings) during the
     meal, on penalty of two Gulden and they and other attending persons should be content
     with half their earnings."
     *Erneuerte Hochzeit=Kind=Tauff= und Leich=Ordnung/ Des Heil. Römischen Reichs Stadt
     Schweinfurt*, 1680: Cij.
16   "Breutigam vnd Braut gehen ohn Spiel zur Kirchen. Alldieweil auch zum vier vnnd
     zwantzigsten/ durch Pfeiffen/ Trummel vnnd andern Seiten spiel/ dadurch die Hochzeiter
     zur Kirchen/ vnd wider davon gefüret werden/ kein ander vortheil vnd nutzen bißdaher
     gestifftet/ dann das der Pracht bey menniglichen zu/ ja gantz vberhand/ genommen/ offt
     die gantze halbe Stadt gleichsamb dadurch zusammen geruffen."
     "Bridegroom and bride go to church without musical accompaniment. Because, point
     number 24, through piping, drumming, and playing of strings to accompany the wedding
     party to church, no other end is achieved than grandeur that has gotten entirely out of
     hand by everyone [such that] often half the city is called together." *Rectoris Vnd Eines*

Within the church, music was similarly regulated, often according to social strata. In Nuremberg, weddings were permitted two choral pieces, one after the vows and the other after the series of biblical readings before the final blessing.[17] In Augsburg, citizens of the highest class were permitted polychoral music, while those of the merchant class were permitted only a single choir; commoners were allowed only simple music accompanied by the organ.[18] Hamburg's wedding ordinances are among the only ones to have been studied in detail for their musical implications: Esther Criscuola de Laix documents the economics and fashions surrounding the city's weddings—Hamburg was one of the few cities that cultivated a flourishing industry of printed ad hoc epithalamia.[19] The practice of printing ad hoc compositions flourished in the early seventeenth century in the hands of composers such as Melchior Franck (ca. 1579–1639), in Coburg; Johannes Christoph Demantius (1567–1643), in Freiberg; Johannes Eccard (1553–1611), in Königsberg; Paul Homberger (ca. 1560–1634), in Regensburg; Georg Quitschreiber (1569–1638), in Jena; and Thomas Selle (1599–1663), in Hamburg. The practice seems to have taken the strongest and longest-lasting hold in the North, where Johann Stobaeus (1580–1646) was remarkably industrious in Danzig and Köngisberg. The tradition continued into the eighteenth century in the hands of Friedrich Gottlieb Klingenberg (d. 1720) and Michael Rohde (1681–1732), who seem to have made quite a business out of providing ad hoc wedding pieces for Prussians in Stettin well into the eighteenth century, long after most central Germans had abandoned the practice.

Commissioned ad hoc pieces paint a rich picture of the sonic world of German weddings. While learned, noble, or high-social-status couples might have commissioned a piece in Latin with a bespoke text, perhaps encoding the names or identities of the couple in an acrostic, many burghers chose texts either from the apocryphal book of Sirach, usually known in English as Ecclesiasticus, or from the Song of Songs for printed epithalamia, if they chose a biblical text at all. Both are books of Wisdom literature; only the latter is part of the Lutheran canon. Ecclesiasticus is primarily concerned with moral instruction, and chapter 26 focuses on wives in particular, which made it moderately popular as a nuptial text in the first decades of the seventeenth century.[20] This text appears dozens of times in print and manuscript choral

Ehrwürdigen CONCILII Revidierte *Kleider / Vorlöbnuß: Hochzeit / Kindtauff /* Rectorats: *vnd* Promotion: *Ordnung*, 1625: 35.

17   *Verneuerte Hochzeit=Ordnung der Stadt Nürnberg*, 1662: Cv.

18   *Eines Wohl=Edlen Hochweisen Raths deß Heiligen Reichs Statt Augspurg*, 1683: 116.

19   Criscuola de Laix, 2010.

20   A setting by Heinrich Schütz for the wedding of Joseph Avenarius and Anna Dorothea Görlitz in Dresden, 21 April 1618, is a fairly typical example of this text as nuptial music:

part books. Its use as nuptial music clearly points to the policing of female virtue that scholars have seen as a consequence of Protestant marriage laws and practices.[21] Settings of texts drawn from the Song of Songs, however, communicated the important connection between marriage and death, masked beneath a pleasurable amorous surface.

In the preface to a 1608 collection of music by Melchior Franck dedicated to the wedding of Philipp Ernst, Count of Gleichen, Spiegelberg, and Pirmond, the great dogmatist Johann Gerhard makes clear that earthly marriage is an opportunity to reflect on the great spiritual marriage to come. He writes before the twenty-four motets of Franck's *Geistliche Gesäng*, which is drawn largely from the Song of Songs, that

> der Ehestand ... ein herrlich Bild der Geistlichen vormählung Christi vnd seiner Kirchen/ ja auch einer jeglichen Gläubigen Seelen/ insonderheit vnd vorgestellet/... Ist demnach in ansehung dessen/ deß sonderbahren *artificis* Herrn Melchior Francken/ Fürstl. Sächs. berümten Capellnmeisters zu Coburgk intens vnd vornehmen zuloben/ Daß er die vornembsten Text auß ermeltem Geistlichem *Epithalamio* nehmen/ dieselbe in artige *composition* bey Hochzeitlichen Ehren vnd Frewdentagen zusingen fassen/ vnd in Druck vorfertigen wollen damit also angehende Eheleut vnd anwesent Hochzeytgäste sich erinnern möchten/ wie man den Ehestand mit rechs Geistlichen Augen/ nicht allein als einen Ehrlichen vnd vnbefleckten stand/ sondern auch als ein Bild der liebe Christi gegen vns anzusehen ... vnd jederzeit daß grosse geheimnuß Christi vnd seiner Braut darinnen vns zum Trost vorgebildet zubedencken/ daß gebe Gott allen Christlichen Eheleuten zuerkennen vnd erhalte seine Heilige Ordnung vnverrückt wider alle Eheschender/ Amen.

Wohl dem der ein tugendsam Weib hat (SWV 20).

Wohl dem der ein tugendsam Weib hat, des lebet er noch eins so lang.

Ein häuslich Weib ist ihrem Manne eine Freude und macht ihm ein fein ruhig Leben.

Ein tugendsam Weib ist eine edle Gabe, und wird dem gegeben der Gott fürchtet, er sei gleich reich oder arm, so ists ihm ein Trost und macht ihn allzeit Fröhlich.

Wie die Sonne, wann sie aufgegangen ist, an dem hohen Himmel des Herren eine Zierde ist, also ist ein tugendsam Weib eine Zierd in ihrem Hause.

How blessed is the husband of a virtuous wife, the number of his days will be doubled.

A home-loving wife is the joy of her husband and provides him a peaceful life.

A good wife is precious thing, reserved for those who fear the Lord; rich or poor, she is a consolation and gladdens him always.

Like the sun when it is risen high in the heavens of the Lord, so too is a virtuous wife an adornment in her house.

(Sirach 26:1–4, 16)

21   Burghartz, 2004: 88–92; Harrington, 1995.

[marriage ... is a magnificent image of the spiritual marriage between Christ and his church, indeed also each individual faithful soul, in particular ... Herr Melchior Franck ... is to be praised most highly, for he has taken this most distinguished text of sacred *epithalamio* and set it in gracious compositions to be sung at nuptial honors and wedding days and set forth in print so that the prospective couple and all wedding guests present may remember to view marriage with the correct spiritual regard, not only as an honorable and pure state, but also as an image of the love Christ has for us ... and to think at all times of the great mystery of Christ and his bride, which is pictured therein for our solace, this God makes known to all Christian wedded people.]

Franck's compositions are rather typical, if delightfully inventive, motets for six to eight voices; they employ vivid musical-rhetorical devices that do not shy away from painting a surprisingly literal picture of the texts. If they were heard with a "correct spiritual regard," as Gerhard claims they lent the service, it must have been through the long exegetical understanding of the book, for the music luxuriates in colorful word painting. "Was ist dein Freund für ander Freunden," for example, is a setting of So 5: 9–16, which includes a full physical description of the male lover: he is "white and ruddy," his hair is "bushy, and black as the raven," his eyes are as those of the dove "by the rivers of waters, washed with milk, and fitly set," his cheeks flower as a bed of spices, and his lips, dripping myrrh, are likened to roses. The rest of his body is compared to precious stones: hands like gold rings with turquoise, a belly like ivory inlaid with sapphires, and legs that are pillars of marble in sockets of the finest gold. Franck's madrigalisms are brief, though imaginative. The curls of his raven-black hair are given quick circular figures in each voice, followed by black-note coloration, *Augenmusik* that only the musicians would see. His rosebud lips part suggestively with a moment of rapid hocketing that stands out in this largely homorhythmic piece (see example 1). Lest the listener or performer be persuaded by these physical glories, Franck supplies a musical reminder of just who this beautiful lover is: "Ein solcher ist mein Freund, ihr Töchter Jerusalem" [Such a one is my lover, you daughters of Jerusalem], set suddenly in triple meter, states that the Holy Trinity gives the definitive answer to the question posed by that opening line of the piece.

The use of triple meter to mark the male lover through musical symbolism is a commonplace of Song of Songs settings, whether expressly marked for weddings or not. Almost every setting of the text in Latin or German uses this device to convey a Christological interpretation. Settings of the Song of Songs thus reminded the listener that while the text might arouse, its great mystery could only be conveyed without words, directly to the soul via music.

FIGURE 6.1 Melchior Franck "Was ist dein Freund für ander Freunden" mm. 54–67

In Mühlhausen, composer and organist Johann Rudolph Ahle (1625–1673) combined metrical symbolism with sober timbres to evoke the final wedding during a nuptial celebration.[22] In 1664 Andreas Schultz, a student of both canon and civic law, married Dorothea Öhme, the daughter of the Mühlhausen *Bürgermeister* Emanuel Öhme. Andreas and Dorothea were fortunate to be among the class of people who could afford original music. While they may well have been escorted to the church with brass instruments, befitting their high social status, once inside, those aural status markers were replaced with funerary tropes, as Ahle composed for them a setting of Song of Songs chapter 3 ("Ich suchte des Nachts") for two vocalists and two violas. The lower strings, chosen instead of violins, evoke a funerary topos, ensuring the correct spiritual regard, as Gerhard advised.

FIGURE 6.2 Johann Rudolph Alhe, *Verlangter Liebster*, Cantus part. Staatsbibliothek zu Berlin-PK
http://resolver.staatsbibliothek-berlin.de/SBB0000C04900000000

---

22   Ahle, 1664.

The text chosen is in the female beloved's voice, as she seeks her lover.

> Ich suchte des Nachts in meinem Bette, den meine Seele liebet. Ich suchte aber ich fand ihn nicht. Ich will aufstehen, und in der Stadt umgehen auf den Gassen und Strassen, und suche, den meine Seele liebet. Ich suchte aber ich fand ihn nicht. Habt ihr nicht gesehn den meine Seele liebet? Da ich ein wenig fürüber kam, da fand ich den meine Seele liebe. Und wil ihn nicht lassen, biß ich ihn bringe in meiner Mutter Hauß in meiner Mutter Kammer.

> [In the night I searched my bed, for him whom my soul adores. I sought him, but found him not. I arose and went out in the city, into the streets and alleys, and sought him, whom my soul adores. I sought him, but found him not. Have you not seen him, whom my soul adores? Then when I had gone a little further, I found him, whom my soul adores. And I will not leave him until I bring him to my mother's house, in my mother's chamber.]

The identity of the beloved sought is marked through a dramatic change in meter whenever he is mentioned. While the meter of the piece is quadruple, characterized by regular flourishes of running sixteenth notes after an upward leaping motif that sets up rather typical counterpoint between the two voices, whenever the text turns to the object of desire, "den meine Seele liebet" [he whom my soul adores] is set in 3/1 with whole notes creating a dramatic and aurally obvious musical separation.

For the musicians playing from the parts, this shift again offers a sort of *Augenmusik*: in the two vocal parts, the first shift to triple meter, on the words "des Nachts in meinem Bette," is rendered in coloration—a visual way to indicate to the performers that a metric shift has taken place, but also drawing attention to the darkness of night in the text. The other metric shifts all accompany the text "den meine Seele liebet," and in every case the notation is white, not colored, representing Christ's holiness and confirming the eschatological orientation of the piece.

The prevalence of Song of Songs settings among ad hoc wedding compositions suggests that motets using this text might well have been performed at other, presumably less high-status weddings for couples who lacked the resources for original compositions. Common citizens might well have enjoyed pieces of a similar kind as a form of musical social aspiration. The relatively high number of small-scale motet settings of the Song of Songs, without instruments and for a small number of singers, in manuscript part books held by a variety of church libraries and inventories, suggests that these works found regular use.[23] And, unlike Ecclesiasticus, the Song of Songs offered a canonic text, with opportunities for both members of the bridal couple to be given implicit moral instruction, and, at least on the surface, to contemplate physical attraction, human affection, and love, factors that may well have prompted some marriages, but that were generally avoided in the official church service. Eros was introduced to the Protestant wedding service at first only musically, under the shared understanding that such erotics addressed not the libidinous fantasies of the newly-weds but every Christian's inevitable death and mystical union with Christ, here modelled in the earthly nuptial couple. During most of the seventeenth century, it was through music that participants were reminded of marriage's eschatological underpinnings and invited to hear a simulacrum of that final wedding.

Bibliography

Agenda, Das ist: KirchenOrdnung/ Wie sich die Pfarrherrn und Seelsorger in ihren Ampten und Diensten halten sollen : Für die Diener der Kirchen In Hertzog Heinrichen zu Sachsen/ U.G.H. Fürstenthumb gestellet / Sachsen, Herzog, Heinrich (Leipzig: Lanckisch, 1658). http://diglib.hab.de/drucke/tk-75/start.htm.

Agenda Das ist Außerlesene Kirchen-Ceremonien: Welche in den Kirchen Augspurgischer Confeßion in üblichem Brauche seyn/ und hin und wieder gleich und ungleich Bey Dem Sacrament der H. Tauffe/ Administration des Herrn Christi Nachtmahl/ Copulation, B .../ die Fehler geändert und auf Begehren geduckt (Frankfurt an der Oder: Völcker, 1697). http://diglib.hab.de/drucke/xb-800/start.htm.

Ahle, Johann Rudolph. *Verlangter Liebster/ Aus dem 3. Cap. des Salomonischen Hochliedes | begehrter massen gesuchet | Mit 2. Sing- und 2. Geigen-Stimmen zur Grund-stimm | zwar eiligst/ jedoch willigst gesetzet/ | Und | An dem/ den 22. Novembris dieses 1664 Jahrs | feyerlich angestelleten | Ehe-Feste* (Mühlhausen: Johann Hüter, 1664). Staatsbibliothek zu Berlin—PK Mus. ant. pract. 4° A 166. http://resolver.staatsbibliothek-berlin.de/SBB0000C0490000000.

---

23 Craig Westendorf has suggested that weddings were the only likely performance outlet for these motets on Song of Songs texts. While weddings are one possible performance context, the biblical text has strong exegetical connections with a variety of liturgical days throughout the year and could have been performed liturgically at any time, as Johann Gerhard explicitly demonstrates in his *Postilla*; see Westendorf, 1987. The number of motets on Song of Songs texts in church collections varies, though settings appear in every collection or archival list. The collection of St. Stephani in Helmstedt, today housed in the Herzog August Bibliothek, boasts the largest number of settings, seventy-one, accounting for nearly 14% of the total collection; see Garbe, 1998.

Burghartz, Susanna. "Ordering Discourse and Society: Moral Politics, Marriage, and Fornication during the Reformation and the Confessionalization Process in Germany and Switzerland." In *Social Control in Europe, 1500–1800*, ed. Herman Roodenburg and Pieter Spierenburg (Columbus: The Ohio State University Press, 2004), 78–98.

Brauner, Sigrid. "Gender and Its Subversion: Reflections on Literary Ideal of Marriage." In *The Graph of Sex and the German Text: Gendered Culture in Early Modern Germany 1500–1700*, ed. Lynne Tatlock (Amsterdam and Atlanta, GA: Rodopi, 1994), 179–98.

Criscuola de Laix, Esther. "Venus's Cupid Commands Me to Sing." *Musica disciplina* 55 (2010), 219–90.

E. E. Rahts Der Stadt Erffuhrt Anno 1653. Ernewerte und verbesserte Hochzeit- Kleider- KindTäufft- und Begräbnüß-Ordnungen (Erfurt, 1653). urn:nbn:de:gbv:3:1-58985.

Eines Wohl=Edlen Hochweisen Raths deß Heiligen Reichs Statt Augspurg Erneuerte Policey=Zierd=Kleider=Hochzeit= Kind Tauf= und Leich=Ordnung (Augsburg: Simon Utzschneider, 1683). HAB Xb 7069 (3).

Erneuerte Hochzeit=Kind=Tauff= und Leich=Ordnung / Des Heil. Römischen Reichs Stadt Schweinfurt (1680). HAB Wa 6249.

Exum, Cheryl J. *Song of Songs: A Commentary*, The Old Testament Library (Louisville, KY: Westminster John Knox Press, 2005).

Franck, Melchior. *Geistliche Gesäng und Melodeyen* (Coburg: Justus Hauk, 1608).

Garbe, Daniela. *Das Musikalienrepertoire von St. Stephani zu Helmstedt: Ein Bestand an Drucken und Handschriften des 17. Jahrhunderts*. 2 vols. (Wiesbaden: Harrassowitz Verlag, 1998).

Gerhard, Johann. *Postilla Salomonœa. Das ist Erklärung etlicher Sprüche auß dem Hohenlied Salomonis auff die Sontägliche vnd vornembste Fest Evangelia durchs gantze Jahr.* [1631] (Jena, 1652).

Harrington, Joel F. *Reordering Marriage and Society in Reformation Germany* (Cambridge: Cambridge University Press, 1995).

Hofstede de Groot, C[ornelis]. P[hilipp]. *Hundert Jahre aus der Geschichte der Reformation in den Niederlanden, 1518–1619*, trans. D. Greeven (Gütersloh: Bertelsmann, 1893).

Karant-Nunn, Susan C. "'Fragrant Wedding Roses': Lutheran Wedding Sermons and Gender Definition in Early Modern Germany." *German History* 17 (1) (1999), 25–40.

Kevorkian, Tanya. "Town Musicians in German Baroque Society and Culture." *German History* 30 (3) (2012), 350–71. https://doi-org.ezproxy.gc.cuny.edu/10.1093/gerhis/ghs048.

Koch, Ernst. "Die Bernhard-Rezeption im Luthertum des 16. und 17. Jahrhunderts." In *Bernhard von Clairvaux: Rezeption und Wirkung im Mittelalter und in der Neuzeit*, ed. Kaspar Elm. Wolfenbütteler Mittelalter-Studien, vol. 6 (Wiesbaden: Harrassowitz, 1994), 333–351.

Murphy, Roland E. *The Song of Songs: A Commentary on the Book of Canticles or The Song of Songs* (Minneapolis: Fortress Press, 1990).

Praetorius, Michael. *Syntagma musicum* volume 2 (Wolfenbüttel, 1619; Kassel: Bärenreiter, 2001 [facsimile edition]).

Rectoris Vnd Eines Ehrwürdigen CONCILII Revidierte *Kleider / Vorlöbnuß: Hochzeit / Kindtauff* / Rectorats*: vnd* Promotion*: Ordnung* (Rostock: Joachim Feuß, 1625). HAB Pd 314 (1–2).

Schnell, Rüdiger ed. *Text und Geschlecht: Mann und Frau in Eheschriften der frühen Neuzeit* (Frankfurt am Main: Suhrkamp, 1997).

Verneuerte Hochzeit=Ordnung der Stadt Nürnberg. wie es mit / und bey den Erbarn und andern verlegten Hochzeiten allhier in der Stadt gehalten werden soll. (Michael Endter, 1662). HAB Gm 3238.

Westendorf, Craig Jon. *The Textual and Musical Repertoire of the Spruchmotette*, Dissertation (School of Music, University of Illinois at Urbana-Champaign, 1987).

Wiesner-Hanks, Merry E. *Christianity and Sexuality in the Early Modern World: Regulating Desire, Reforming Practice*. Christianity and Society in the Modern World (New York: Routledge, 2000).

Wirth, Sigrid. *Weil es ein Zierlich vnd lieblich ja Nobilitiert Instrument ist: Der Rosonanzraum der Laute und musikalische Repräsentation am Wolfenbütteler Herzogshof 1580–1625* (Wiesbaden: Harrassowitz, 2017).

CHAPTER 7

Emblematic Virtues: The Orations for Ferdinand Carl and Sigismund Franz, Archdukes of Tirol

Cornelia Niekus Moore

The early modern European perception of the human makeup embraces the idea that a person's character should be an amalgam of virtues, to be formed and enhanced by Christian edification and self-improvement (Schleier, 1973; Bautz, 1999; Bejczy, 2008). Derived from Aristotle's idea of virtues, which was then Christianized during the medieval centuries, this notion manifested itself in the literature written for children, for women, and for men. Some of the genres in which virtuous living was propagated were (1) the "Mirrors of Princes" (*Fürstenspiegel*), whose mostly burgher authors portrayed their visions of the necessary virtues of the ideal ruler (Müller, 2005); and (2) the funeral sermons and orations where the preacher took stock of how far a person had come in this noble and necessary endeavor, thereby composing his own princely mirror (Boge/Bogner, 1999; Moorc, 2006).[1] In early modern Germany, both genres were anti-Machiavellian to the core, which is understandable given the German authors' notion that actions should be guided by a ruler's virtues rather than political motives (Durchhardt, 1991: 29; Moore, 2013). Or, as Bidermann writes, "Trolle sich dann nur fort die rohe Grausamkeit des Gottlosen Macchiavelli, als welche sich erkühnet hatte/ die Fürstliche Tugend zu verschreyen, gleich wäre sie undüchtig zu vollstendiger Beherrschung" [Slink away, you brute cruelty of the godless Machiavelli, who was so bold as to denounce the virtue of a ruler, as if it were incapable of total control.][2] It is understandable that Machiavelli's political expediency, based on the biographical accounts of famous people, would clash with the virtue-based biographical reflections of the eulogists (Birely, 1990, 217–42).

The title page of the funeral book under discussion provides, in true Baroque fashion, an extensive account of content, occasion, and printing details: *Ehren=Gebäu Oesterreicher Helden-Tugenden/ Mit welchen weilandt der Durchleüchtigste Fürst und Herr/ Herr Ferdinandus Carolus Ertzherzog zu Oesterreich etc etc. in Lebens zeiten herrlich gezieret ware. Bey deroselben*

---

1 I thank the librarians of the Herzog August Bibliothek, who always assist me in my searches.
2 *Ehren-Gebäu* (hereafter *EG*), p. C2.

© KONINKLIJKE BRILL NV, LEIDEN, 2023 | DOI:10.1163/9789004682245_009

Ertzfürstlichen Traur=Gerüst/ unnd Leichbegängnuß/ in nachfolgender Lobred und Sinn=Bildnussen vorgestelt Von P. Ernesto Bidermanno Soc. Iesu Ertzfürstlicher Hofprediger. Zu Ynßprugg in der Kirchen Soc. Jesu Im jar M.DC.LXIII *Monats Martij den iii. Superiorum permissu. Getruckt zu Ynsprugg/ Hieronymo Paur, Hofbuchtruckern* (1663). (Fig. 7.1) We learn that this is a *Lobrede*, an oration, a laudation. The funeral was for Ferdinand Carl, Archduke of Austria (1628–1662), ruler of Tirol and a nephew of the Austrian emperor, who had died 30 December 1662 (Boge/Bogner, 1990: 401). The funeral took place on 3 March 1663, two months after he had passed away, and time had been allotted to present the oration during the obsequies. The speaker was Ernst Bidermann, a Jesuit preacher at the Innsbruck court. After the funeral the oration was printed by Hieronymus Paur in Innsbruck. The illustrations, by Matthaeus Küsell of Augsburg, were then added, and the books were distributed in a limited edition to family, other royals, and dignitaries. I have located five copies extant in Germany: three in Munich,[3] one of which has been published on the internet as well as on microfiche; one in Augsburg;[4] and one in Wolfenbüttel.[5] They are not identical. The copies in Munich and Augsburg have eleven illustrations, whereas the one in Wolfenbüttel has one. This copy, a fold-out print, shows a *castrum doloris*, a funerary monument—that is, a large frame covered with paper and parchment, on which statues and images had been placed, celebrating primarily the glory of the house of Habsburg. There is no image of the deceased.[6] The title of the oration, *Ehren-Gebäu Oesterreichischer Helden-Tugenden* (Monument in Honor of Heroic Austrian Virtues), tells us that the speaker will construct in words what the *castrum doloris* did in wood and paper, and that the illustrations aid in the construction of this verbal edifice. Occurrences like funerals and weddings were powerful reminders to subjects and foreign powers alike of the staying power of the dynasty. Orations like the one discussed here contributed to this goal.

A *Lobrede*, a laudation, was a classical rhetorical exercise, resurrected in the Renaissance, in which learned men praised either a ruler or a colleague. It is a defined genre, related to the argumentation, which allows the speaker to foresee opposing arguments which can then be defeated. An extensive laudatory

---

3 VD17 12:123458U. Zentralinstitut für Kunstgeschichte: SB 277/14 R (copy not complete), BSB: 2 P.o.germ. 3, and BSB: Res/2 Or. Fun 123 (also in microfiche), digitalized by the Münchener Digitalisierungszentrum: Digitale Bibliothek. See: https://www.digitale-sammlungen.de/en /view/bsb10943407?page=,1.

4 Universitätsbibliothek Augsburg: 02/XIII.8.2.303 angeb.1.

5 Herzog August Bibliothek Wolfenbüttel (hereafter HAB): Xb 4° 212. The missing illustrations could be those now available in the Virtuelles Kuperstichkabinett of the HAB.

6 See the article by Sara Smart in this volume for another example of a *castrum doloris*.

Ehren-Gebäu

Oesterreichischer Helden-Tugenden/

Mit welchen weilandt der

Durchleüchtigste Fürst / vnnd

Herz / Herz

FERDINANDVS

CAROLVS

Ertzhertzog zu Oesterreich/2c. 2c.

in Lebens zeiten hertzlich gezieret ware.

Bey deroselben

Ertzfürstlichen Traur-Gerüst / vnnd
Leichbegängnuß / in nachfolgender Lobred
vnd Sinn-Bildnussen vorgestelt

Von

P. ERNESTO BIDERMANNO Soc. Iesu

Ertzfürstlichen Hofprediger.

Zu Ynßprugg in der Kirchen Soc. Jesu
Im Jar M. DC. LXIII.
Monats Martij den III.

Superiorum permissu.

Getruckt zu Ynßprugg/ bey Hieronymo Paur Hofbuchtruckern.

FIGURE 7.1   Title page, Ernst Bidermann, *Ehren-Gebäu* (1663). HAB: Xb 40 212.
Rpt with permission

biography of the subject is the framework—indeed, the primary purpose—of an oration, which, in the case of a laudation for the deceased, also includes a lamentation and a consolation. Comparisons with classical and biblical figures were par for the course. The speaker could earn the admiration of his audience by surprising comparisons, or textual emblems, which then require long intricate explanations. A *Lobrede* is not, however, a sermon. It is a secular feature, which here had entered a religious ceremony. Time had been allotted, probably after the Mass of Souls, to give this laudation for a ruler (Moore, 2006: 32–34). Catholic authorities frowned on such intrusions, and most Catholic orations were presented separately from the actual funeral mass. But for an archduke, exceptions could be made. The given task was not to invent a new genre but to do well within the known tradition.

There is no reference to a portrait. Indeed, there is none, but the title page expressly states that the deceased will be presented in the text and in the *Sinn-Bildnissen*, the emblems (Daly, 2014: esp. 185–220).[7] Together they form the "portrait" of the archduke—a theater, a stage, a construct on which to present the virtues of the deceased, to honor his memory and to provide an example for the living: "Theatre oder Schau-Bühnen/ auf welche die unsterblichen Tugenden der Abgestorbenen teils zu einem beständigen Angedencken/ teils zu einem Beyspiel der Nachwelt vorgetragen werden" (*EG*, p. B2).

A discussion of virtues occurs in almost all funeral sermons and orations, indicating that virtue was indeed the way a person was judged. In this oration, however, the orator makes it clear from the outset that a discussion of the duke's virtues is not just part of the oration; it is the main part, the only topic. There is no list of illustrious forefathers, no mention of parents or a spouse. Anecdotes about the ruler's life are only told as they support a particular virtue. Even the traditional recounting of the deathbed scene is told as it relates to the virtue of felicity. Later historians have described Ferdinand Carl as a weak ruler, a spendthrift who squandered his own wealth and the state coffers and relinquished territory for a price (Stolz, 1955: 546–51). He was married to Anna de Medici (1616–1676), his mother was Claudia de Medici (1604–1648), and these relations continued to live in the splendor they had known in Tuscany (Weiss, 2011). They were great patrons of the arts and supported lavish theatrical productions. Parts of their art collections, in which they featured prominently themselves, still enrich the Vienna museums (Haag, 2009).

---

7 I thank Mara Wade for initiating me into the vast world of emblems and, especially, into the many collections now available on the internet.

The *Lobrede* is occasional literature. The speaker is given a task, and he organizes his oratory accordingly: in this case, the praise of a spendthrift but kind ruler. According to the speaker, Ferdinand Carl's virtues were clemency, munificence, fortitude (but not cruelty), piety, and—in his preparation for death—felicity. With the exception of Felicity, these are social virtues, character traits that assured a benevolent position toward his subjects. It is not surprising to find that these virtues (among others) were also those advocated in the German advice literature for rulers of the time. The authors of these "Mirrors of Princes," who similar to the Jesuit Ernst Bidermann were burgher clerics with court experience and liked to emphasize those character traits that would benefit subjects like themselves. Rainer Müller has called this prescribed behavioral packet for rulers a *Tugendkorsett* (a virtue corset) (Müller, 2004: 152; Müller, 2005).

Having selected the five virtues that make for an ideal ruler—in this case, Ferdinand Carl—the speaker now finds emblematic comparisons that relate to appropriate incidents in the archduke's life. For instance, in the section about clemency, he compares the archduke to a fountain dispensing clemency, noting that he would forgive a subject for stealing, saying the thief needed the food. This composite of the archduke's virtues does not contradict the portrait that later historians have painted, but the palette changes somewhat.

Many of the funeral books, even those of royalty, do not have illustrations, except for a portrait, but in this case and others in the Habsburg dynasty, the decision must have been made to add emblematic illustrations. This gives the emblems an extra impetus, reinforcing the virtue catalogue in the text. Together they are a composite of the ruler's personality. As the author states at the outset, "statt der Sinnbilder unserer Sterblichkeit/ lebhafte Abbildungen der Ertzfürstl. Wohltaten und Verdiensten" [rather than emblems about man's mortality, they are representations of the archducal virtues], which, again, is in the spirit of an oration rather than a funeral sermon (*EG*, p. B). To be sure, the content of the oration was flexible. Still, the deviation from a biographical chronology puts the emphasis on the virtues. The illustrations, which portray these virtues—to the exclusion of anything else—reinforce this singularity.

The printer who signed the print of the *castrum doloris* was Mattheus Küsell (1629–1681) of Augsburg. (Fig. 7.2) He was well versed in various media but was especially known for his engraved portraits and his stage designs. His brother Melchior (1626–1688), married to a daughter of Matthaeus Merian the Elder, had an engraving shop of his own and one of Melchior's daughters married another engraver. More than one family member, including daughters, could contribute to a project, and this collection of emblems shows various hands (Thieme

FIGURE 7.2 Fold-out *castrum doloris* in: Ernst Bidermann, *Ehren-Gebäu* (1663). Engraver
Matthaeus Küsell. HAB: Xb 4° 212. Rpt with permission

Becker, 1928: 22, 73–76; Hollstein, 1977, 19:199–224, 20:9–126; Appuhn-Radtke, 1997: 788; Augustyn, 1997: 801, 808, 825; Künast, 1997: 1246, 1257).[8]

The first virtue to be attributed to Ferdinand Carl is *clementia*, meaning "clemency" or "gentleness." Like the other virtues, it has two emblems. (Figs. 7.3–7.4) The *subscriptiones* read *fortiter et suaviter* and *forte dulcedo*, which both translate as strength with gentleness. I have not found these specific Latin designations elsewhere in the emblem literature, which suggests that all *subscriptiones* were taken from Bidermann's text, where they are mentioned and explained with detailed imagery (*EG*, p. C). Both depict mastery over wild beasts. In one, Orpheus tames animals by playing his harp. From the close resemblance between text and illustrations, one could infer that the printer had the full text of the sermon in front of him when designing the engravings, that they were made in the timespan between the actual funeral and the publication of the funeral book, and that they were not shown in the church during the funeral, as was sometimes the custom. The three months between the death of the archduke and the funeral would have been a short timespan to write a sermon, to get the imprimatur from secular as well as religious authorities, to send a copy of the sermon to Augsburg, and to get the nine engravings, even if more than one person was working in the engraver's shop. The publisher (Paur in Innsbruck) must have fitted the paper copies of the emblems (which he received from Augsburg) between the gatherings of the folio funeral book, because the emblem illustrations do not always correspond to the opposing text page. This would also explain the different numbers of emblem figures in the various copies.

This image of clemency is not original. There is a similar emblem in Rollenhagen's classic emblem book, where David is the musician (Rollenhagen, 1611: 53). It is supposed to depict the power of music, but Küsell's emblem gives a different rendering of the image, based on the text. All emblems are framed by gorgeous borders, a trademark of Küsell's shop. Although the images show the relative simplicity of the emblematic tradition, the borders give an indication that this is a different age.

The next virtue of the prince toward his subjects extolled is *munificentia*, or "largesse." Here again there are two emblems. (Figs. 7.5–7.6) The *subscriptiones* read, *Quo abundant eo exundat* (to disperse abundance) and *o pulchrum sine foenore* (o richness without avarice). The first emblem shows a woman dispensing generosity from a pedestal, a rather common emblem. It has a classic frame. For the second emblem, the engraver had a model to follow. The

---

8 Daughters of Matthäus Küsell: Maria Magdalena (active 1688–1702), who produced a *Blumenbüchlein*; Maria Philippina (1676–1705); Johanna Christina (b. 1665).

FIGURE 7.3 One of two emblems depicting "Clementia." In: Ernst Bidermann,
Ehren-Gebäu (1663). Engraver Matthäus Küsel. München, Bayerische
Staatsbibliothek—2 P.o.germ. 3
© BAYERISCHE STAATSBIBLIOTHEK

FIGURE 7.4   One of two emblems depicting "Clementia." In: Ernst Bidermann, *Ehren-Gebäu*
(1663). Engraver Matthäus Küsel. München, Bayerische Staatsbibliothek—
2 P.o.germ. 3
© BAYERISCHE STAATSBIBLIOTHEK

FIGURE 7.5 One of two emblems depicting "Munificentia." In: Ernst Bidermann, *Ehren-Gebäu* (1663). Engraver Matthäus Küsel. München, Bayerische Staatsbibliothek—2 P.o.germ. 3
© BAYERISCHE STAATSBIBLIOTHEK

FIGURE 7.6   One of two emblems depicting "Munificentia." In: Ernst Bidermann,
Ehren-Gebäu (1663). Engraver Matthäus Küsel. München, Bayerische
Staatsbibliothek—2 P.o.germ. 3
© BAYERISCHE STAATSBIBLIOTHEK

recently published *Fama Prognostica*, celebrating the birth of Maximilian Emmanuel II (1662–1726) has an emblem of a fountain. Adaptation, in this case, is the highest form of flattery. The rows of poplars creating perspective may have been adapted from the older print, but the Cupid carrying the earth is an original addition. In the *Fama*, the emblem stands for *magnificentia*. Bidermann emphasizes that in his oration, it stands for largesse, generosity, and support of the *oeconomia*, as more fitting to the actions of this ruler (Collegium Monacensis, p. Df).

The first emblem's *subscriptione* for Fortitudo reads *Rex erat quia rexerat*, a king's crown was his reward. (Figs. 7.7–7.8) In the text, much is made of the absence of *Zorn* (anger or wrath). It appears to have been the royal attribute that was most feared. (Collegium Monacensis, p. D3) The emblem depicts Alexander taming his horse, Bucephalus, but without physical punishment. The second emblem (*sic martem sine marte sub egit*) shows Alcibiades, who had his shield emblazoned with the picture of Eros rather than Mars (Collegium Monacensis, p. C1). Bidermann refers to the archduke relinquishing territory rather than prolonging a war. Thus, a perceived weakness is turned into a virtue.

Pietas (Piety) also has two emblems, two *subscriptiones*: *hoc tuta sine* and *omne tulit punctum*. (Figs. 7.9–7.10) The latter is a quotation from Horace's *Ars Poetica* and refers to the mixing of the useful with the pleasurable. In the last two sections, Bidermann goes into lengthy description: first, of the archduke's personal piety and his participation in Catholic rituals, like the Mass and processions, especially those on the Feast of Corpus Christi, his devotion to the Virgin Mary, and his exemplary death (Collegium Monacensis, p. E2f). The discussion of piety and the deathbed scene are the most important sections in all funeral literature. They assure the grieving family that the deceased has achieved eternal salvation. Until this point in the oration, most of the examples and references were taken from the classics, as befits the secular genre, but now the oration turns to the duke's Christian piety as befits a eulogy. Bidermann mentions two secure castles for the pious: the Eucharist and the Virgin Mary, but it is the engraver's idea to turn these into the two pillars associated with Charles v and the house of Habsburg, which Bidermann had mentioned on his opening page (Collegium Monacensis, p. E3).[9] One pillar has a statue of the Virgin Mary; the other shows a monstrance. There are many ships in emblem literature, most of which are so flimsy that one would not want to embark on them. This, by contrast, is a sturdy ship, going to a secure harbor, or—as in

---

9 For references to the columns see Daniel de la Feuille, *Devises et emblems anciennes et modernes* (1691).

FIGURE 7.7   One of two emblems depicting "Fortitudo." In: Ernst Bidermann,
            Ehren-Gebäu (1663). Engraver Matthäus Küsel. München, Bayerische
            Staatsbibliothek—2 P.o.germ. 3
            © BAYERISCHE STAATSBIBLIOTHEK

FIGURE 7.8 One of two emblems depicting "Fortitudo." In: Ernst Bidermann, *Ehren-Gebäu* (1663). Engraver Matthäus Küsel. München, Bayerische Staatsbibliothek— 2 P.o.germ. 3
© BAYERISCHE STAATSBIBLIOTHEK

FIGURE 7.9 One of two emblems depicting "Pietas." In: Ernst Bidermann, *Ehren-Gebäu* (1663). Engraver Matthäus Küsel. München, Bayerische Staatsbibliothek— 2 P.o.germ. 3
© BAYERISCHE STAATSBIBLIOTHEK

FIGURE 7.10   One of two emblems depicting "Pietas." In: Ernst Bidermann, *Ehren-Gebäu*
(1663). Engraver Matthäus Küsel. München, Bayerische Staatsbibliothek—
2 P.o.germ. 3
© BAYERISCHE STAATSBIBLIOTHEK

similar emblems depicted by Henkel/Schöne (1967, vol. 1: 455)—symbolizing the certain before the uncertain. For the second emblem, the engraver is more or less on his own, with an emblem showing the traditional symbols of Cupid with an arrow, and a heart with the symbol of Christ.

The last section, which centers on felicity and refers to the archduke's death, contains two emblems, whose images were likely chosen by the engraver. (Figs. 7.11–7.12) One shows a ship on a pole, again in a secure harbor (the subscription is a reference to Noah's ark), and the second depicts Archduke Ferdinand Carl flying to heaven in a chariot, pulled by two eagles, and dropping his earthly crown because he will receive a heavenly one. Again, the choice of imagery was probably that of the engraver. They are unlike other Jesuit images of death, which tend to include skeletons and other memento mori elements (Dimler, 2014). This reinforces the emphasis on the archduke and the role that his virtues play in his conduct during life, including in its final moments.

Bidermann and his courtly audience must have liked the format. Two years later, when Ferdinand Carl's successor Sigismund Franz died, he followed the same procedure, with an oration entitled *Ehren-Crone Unsterblicher Helden-Tugenten Mit welchen deß ... Herrens Sigismund Francisc/ Ertzhertzogens zu Oesterreich. ... Preyß-würdiger Lebens Wandel herrlich gezieret ware: Bey dem hochansehlichen Traur-Gerüste/ Warmit ... Leopoldus 1. Die Leich-Begängnuß Ihres Herren Veteren allergnedigst geehret haben* (Bidermann, 1665).[10] (Fig. 7.13) A *castrum doloris* was again constructed. (Fig. 7.14) This time it featured a life-size statue of a kneeling Sigismund Franz, who had made a concerted effort to put the archduchy on a better financial footing and had reined in some of the court's excesses. He did not live long enough to see through his initiatives, but the selection of his virtues in the oration paid homage to these attempts: they include justice, equanimity, and prudence. The ten pairs of emblems feature ten virtues, and, again, they take the *subscriptiones* and their subject matter from the text. But the proudly sailing ships, Alexander and his horse, and Alcibiades and his sword are gone. They have been replaced by Cupids executing the virtuous actions described in the text, like the Cupid planting seeds in the emblem for munificence (generosity). (Fig. 7.15) One could infer that the engraver did not need and might not have had the entire text of the oration, but just the assigned virtues and the *subscriptiones*. Thus, the emblems may have arrived in time for copies to be hung in the church as posters (*affixiones*),

---

10   Munich: Bayerische Staatsbibliothek: Res 2 Or. fun. 362. See Boge/Bogner, 1990: 410–11.

FIGURE 7.11   One of two emblems depicting "Felicitas." In: Ernst Bidermann, *Ehren-Gebäu* (1663). Engraver Matthäus Küsel. München, Bayerische Staatsbibliothek— 2 P.o.germ. 3

© BAYERISCHE STAATSBIBLIOTHEK

FIGURE 7.12   One of two emblems depicting "Felicitas." In: Ernst Bidermann,
                Ehren-Gebäu (1663). Engraver Matthäus Küsel. München, Bayerische
                Staatsbibliothek—2 P.o.germ. 3
                © BAYERISCHE STAATSBIBLIOTHEK

Ehren=Crone

Unsterblicher Helden=Tugenten/

Mit welchen deß weyland

Durchleüchtigsten Fürstens / vnnd

Herzens / Herzens

Sigismund Francisc/

Ertzhertzogens zu Oesterzeich/ꝛc. ꝛc. Preyß=würdiger
Lebens Wandel herzlich gezieret ware.

Bey dem hochansehlichen Traur=Gerüste/

Warmit

Ihro Röm: Kaiſ: May:

LEOPOLDVS I.

Die Leicht=Begängnuß Ihres Herzen Veteren
allergnedigſt geehret haben.

Durch P. Erneſtum Bidermannum Societ. I E S V
in nachgeſetzter Lobred/vnd Sinn = Bildnuſſen vorgeſtelt.

Zu Ynſprugg in der Kirchen Soc. I ᴇ s v im Jar M. DC. LXV.
Monats Septembr. 18.

_____

Superiorum permiſſu.

Getruckt zu Ynſprugg/bey Hieronymo Paur Hoffbuchtruckern.

BS**B**

FIGURE 7.13   Title page, Ernst Bidermann, *Ehren-Crone* (1665). München BSB:
Res 2 Or.fun. 362

BSB

FIGURE 7.14
Fold-out *castrum
doloris* in: Ernst
Bidermann,
Ehren-Crone (1665).
Engraver Matthaeus
Küsell. München BSB:
Res 2 Or.fun. 362

FIGURE 7.15   One of two emblems depicting "Munificentia." In: Ernst
Bidermann, *Ehren-Crone* (1665). Engraver Matthaeus Küsell.
München: SBS: Res 2 Or. Fun. 362

although it is doubtful that the black-and-white folio-sized pieces would have
made much of an impact in the highly ornate Jesuit church in Innsbruck.
The uniformity is enhanced and offset by the magnificent borders, which are
varied slightly from picture to picture—half of them in the more classical
square frames and the other half in round ones. The last emblems are elaborate tributes to the House of Habsburg, such as the final emblem, depicting a
genealogical tree. (Fig. 7.16) Since Sigismund Franz left no descendants, the

FIGURE 7.16   One of two emblems depicting the Habsburg dynasty.
In: Ernst Bidermann, *Ehren-Crone* (1665). Engraver
Matthaeus Küsell. München: SBS: Res 2 Or. Fun. 362

territory was reincorporated into the Austrian lands and ruled by the emperor, who, as the title page states, had arranged the obsequies. There has been an ongoing discussion about how much explanation an emblem needs when it refers to stories that might be part of a cultural tradition (Daly, 2014: chapter 8). The emblems in the second oration would require fewer "footnotes," but they still clearly illustrate the virtues they refer to.

Initially, copies of these lavish funeral books would have been seen by fewer people than attended the funeral services, but these printed versions of oral presentations materialized the spoken emblematic texts, enabling them to last through the ages. The cooperation between author and engraver, between text and illustrations, succeeded in producing books containing the biographies and characters of Ferdinand Carl and Sigismund Franz, which in their execution stand as worthy monuments for these rulers.

Bibliography

Appuhn-Radtke, Sibylle. "Augsburger Buchdrucker und Verlagswesen im 17. Jahrhundert." In *Augsburger Buchdruck und Verlagswesen von den Anfängen bis zur Gegenwart*, eds. Helmut Gier and Johannes Janota (Wiesbaden: Harrassowitz, 1997), 735–90.

Augustyn, Wolfgang. "Augsburger Buchillustration im 18. Jahrhundert." In *Augsburger Buchdruck und Verlagswesen von den Anfängen bis zur Gegenwart*, eds. Helmut Gier and Johannes Janota (Wiesbaden: Harrassowitz, 1997), 791–862.

Bautz, Michaela. *Virtvtes. Studien zur Funktion und Ikonographie der Tugenden* (Berlin: Dissertation.de, 1999).

Bejczy, István, ed. *Virtue Ethics in the Middle Ages. Commentaries on Aristotle's Nicomachean Ethics, 1200–1500* (Leiden: Brill, 2008).

Bidermann, Ernst. *Ehren=Gebäu Oesterreicher Helden-Tugenden/ Mit welchen weilandt der Durchleüchtigste Fürst und Herr/ Herr Ferdinandus Carolus Ertzherzog zu Oesterreich etc etc. in Lebens zeiten herrlich gezieret ware. Bey deroselben Ertzfürstlichen Traur=Gerüst/ unnd Leichbegängnuß/ in nachfolgender Lobred und Sinn=Bildnussen vorgestelt Von P. Ernesto Bidermanno Soc. Iesu Ertzfürstlicher Hofprediger. Zu Ynßprugg in der Kirchen Soc. Jesu Im jar M.DC.LXIII Monats Martij den iii. Superiorum permissu* (Innsbruck: Hieronymus Paur, [1663]).

Bidermann, Ernst. *Ehren-Crone Unsterblicher Helden-Tugenten/ Mit welchen deß ... Herrens Sigismund Francisc/ Ertzhertzogens zu Oesterreich. ... Preyß-würdiger LebensWandel herrlich gezieret ware: Bey dem hochansehlichen Traur-Gerüste/ Warmit ... Leopoldus I. Die Leich-Begängnuß Ihres Herren Veteren allergnedigst geehret haben* (Innsbruck: Hieronymus Paur, 1665).

Bireley, Robert. *The Counter-Reformation Prince. Anti-Machiavellianism or Catholic Statecraft in Early Modern Europe* (Chapel Hill: University of North Carolina Press, 1990).

Boge, Birgit, and Ralph Bogner. *Oratio Funebris*. Chloe, Vol. 30. (Amsterdam: Rodopi, 1999).

Collegium Monacensis SJ, ed. *Fama Prognostica* (Munich: Lucas Straubius, 1662).

Daly, Peter M. *The Emblem in Early Modern Europe. Contributions to the Theory of the Emblem* (London and New York: Routledge, 2014).

Dimler, Richard. "Jesuit Emblems of Death." In *Emblems of Death in the Early Modern Period*, eds. Monica Calabritto and Peter Daly (Geneva: Droz, 2014), 269–86.

Duchhardt, Heinz. "Das protestantische Herrscherbild." In *Das Herrscherbild im 17. Jahrhundert*, ed. Konrad Repgen (Münster: Aschendorff, 1991), 26–42.

Haag, Sabine. *Ferdinand Karl, ein Sonnenkönig in Tirol. Eine Ausstellung des Kunsthistorischen Museums Wien Schloss Ambras* (Vienna: Kunsthistorisches Museum, 2009).

Henkel, Arthur, and Albrecht Schöne. *Emblemata: Handbuch zur Sinnbildkunst des XVI. und XVII, Jahrhunderts* (Stuttgart: Metzler, 1967).

Hollstein, F. W. H. *German Engravings, Etchings, and Woodcuts*. 98 vols. (Amsterdam: Van Gendt & Co, 1977).

Kern, Margit. *Tugend versus Gnade. Protestantische Bildprogramme in Nürnberg, Pirna, Regensburg und Ulm* (Berlin: Mann, 2002).

Künast, Hans-Jörg. "Dokumentation: Augsburger Buchdrucker und Verleger." In *Augsburger Buchdruck und Verlagswesen von den Anfängen bis zur Gegenwart*, eds. Helmut Gier and Johannes Janota (Wiesbaden: Harrassowitz, 1997), 1205–340.

Moore, Cornelia Niekus. *Patterned Lives, The Lutheran Funeral Biography in Early Modern Germany* (Wiesbaden: Harrassowitz, 2006).

Moore, Cornelia Niekus. "Spiegel weiblicher Tugenden. Die Fürstin als Vorbildliche." In *Der Hof, Ort kulturellen Handelns von Frauen in der Frühen Neuzeit* (Cologne: Böhlau, 2013), 100–115.

Müller, Rainer A. "'Die Oeconomia ist eine Monarchia.' Der Deutsche Fürstenhof der Frühmoderne als Objekt der Hausväter und Regimentsliteratur." In *Hof und Theorie*, eds. Reinhardt Butz et al. (Cologne: Böhlau, 2004), 145–63.

Müller, Rainer A. "Der (deutsche) Fürstenhof als Thema der Fürstenspiegelliteratur der Renaissance (1450–1570)." In *Der Innsbrucker Hof*, eds. Heinz Noflatscher et al. (Vienna: Oesterreichische Akademie der Wissenschaften, 2005), 31–53.

Rollenhagen. Gabriel. 1611. *Sinn-Bilder. Ein Tugendspiegel*. Ed. Carsten-Peter Warncke. Dortmund: Harenberg. 1983.

Schleier, Reinhart. *Tabula Cebetis, oder Spiegel des menschlichen Lebens darin Tugent und Untugent abgemalet ist. Studien zur Rezeption einer antiken Bildbeschreibung im 16. und 17. Jahrhundert* (Berlin: Mann, 1973).

Schmidt, Wilhelm Adolf. "Küsell, Matthäus." In *Allgemeine Deutsche Biographie*, vol. 17 (Leipzig: Duncker & Humblot, 1883), 434.

Stolz, Otto. *Geschichte des Landes Tirol*. Vol. 1 (Vienna: Tyrolia Verlag, 1955).

Thieme, Ulrich, and Felix Becker. *Allgemeines Lexikon der bildenden Künstler von den Antiken bis zur Gegenwart.* Vol. 22. (Leipzig: Seemann, 1928).

Weiss, Sabine. "Claudia und Anna de' Medici, Kunst- und Kulturtransfer Florenz— Innsbruck—Wien (1626–1676)." In *Die Frauen des Hauses Medici. Politik, Maezenatentum und Rollenbilder (1512–1743)*, ed. Christina Strunck (Petersberg: Imhoff, 2011), 117–32.

CHAPTER 8

The Concept of Heraldry in Sixteenth- and Seventeenth-Century German-Speaking Territories as Seen through the Lens of Printed *Wappenbücher*

Kathleen Smith

1 Introduction

While the first "King of Heralds" was appointed as early as 1290 in England and Richard III founded the College of Arms in 1484,[1] the Holy Roman Empire did not have a similar central college or governing body. The sole consensus on the practice of heraldry in German areas consisted of standards that had been adopted in the thirteenth century.[2] Because there was no strong central governmental authority in the German-speaking regions of the Holy Roman Empire, the practice of arms in those areas developed independently; for example, there was middle-class use of arms starting in the fourteenth and fifteenth centuries without opposition, as well as noble arms being granted to families without territory.[3]

This comparative openness in the Germanic heraldic system is fascinating and ripe for closer investigation, particularly since it has been portrayed so negatively in prior historiography. Writing in 1912, Erich Gritnzer points to several factors that led to what he terms the "Niedergang" [decline of heraldry] in the German lands: the invention of guns;[4] the resulting changes in noble games and the end of tournaments in 1550, turning the heraldic shield into a wall decoration or decorative element;[5] the descent of heraldry into rigid rules and overly detailed arguments; and, finally, the "allgemeine Verbreitung" [general spread] of arms, which Gritzner claimed could be easily purchased.[6]

---

1 Filip, 2000: 40.
2 Filip, 2000: 41.
3 Gritzner, 1912: 72.
4 See the discussion of "Feuerwaffen" in Gritzner, 1912: 75.
5 Gritzner, 1912: 76.
6 "[D]ie allgemeine Verbreitung des Wappens; es erheischte die Mode, dass jeder halbwegs zu Amt und Wuerden Gekommene ein Wappen haben musste. Ein solches erreichte er aber entweder durch die Erlangung der Ratsfaehigkeit in den Staedten oder aber durch die

© KONINKLIJKE BRILL NV, LEIDEN, 2023 | DOI:10.1163/9789004682245_010

This is not to say there was no attempt to police or restrict the adoption of arms among the citizens of the Germanic lands. Indeed, the *Wappenverleihung*, or granting of arms, was an important source of income for the Holy Roman Emperor, and those who had their arms recognized by the emperor theoretically had the assurance that under imperial protection, no one else could use the same arms. However, without the comparably strong and centralized/local authority of the British or French crown, the Holy Roman Emperors were unable to police the adoption of arms as closely as their counterparts. Gritzner states that in particular this "Wappenhandel" [trade or commerce in coats of arms] led to the disgrace of heraldry since it resulted in the overornamentation of arms: their aesthetic effect became less clear, and he claims that in the end, only the ancient nobility had "a simple coat of arms with one field and a helmet with a simple decoration."[7]

Though the study of heraldry is today relegated to the category of "auxiliary science,"[8] and further situated within paleography, heraldry can be used to interpret and reveal much about the society in which it exists. The ability to recognize and identify heraldic arms was a useful skill for people in all walks of life in earlier periods. One clear demonstration of this is the proliferation of inexpensively printed heraldic manuals and guides that appeared in the German-speaking territories in the sixteenth and seventeenth centuries, once printing technology had advanced to the point at which it became practical to produce them.

Despite the widespread availability of these *Wappenbücher*, studies tend to focus on manuscript rolls of arms, which they interpet visually and iconographically. The few existing studies of *Wappenbücher*, moreover, largely focus on the ancillary aspects, such as the printers involved. In this paper, I take a preliminary look at prefatory material, dedications, and other textual evidence to examine how heraldry was depicted by those who produced these printed books. Unlike the elaborate manuscript rolls of arms that have survived,

---

allmaehlich sich ausbildende urkundliche Wappenverleihung seitens des Kaisers oder der von ihm beauftragten Personen, mit Hilfe klingender Muenze": Gritzner, 1912: 76.

7 "[K]urz, die Wappen wurden im Weiterverlauf der Zeit immer ueberladener und ihrer aesthetischen Wirkung unklarer und unuebersichtlicher. Man konnte schliesslich Wappen mit einem Felde und einem Helme mit einfacher Helmzier fast nur noch bei dem Uradel finden, dem es nicht aufgefallen war, sein Stammwappen zu veraendern": Gritzner, 1912: 77.

8 In Hiram Kümper's thorough compendium and textbook for studying the "Historischen Hilfswissenschaften," [auxiliary sciences in the field of history] for example, coats of arms are primarily described as useful for identification purposes, as a type of coded language that assumes a direct correspondence between signifier and signified that allows for meaning to be deciphered; see Kümper, 2014: 294–308. *Wappenbücher*, therefore, are useful as tools to decipher armorial bearings but are not presented as texts for analysis in and of themselves.

heraldry books were produced in large numbers and would have been accessible to German speakers who could afford them. Centering heraldry books, as opposed to manuscripts, shows how heraldry was understood by a much larger community. Perhaps more significantly, the documentary materials contained within these books reveal individual artistry and artistic choices. The artists display their individual expression and self-representation within frameworks bound by tradition and heritage. They saw and represented themselves within a long tradition that served a variety of purposes, from defending against the Turks to shaping citizens. By examining the introductions, prefaces, dedications, and other textual evidence found in printed heraldic guides by Johann Siebmacher and five other notable printer/creators, this paper explores the meaning of heraldry for these publishers and artists, and how they represented their own positions within broader systems of meaning.

First, however, I wish to discuss a few of the misconceptions about the nature of heraldry, particularly *Wappenbücher*, and how this subject is being addressed by modern scholars interested in reevaluating it critically.

In the introductory chapter in a volume of conference essays entitled *Heraldic Artists and Painters in the Middle Ages and Early Modern Times* (2018), Torsten Hiltmann explicitly situates heraldry's neglect as a field of study in three misunderstandings related to the representation of who was able to handle heraldry and for what purposes. He states that 1) "coats of arms are often presented as a mere means of identification"; 2) "heraldry [is presented as] almost exclusively a sign of the nobility"; and 3) "the prevalent idea that the proper handling of heraldry was the business of a small group of specialists, namely the heralds."[9] He goes on to reject these misconceptions and to state that "heraldry was a widespread means of communication" that "lent itself to a wide variety of different communicative purposes."[10] In encouraging more attention to be paid to who used heraldic forms of communication and how they were implemented, Hiltmann writes that we can learn much about heraldry as a social and cultural phenomenon, in addition to gaining insights into late medieval and early modern culture and society. These discussions focus primarily on the manuscript rolls of arms, but the same points can be applied to the less expensive printed works.

As Hiltmann explains in a 2011 article, armorials represent a rich scholarly resource but it is essential to understand their structure, purpose, and origins—the context that is often missing in the modern understanding of armorials, and of heraldry in general—in order to more accurately examine

---

9   Hiltmann, 2018: 11–12.
10   Hiltmann, 2018: 12.

them.[11] Most surviving German armorials are arranged by rank and hierarchical order, instead of marches of arms based on regions or territories, in order "to put the world in one book."[12] These texts attempt to make sense of the world in which their creators and artists lived, rather than reflecting it for later readers. "There is quite simply no such thing as an armorial with a clearly ordered portrayal of the existing social order, complete with all ranks and distinctions and qualifying as an uncompromised and rich source for research. It remains a desideratum—as indeed it was for contemporaries."[13] There is also no such thing as a static, unchanging heraldic bearing, since they evolve over time. Arms often originate in family traditions and are influenced by regional or prevailing fashions, with meaning being attributed later. Another later addition is a motto to connect meanings,[14] and arms could be marshalled or combined to display and lay claim to territories and royal possessions. Many decorative elements, such as crowns, may simply be ornamental—or they might convey meaning in later periods, similar to colors. This complex system of meaning was well known to and used by the contemporary authors and artists who created heraldic works of all kinds, as Hiltmann argues: "[t]hese texts deal in the imaginary. They are seemingly normative but have no great impact on reality. This was already evident to heraldic authors at the end of the sixteenth century."[15] Indeed, "rolls of arms [...] are documents of prevalent assumptions, not empirical images of the inhabited world."[16] The modern interpretation of the manuscript heraldic works that have survived reduces them to an unsophisticated, normative system of identification via one-to-one correspondence, in which variations in armorial bearings are perceived as factual errors. Few of these elaborate armorial rolls are accessible today, but the many printed books of heraldry that were created in greater numbers are also available to us in larger numbers, and they have much to reveal about the societies and the social structures in which they arose. These books resist easy classification since they functioned within a world of symbols—the emblematic imagery of the German-speaking territories of the sixteenth and seventeenth centuries is intricately complex and open to various interpretations, and there are clear connections to an emblematic understanding in the printed book of heraldry that arose during this time.

---

11   Hiltmann, 2011: 157–198.
12   Hiltmann, 2011: 186–187.
13   Hiltmann, 2011: 186.
14   Hiltmann, 2011: 188.
15   Hiltman, 2011: 189.
16   Hiltman, 2011: 197.

2   The Printed *Wappenbücher* of the Sixteenth and Seventeenth Centuries

The importance and prevalence of manuscript *Wappenbücher* up until the sixteenth century can be attributed to factors such as the expense, knowledge, and artistry involved in their production. Early printing technologies did not have adequate methods to depict and reproduce the complicated patterns, intricate details, and, above all, the palette of colors necessary to create catalogues of heraldry.

With the development of printing, however, came numerous versions and approaches to the *Wappenbuch* in the Germanic context. There was clearly a market for these works, as is recognized and described by their creators. Their authors, artists, and publishers also describe their own motivations for working in this area that seems to have been coded as belonging to the upper classes; they have a variety of disclaimers, justifications, and explanations for why they have chosen to publish a work of heraldry. This perceived ambivalence and uncertainty is overcome in all cases by the stated desire to improve the citizenry and to advance knowledge; the voracious market for these works no doubt played an important role.

To learn more about the concept of heraldry as interpreted by German printers and publishers of the sixteenth- and seventeenth-century, it is useful to explore some of the early printed *Wappenbücher*, starting in 1555 and moving chronologically forward to Siebmacher, whose book was so influential that it became the standard. The books that include an introduction or preface or supplemental material written by the publisher or artist often contain valuable information about the perceived purpose and goals of the work, yet this material is rarely scrutinized. What did these artists and publishers claim that they were doing, in their own words? Did it align with our understanding of the ways in which heraldry was used at the time?

3   Virgil Solis and His 1555 *Wappenbüchlein*

One notable printed heraldic guide appeared in 1555 from the German printmaker and engraver Virgil Solis (1514–1562), who employed Jost Amman in his workshop. His book follows a processional structure, beginning with a dedication page in Latin to the emperor, the pope, and the electors and imperial nobility followed by an elaborate full-page depiction of the armorial bearing of the Holy Roman Emperor, followed by a page with the twelve arms of Ferdinand's ancestral claims (Hungary, Bohemia, Dalmatia, Croatia, Slavonia,

Hispania, Austria, Burgundy, Brabant, Steyr, Carinthia, and Carniola). The arms of kingdoms like France, Sweden, Denmark, Scotland, and so on, follow. In order to emphasize the historic nature of arms, the author then describes the "first three coats of arms" in the world—those of "Abysey, Ganamevs, and Sabitey"—and then those of the three biblical kings Caspar, Bathasar, and Melchior. The description moves on to foreign kingdoms such as Bethlehem and Anthiopia before listing the coats of arms of the German electoral princes and then proceeding down through the ranks of German society. Afterward comes the Pope, and then the cardinals and bishops, and then the holders of lower clerical ranks. Next are the German cities.

Following the arms and a nota that describes the color code, at the end of the book, the author concludes with a disclaimer of sorts, in case anyone is offended that he did not seek permission to print his book:

> Wiewol ich dise Wappen (one yemandts verllayerung) meynes höchsten vermügen un[d] fleyß gemacht hab. So ist demmach an meiniglich was Eeren Wirden-Standts oder wesens diesem mein hochfreündtlich bit wollen in solch mein mühe un[d] arbeit gefallen lassen. Und ob etwan ainiger mangel an einem wappe[n] oder desselbe[n] farben gefünden würde, dasselb in keinem ungüten aüfnemen. sonder dasselb nach seinem gefallen korrigiern und endern. das bin ich umb einen yeden (seinem Standt nach) in aller gebüer und freündtschafft Züüer schülden verbüetig unnd willig.[17]

> [Why I gave these Arms my highest ability and effort (without anyone's support). So is the following my very cordial plea that Honor, Worth-Standing or Manners will be pleased by my labors and work. And if somehow any coat of arms is found to be lacking or its colors, please don't take this badly, but instead correct and change it accordingly. For this I am willingly indebted to every person (according to his social status).]

Solis's practical orientation is clear; if there is a correction to be made, the information provided by his readers will serve as a corrective. The implication is that there is no higher body or authority that needs to be consulted, nor do the self-reported corrections to this hierarchy need to be confirmed by other authorities. Solis serves as the referee, and the corrections should be made to him. However, the reader is also asked to participate by adding the proper colors to the black-and-white templates in the book. These artists, printers,

---

17 Solis, 1555: 52. Unless otherwise noted, all translations are by the author.

and publishers do not refer to a higher heraldic authority or even to French or English sources; instead, their work is framed as a collaborative effort involving the readers.

4 Martin Schrot and His *Wappenbuch des Heiligen Römischen Reichs* in 1551, 1576, and 1580

The Augsburg engraver Martin Schrot published another notable heraldic guide, his *Wappenbuch des Heiligen Römischen Reichs, und allgemainer Christenheit in Europa*, in 1576 and a revised edition in 1580. This work is dedicated to another member of the nobility, Rudolph the Holy Roman Emperor, and Schrot (although listed as "Adam Berg" at the end of the *Vorrede*) begins by quoting Cicero about how we are born to serve others and our Fatherland ("wir uns nit selb geboren seind, sonder andern und sonderlich dem Vatterland"), adding that knowing the illness is half the cure, before he comes to his main point. He is producing this book of German heraldry, he writes, in order to call all Christians to account:

> So hab ich vor diser zeit etlicher Heupter der Christenheit Wappen in ein Buch zusamen wöllen bringen, dabey alle und ieder Christ für augen bey den stillschweigenden wappen sehen künde, wie weit sich vor der zeit die Christenheit erstreckt hab, auch in was enge sie ietzt getriben, und daneben den sachen ferrer nachdencken, was die ursachen seind, daß das Römisch Reich, welches sich bey anderer Völckern Regierungen so weit erstrecket aber bey unser der Teutschen Regierungen solcher gestalt wie ietzt zusehen geschmälert worden, so doch Teutsche Nation biß daher allenthalben den Namen und das lob der redlichen mannligkeit und streitbarkeit gehabt.

> Thus I have long wanted to bring together in a book many Arms of the Heads of Christentum, so that each and every Christian could see for his own eyes through the arms (themselves silent) how far before the time of Christianity they reach, also to what narrow purposes they are now put, and, accordingly, could think more deeply about the reasons why the Roman Empire, which spread its dominion so far out over other peoples has been reduced to such a form as the present by our German Government, so however the German Nation has had until now the name and the praise of eloquent manliness and ambition.

Schrot's book is intended to bring to the attention of all Christentum the prob-lems of the German lands ("mangel, fehl oder abgang unsers lieben Vatterlands, der Teutschen Nation"). Christianity needs a wakeup call in order to be aware of its own decay. His preface repeatedly emphasizes the "mangel" [deficiency] in German society, and how the people need to be made aware of this prob-lem. The Christian leaders must stand together in unity and Christian solidar-ity "freundlich unnd Christlich mit einander zusammen hielten, und nit also sich von einander theilen und trennen liessen," and all of Christianity must be warned against the horrible tyranny of the Turks ("erschröckliche Tyranney des Türken"). The next preface is directed to the Christian reader, particularly to the *Teutsche Nation,* and he opens by repeating his refrain, drawing atten-tion to his reasons: "nemlich damit allen menschen gleich als in einer tafeln für augen stehe, wie weit unnd fern sich vor diser zeit das Römisch Reich auch Christenthumb erstrckt hat" [namely, so that all people can see, as clearly as though it were written on a tablet before their eyes, how distant and remote Christianity has spread from the time of the Roman Empire]. A long lament follows about the holy land, accompanied by comparisons with the suffering of Christ. Schrot feels no need to apologize for any perceived transgression in printing this work, nor does he show fealty to the Pope or the Catholic Church in general. This work is fully steeped in the teachings of Martin Luther and the Reform movement.

5 **Sigmund Feyerabend and His *Wapen und Stammbuch* in 1579 and 1589**

Sigmund Feyerabend (1528–1590), one of the most important prints and pub-lishers in Frankfurt, published his *Wapen und Stammbuch Darinnen der Keys. Maiest. Chur und Fürsten/ Graffen/ Freyherrn/ deren vom Adel/ ec. Mit kunst-reichen Figuren/ durch den weitberühmpten/ Josten Ammen gerissen/ sampt iren Symbolis, unnd mit Deutschen Reymen geziert* in 1579, with another ver-sion in 1589.[18] The book features woodcuts by Jost Amman (Zurich 1539–1591 in Nuremberg).[19] This printed work is dedicated to Sigmund Heldt (also

18   Benzing, 1961: 119.
19   Although this book is often attributed to Jost Amman, such as in the 1881 facsimile reprint
      edition, Feyerabend clearly sees himself as the author and creator. The reprint of this
      work is listed in the Bibliography under Amman, since that is how it was listed in the
      facsimile reproduction.

written Held or Helt) (1528–1587), who created the elaborate manuscript called the Heldt'isches Trachtenbuch, including 867 colored drawings created in Nuremberg between 1560 and 1580 and is currently in the collection of the Kunstbibliothek of the Staatliche Museen zu Berlin.[20]

In the beginning of his dedication, Feyerabend makes his purpose clear and unmistakeable by setting one expression in larger type so that it stands out from the rest: "Die Kunst hab keinen Feyndt ohn den unwissend oder unverstendigen" [Art has no enemy other than the ignorant and those void of understanding]. He praises the useful art of printing and its ever-increasing improvement, which, unfortunately, is not recognized by the majority, who pay more attention to the untalented and deceptive than they do to those with experience and skill. Music and poetry are cited to illustrate Feyerabend's example of arts that have been almost ruined by unskillful practicioners. From printing, Feyerabend moves to lamenting the lack of appreciation shown to those who draw images, paint, and engrave copper. He cites Alexander the Great; King Attalus, the ruler of Pergamon; King Demetrius of Macedonia; Julius Caesar; Hortensius, orator of Rome; and other examples from Pliny the Elder as those who prized the skill of painting and paid large sums of money for paintings.

Feyerabend's dedication then explains that since childhood he has been interested in the proper use of arts like printing and painting to serve good and useful German authors; beginning with biblical writings and moving to historical accounts and the poets, out of love for such artistry and to honor and serve all men who love honor, he writes, he is publishing a book he put together in Latin and "our" German language and decorated with the arms of many distinguished gentlemen, starting with the Holy Roman Emperor but including electoral princes and counts, barons, and other well-known nobles and distinguished dynasties in the cities.

He writes that he wants to dedicate this book to Heldt because he (Feyerabend) knows that Heldt is a particular lover of good art and himself created a remarkable book with beautiful figures and arms. For this reason, Heldt would certainly appreciate Feyerabend's book, especially the interpretations in German ("die Deutung, so in den Teutschen reimen herzu setzt"). This dedication is all the more relevant since Feyerabend is well aware that he has taken some liberties in terms of his heraldic depictions:

---

20   Heldt, 1560–1580. Some of the images are available through the SMB Online Collections Database: http://www.smb-digital.de/eMuseumPlus?service=ExternalInterface&module =collection&objectId=2042949&viewType=detailView.

Unnd da solche deutung nicht nach eines jeden Kopff und Sinn gestellet wer das beste helffen fürwenden. Dann nach dem offtermals seltzsame deutung der Wapen mögen fürfallen die auch wol denen selbst so die Wapen führen offt unbewußt so habe ich auff schlechter und einfaltiger deutung beruhen und alles so viel müglich auff die Tugend, Ehrbarkeit, und Gottesforcht richten wöllen. Versehe mich jedoch und verhoffe gentzlich ein auffrichtiges und ehrliebhabendes Herz werd diese meine mühe ungetadelt lassen.[21]

[And that such interpretation will not be pleasing to all minds and feelings, which is the best to be used. For, according to the frequently peculiar interpretation of the arms, it may come to pass that those themselves who bear the arms are often unaware of their meaning, and therefore I have been motivated by these bad and simple interpretations and have oriented everything as much as possible on Virtue, Honesty, and the Fear of God. Forgive me in any case and I hope fervently that a sincere and honesty-loving heart will leave my hard work uncriticized.]

The actual images in the book confirm that Feyerabend has indeed taken some liberties in the matter of interpretation and placement. Many of the images of the heraldic arms are interleaved with emblems that appear to have no easily decipherable connection without access to other contexts. To list some examples: the Kurfürst von Köln is paired with Temperantia, the Pfaltzgraf bey Rheyn with Charitas; the Kurfrst von Sachsen with Jason and Medea; the Herzog von Braunschweig with "Abscheid eines Hofmanns von seiner geliebten" [the parting of a courtier from his beloved]; the House of Freymonii with Medea alone; D. Johan Wimphelingius with Jason and Medea (again); Die Stallberger with "Eins Vatters Testament" [a father's will]; the D. Fichardt with Temperantia again; and so on. This juxtaposition reinforces the connections between emblems and heraldic bearings, at least from the perspective of an artist and printer who works with visual material in a variety of genres, and it would be fascinating to look at how print and manuscript emblem books during this time are often interleaved with armorial bearings in a variety of ways.

One illustration of the complexity faced by these publishers, printers, and artists can be seen in Feyerabend's approach to his own armorial bearing. The arms of "Die Feyrabendt" (Figure 8.1) and "S. Feyrabendt" (Figure 8.2) both feature a shield with a lion rampant facing to the left of the reader (right in heraldic imagery), but there are notable differences in the images. For the purpose

---

21   Feyerabend, 1881.

Die Feyrabendt.

Schauw an im dreyferbigem Feldt /
Ein edler Löw sich keck darstelt.

Eins edlen Löwen tapfferkeit /
Ein einig Klaw leichtlich anzeigt.

Also der Stamm der Feyrabendt /
Allein auch hierauß wirt erkennt.

Daß sie allzeit nach Ehren streben/
Vnd der Tugend mit ernst thun pflegen.

145

FIGURE 8.1 "Die Feyrabent"
FROM JOST AMMAN, *WAPEN UND STAMMBUCH* (1589), #153 ON PAGE 145 FROM THE
DIGITAL EDITION AT HATHITRUST, HTTPS://HDL.HANDLE.NET/2027/UIUG
.30112118724530

S. Feyrabendt.

Diß Wappen vilen wol bekandt /
Führt Sigmund Feyrabendts standt.

Im Buchhandel führ ich mein Lauff /
Wer mir nachfolgt / muß sehen drauff.

Deß Glücks von Gott / wie er mirs geit /
Thu ich erwarten allezeit.

Vnd steht in seiner Macht auff Erd /
Ob ich Bischoff oder Bader werd.

[51]

FIGURE 8.2 "S. Feyrabendt"
FROM JOST AMMAN, *WAPEN UND STAMMBUCH* (1589), #159 ON PAGE 151. THIS IMAGE
TAKEN FROM THE DIGITAL EDITION AT HATHITRUST, HTTPS://HDL.HANDLE.NET/2027
/UIUG.30112118724530

of this paper, which explores the understudied textual apparatus surrounding the heraldic images focus is on the texts surrounding each image and what they reveal.

Die Feyrabent
Schauw an im dreyferbigem Feldt
Ein edler Löw sich keck darstelt.
Eins edlen Löwen tapfferkeit
Ein einig Klaw leichtlich anzeigt.
Also der Stamm der Feyrabendt
Allein auch hierauß wirt erkennt.
Daß sie allzeit nach Ehren streben
Und der Tugend mit Ernst thun pflegen.

[Look at the three-colored field
A noble Lion displays itself boldly
The bravery of a noble Lion
One single claw lightly outstretched.
Thus the lineage of Feyrabendt
Only through this is it recognized,
That they all times strive for Honor
And Virtue with Ernestness tend.]

S. Feyrabendt
Diß Wappen vilen wol bekandt
Führt Sigmund Feyerabents standt.
Im Buchhandel führ ich mein Lauff
Wer mir nachfolgt muß sehen drauff.
Deß Glücks von Gott wie er mirs geit
Thu ich erwarten allezeit.
Und steht in seiner Macht auff Erd
Ob ich Bischoff oder Bader werd.

[This Arm known to many
carries Sigmund Feyerabent's status.
In the book trade I purchased my career
Whoever follows me must look thereupon.
That God's fortune will determine my fate
I expect always.
And it is within His Power on Earth
Whether I become a bishop or a barber.]

In these two depictions of Feyerabend's arms, both those of his "Stamm," that is his family dynasty, and those to whom he relates himself as an individual, heraldry informs all levels of German society (not only the nobility and upper classes), and is deeply interconnected with other systems of visual meaning. It is both clear and opaque. Feyerabend's two heraldic arms are "known to many" and "recognized," while simultaneously requiring that he provide textual explanation and decryption. His authority to decode his own arms springs from his experience, knowledge, and skill as an artist, rather than from his position as the bearer of those arms or as a specialized herald.

6 Georg Brentel (1525–1610) and His *Wappenbuch* of 1584

This book starts off with a printed and handcolored coat of arms of Philip Ludwig Pfalzgrave bey Rheyn, Herzog in Bayrn, Grave zu Feldentz und Sponheim, and it is dedicated to all noble ranks of the Holy Roman Empire and the Teutscher Nation. In his introduction, the author makes reference, and compares his own purpose, to that of Peter Fleischman zu Franckendorff and his description of the attendees of the 1582 Reichstag. This *Wappenbuch* is specifically directed toward the nobility, which in comparison with some of the other examples discussed in this paper, demonstrates the author's desire to appeal to a limited audience:

> Welliches Werck ich in die zwey Jarlang zusamen getragen und nicht mit geringem costen in Holz schneiden lassen unnd auß sondern bedencklichen ursachen (Weil ich gesehen das under dem Adel hin und her die Geschlecht verwandelt Also das nicht alle ihres alten herkommens so im Land Schwaben wonen Schwaben sondern dißweylen Francken iha auch Bayren und Reynländer seyen.) Deren Vier Land Schlecht unnd Wappen souil mir deren zubekommen immer müglich gewesen in Vier besondere underschiedliche Bücher abgetheilet unnd gestellt. [...] Unnd da ich bißweylen inn den Namen Wappen Farben oder anderm geirret oder sonsten was außgelassen were worden, dasselbig meiner unwissenheit einfalt und unverstand zuzuschreiben. Dan[n] ein solches einem ieden er sey hohes oder Niderstandts Geistlich oder Weltlich an seiner Würde Ehren Stand und wesen keins wegs preiudiciert noch nachtheilig sein soll.

This work that I have brought together in two years and had cut in woodcuts at no small cost, and for such a critical cause (because I had seen that among the Nobles here and there the dynasties change, and not all remain in their land of origin so that only Swabians reside in the Land of the Swabia On the contrary, there are also Franks, Bavarians and Rhinelanders). These four lands, families and arms should, in my opinion, always be divided and presented in four different books if possible. [...] And if I have been mistaken in the Name, Arm, Color, or if I otherwise have left anything out, such should be attributed to my ignorance, simplicity, and lack of sense. Because no one should be prejudiced or disadvantaged in his worth, honor, status, and way [wesen], be he of high standing or low, spiritual or secular.

Suitably for someone who wishes to emphasize German governance and the power of the princes, Brentel has chosen to depict powerful (male) rulers such as Rudolph II, Holy Roman Emperor. The first noble family is the House of Austria,[22] and it is not until much later[23] that we see the arms of the Holy Roman Emperor and the Reichsstaat. The coats of arms grow increasingly complex and soon cannot be confined to single pages as the book continues. Those prints that have been filled in are elaborately hand-colored—Brentel does not print a color register or key—and we see more families represented. The book ends with an index of family names of the Four Lands ("Schwaben, Francken, Bayren, and Rheinstrom").

This expensive book contains beautiful and detailed woodcut images of the heraldry, and it clearly comes from an artist who knows the practice of heraldry well: elements such as the crest are very important in conveying profession, status, and other information not in the shield itself. This book is much more a register of the individual people than the families, as is shown in the descriptions of the arms as linked to the current bearer, such as "Carolus, von Gottes Gnaden Ertz-Herzog zu Osterreich, Herzog zu Burgundi, zu Steir, Kaernten, Crain, und Wirttemberg, Graf zu Tirol und Goertz," etc.[24] The audience would likely be limited to those able to afford this book, mainly nobility and wealthy members of the middle class, and the purchasers would almost certainly have a court artist or hire an artist to complete the arms.

---

22   Brentel, 1584: image 33.
23   Brentel, 1584: image 133.
24   Brentel, 1584: 31. Since these dynastic connections and claims shifted over time, it would
      be interesting to explore if these printers and authors who were working with heraldic
      guides (and therefore presumably more sensitive to such nuances) changed their dedica-
      tions to address the variety of titles that each individual member of the nobility held over
      time, or whether this sensitivity was simply a necessity for all printers and artists in this
      period, particularly those who hoped for noble patronage.

7 Kaspar Hennenberg's 1595 *Erclerung der Preussischen grössern Landtaffel oder Wappen*

Hennenberg's book, dedicated to Georg Friedrich, Margraf zu Brandenburg in Preußen, begins by describing how God created the human body out of many well-formed limbs, each in its right place, and then compares these to how each person is assigned a suitable "Geschafft und Ambt," or "job and life." Each piece is essential to the whole. Hennenberg then quotes the apostle Paul, who writes in his First Letter to the Corinthians that God has assigned to each "sein besondere Gabe/Ampt/Beruff und Standt," meaning that we, as members or limbs of the body of Christ, must serve another and help one another. Hennenberg then points to the ruling classes and nobility as having been confirmed in this position, "das sie die Herrn und Haupter darueber sein sollen" [that they should be the lords and rulers over it]:

> Damit ich auch nun eine zimliche raume zeit hero umbgegangen biß ich solches alles in ein Buch/wie die Binen ihr Konig im Binkorb zusamen gebracht/ das sich also der Leser an einem iedern ort zuerinnern wie es vor alters allda zugegangen und gestanden habe.

> [I have spent no little time engaged with this, until I brought everything together in a book, like the bees their king in the beehive, so that the reader can be reminded in each place how it was ages ago.]

Images of noblemen begin on page 199, with the fifteenth-century figures Ludwig von Erlingshausen and Heinrich Reuzss Herr von Plawen (each with simple arms, such as the eagle and the lion). In this book, the arms are treated as immutable historical facts, without much thought to how they are created or adapted. Heraldic bearings are characteristics related to the nobility, explained by and for the nobility. The world has been ordered by God into the ranks as Henneberg lists them, and all fit together as parts of the whole. Yet the book's audience is not limited to the nobility, since it also functions as a reminder of the role of nobility directed to all members of the social order, and Henneberg never questions his ability to create this guide for the good of all.

8 Johann Siebmacher's *New Wapenbuch* (1605–1609)

The most popular and most successful German Wappenbuch by far was Johann Siebmacher's *New Wapenbuch*, which became synonymous with reference works for the study of arms. This book was a runaway best seller. As Horst Appuhn describes it in his afterword, Siebmacher's work superseded its predessesors in its detailed depictions and its comprehensive contents of 226 plates with 3,471 arms. According to Appuhn, this book was "ein Neubeginn, der für die Heraldik oder Wappenkunst erstmals eine solide Basis legte" [a new beginning that for the first time laid a solid basis for Heraldry or Wappenkunst].[25] The original edition was a small book printed in black and white, with the expectation that readers would color in the illustrations themselves (few surviving copies were colored in by their owners, however.)

Let us look more closely at Siebmacher and his accomplishment. Johann Ambrosius Siebmacher was born into a family of tinsmiths (Kannengießer) around 1561 in Nuremberg; he trained as a tinsmith but also as an etcher (Radierer). Siebmacher illustrated many works, including emblem books, numismatics, maps, and city views—in particular, however, he became known for his pattern books for etching and needlework.[26] His *Schön Neues Modelbuch von allerleÿ lustigen Mödeln naczunehen Zuwürcken unn Zustikken* (1597) was the first model book with patterns in copperplate etching and was very successful.[27]

He turned his interest to heraldry in 1596 with a small work: a nineteen-plate pattern book. This was followed by the two-part *New Wapenbuch. Darinnen deß H. Röm. Reichs Teutscher Nation ...* in 1605 and 1609. In 1612, after his death, his widow published another edition of both parts, with new editions and expansions coming in 1657, 1668, 1705, 1734, 1753–1806 (with twelve supplement volumes), and in 1855 an expanded edition of 119 volumes with over 130,000 arms represented.[28] The editions following his death appeared under different editors and names, but the term "Siebmacher" is used to refer to the whole, with the "Alte Siebmacher" used to differentiate between the edition published during Siebmacher's lifetime, whichconsisted of one volume.

How did Siebmacher himself describe his activity in creating this authoritative *Wappenbuch*? In his introduction, Siebmacher mentions that his primary interest in publishing this work is usefulness. Others printed shields, *Wappen*, and genealogies before him, but they were not complete, so he searched in "Kirchen, Cloestern, Bibliotheken, bey den Grabstaetten und andern publicis & privatis locis & personis" [churches, cloisters, libraries, at gravesites, and

---

25   Appuhn, 247–48.
26   Tacke, 2010: 35.
27   This work is available online at the BSB: https://bildsuche.digitale-sammlungen.de/index .html?c=viewer&bandnummer=bsb00026001&pimage=0&v=5p&nav=&l=de.
28   For an extensive list of editions, see www.drbernhardpeter.de/Heraldik/seite53siebhtm.

other public and private locations and persons] to bring many to light. He knows that he will be criticized for his work, but he requests that the detractors and interpreters ("Verleumbder und Deuter") leave off mocking and criticizing his work until they can do better, at which point he will be happy to concede to them.[29] Later editions of the work quickly expanded, since anyone who wished could send a listing of a coat of arms to be included.

Siebmacher also directly indicates an awareness of the market for his book when he states that he was aided in his work by those who will benefit from it: "Zur Beförderung dieses meines Thun und Buchs haben mir viele fürtreffliche Personen, als sie vermerckt daß es zur Hinlegung vieler Strittigkeit in Beweisung der Sipschaften, in Lehenentpfengnussen, in Erbfällen und andern sehr dienst und fürträglich sehr gute Befürderung und Hülff gethan" [Nobles helped me when they realized my work could be useful for solving disagreements in cases of inheritance, and other legal matters]. However, Siebmacher is covering his bases when he hopes that nobody suffers from the order and arrangement of this, his private work, in regard to their dignities, honors, reputation, and worth ("praecedentz, reputation, dignitet, Ehren, Herkommen, Standt und Wirden").

It is noticeable that one use Siebmacher does not mention in his introduction is as a pattern or model book—a use he would have been well familiar with. There is a register of names, which would aid in searching for particular families or cities that are known, but would not be of help in searching for a coat of arms whose name is not known.[30]

The plates themselves are printed in black and white, with the colors "tricked" or represented in abbreviated form with the first letter of the name of the correct color. The later technique of hatching to indicate tincture, or colors and patterns, is attributed to Silvestro de Petra Sancta, a Jesuit priest and heraldic scholar who took his hatching system from illustrators and engravers in the Netherlands and published it in his *Tesserae gentilitiae* of 1638. Such systems allowed readers to color in the arms themselves.

One common element of the printed *Wappenbücher* intended for a non-noble readership is their explanatory focus and the practical apparatus for encouraging their audience to color in or draw the coats of arms themselves.

---

29   Siebmacher, 1999: 12.

30   As Ottfried Neubecker points out in the introduction to his *Großes Wappen-Bilder-Lexikon* (1992), "Die seit dem frühen 17. Jahrhundert entstandenen gedruckten Wappelsammlungen vermerken zwar bei ihren tabellarischen Uebersichten, ob die Familien, deren Wappen dargestellt sind, einer adeligen, einer patrizischen, einer ehrbaren oder einer bürgerlichen Familie gehören, lassen aber die Frage offen, wie man ein Wappen identifizieren kann, dessen Herkunft man nicht kennt": Neubecker, 1992: viii.

These works were intended for a wide readership with an interest in heraldry but no first-hand experience with it, and no pre-existing knowledge or expertise is required or assumed. They are remarkably transparent for treating such a complicated and intricate subject. Indeed, these books are clearly presented as the works of their authors, as expressions of skill and knowledge, but they are not intended to obscure or complicate the subject matter—rather, their goal is to simplify and popularize it.

9   Conclusion

Wappenbücher and the complicated subject matter they contain deserve wider study in the cultural context of the period, as do the networks of transmission and communication they preserve and perpetuate, as well as the manner in which they participate and represent themselves within those systems. For those who are looking for evidence to confirm a pre-existing belief that heraldry in German-speaking regions underwent a decline during the sixteenth and seventeenth centuries, these printed armorial guides could perhaps be interpreted as supporting evidence, given that there is no single cohesive narrative history of heraldry, its meaning and purpose, to be found in them. If, however, readers open their eyes to what is actually present in these printed works, they will encounter a dazzling array of purposes and meanings, each worthy of further exploration. It is the difference between prescriptive grammars, which aim to set rules and determine proper usage, and descriptive grammars, in which the actual language being used is documented and not judged. Those German scholars in the mid-eighteenth century and beyond desperately wanted these *Wappenbücher* to be prescriptive, rather than descriptive.

Viewing the above works as imperfect historical records, however, reduces their complexity and limits their value as representations of a transitional period from manuscript to print. One of the major recurring themes to be found in them is the democratization of the study of heraldry, in the sense that these creators/artists/publishers are in the position of explaining and clarifying not only what heraldry is and what it does but also why they themselves, as non-nobles, can be printing and creating these reference works.

There is so much to be done with these printed heraldic manuals. A fuller study is needed of the techniques each book uses in dealing with the complexities and technical challenges of translating its subject matter into a printed book. For example, Martin Schrot's book includes an extensive register of colors for the arms, while others, such as Siebmacher's, include a color key indicated by tiny letters printed onto the arms. The Jost Amman work has no colors listed. Another area of interest is the organizational principles of these works, and how such complicated subject matter is dealt with. As Hiltman notes, these are aspirational works rather than exact duplicates of the social order, so it is particularly relevant to study how the arms are grouped, who is included/ excluded, and how the depictions themselves vary, particularly with an eye not toward evaluating them for accuracy but toward comparing them and exploring the variations as a positive feature. These encyclopedic catalogs of armorial bearings have much to tell us about the world of the sixteenth and seventeenth centuries—not only about the heraldic symbols in them, but about the fascinating and multilayered world of those who bore them and those who negotiated their meaning.

Bibliography

Amman, Jost. *Jost Amman's Wappen & Stammbuch.* (Munich: Hirth, 1923). https://hdl.handle.net/2027/uiug.30112118724530.

Appuhn, Horst. "Johann Siebmachers Wappenbuch. Nachwort des Herausgebers." *Johann Siebmachers Wappenbuch von 1605. Herausgegeben und mit einem Nachwort von Horst Appuhn.* (Munich: Orbis, 1999): 247–255.

Benzing, Josef. "Feyerabend, Sigismund." *Neue Deutsche Biographie* 5 (1961), 119 [online version]. https://www.deutsche-biographie.de/gnd118683527.html#ndbcontent.

Brentel, Georg. *Wappenbuch & Zier Ihren Ro. Kay. May. sampt Chur und Fursten Geistlichs unnd Weltlichs Standts Wappen/fuernemlich aber deren/ so auff verschinem Reichstag zu Augspurg im Jar 1581 gehalten/selbs Personlich erschinen/ Auch deren Abwesenden/so ihre Gesandten alda gehabt/ souil deren zubekommen mueglich gewesen/ordenlich begriffen. Hierzu seind auch neben der Rom. Kay. May. und Chur/ auch der Stifft sampt mehrertheil der Reichstaett/Dessgleichen der Vier Land/sampt derselben Grauen/Herzen und Adelspersonen Wappen gesetzt worden. Alles mit sonderm Fleiss zusamen getragen/Artlich/Gruendlich und eigentlich fuergemalet/In Sechs Buecher abgetheilet/sampt einem zu ruckh angehenckten ordenlichen Register der Vier Land/ und in verlegung Georgen Brentels Burgers und Malers zu Laugingen in Truck verfertiget* (Laugingen, 1584). https://mdz-nbn-resolving.de/bsb00083990.

Feyerabend, Sigismund. *Wapen und Stammbuch Darinnen der Keys. Maiest. Chur und Fürsten Graffen Freyherrn deren vom Adel ec. Mit kunstreichen Figuren durch den weitberühmpten Josten Ammen gerissen sampt iren Symbolis, unnd mit Deutschen Reymen geziert* [...] (Frankfurt, 1579).

Feyerabend, Sigismud. "Vorrede." In *Jost Amman's Wappen & Stammbuch*, facsimile reprint (Munich: Georg Hirth, 1881).

Filip, Vaclav Vok. *Einführung in die Heraldik* (Stuttgart: Franz Steiner, 2000).

Gritzner, Erich. "Heraldik." In *Grundriss der Geschichtswissenschaft. Zur Einfuehrung in das Studium der deutschen Geschichte des Mittelalters und der Neuzeit, Vol. 4 Sphragistik, Heraldik, Deutsche Muenzgeschichte* (Leipzig and Berlin: B. G. Teubner, 1912).

Heldt, Sigmund. *Abconterfaittung allerlei Ordenspersonen in ihren klaidungen und dan viler alter klaidungen, so vor zeiten von Fursten, Furstin und Herrn, auch Burger und Burgerin, alhie zu Nurmberg und vilen andern orten getragen sinnt worden, Und an eins theils orten noch getragen werden. Desgleichen allerlei Turnier und Gestech von Hohen und Nidern Stenden.* [...] (Nürnberg, 1560–1580).

Hennenberg, Kaspar. *Erclerung der Preussischen grössern Landtaffel oder Wappen, Mit leicht erfindung aller Stedte/Schloesser/Flecken/Kirchdoerffer/Orter/Stroeme/Fiesser und See so darinnen begriffen. Auch die erbauuage der Stedte und Schloesser/ ihre zerstoerunge und widerbauung. Sampt vielen schoenen auch Wunderbarlichen Historien/ guten und boesen loeblichen und schentlichen Wercken unnd Thaten/Sampt derselbigen Straff und belohnung/so darinnen geschehen: und wunderlichen Mirackeln/ welche in Preussen zum theil sein/ oder sich darinnen zugetragen haben/nuetzlich zu lessen. Auch mit feinen contrafeiten Figuren gezieret. Aus Alten und Newen Scribenten colligiret/wie dann auch dabey verzeichnet* (Königsberg in Preussen, 1595).

Henning, Erkart, and Gabriele Jochums. *Bibliographie zur Heraldik. Schrifttum Deutschlands und Österreichs bis 1980* (Vienna: Böhlau, 1984).

Hiltmann, Torsten, and Laurent Hablot, eds. *Heraldic Artists and Painters in the Middle Ages and Early Modern Times* (Ostfildern: Thorbecke, 2018).

Hiltman, Torsten. "Arms and Art in the Middle Ages. Approaching the Social and Cultural Impact of Heraldry by its Artisans and Artists." In Torsten Hiltmann and Laurent Hablot, eds., *Heraldic Artists and Painters in the Middle Ages and Early Modern Times* (Ostfildern: Thorbecke, 2018): 11–23.

Hiltman, Torsten. "Potentialities and Limitations of Medieval Armorials as Historical Source. The Representation of Hierarchy and Princely Rank in Late Medieval Collections of Arms in France and Germany." In Thorsten Huthwelker, Joerg Peltzer, and Maximilian Wemhoener, eds., *Princely Rank in Late Medieval Europe: Trodden Paths and Promising Avenues* (Ostfildern: Jan Thorbecke, 2011): pp. 157–198.

Kümper, Hiram. *Materialwissenschaft Mediaevistik: Eine Einführung in die Historischen Hilfswissenschaften* (Paderborn: Ferdinand Schöningh, [2014]).

Neubecker, Ottfried. *Grosses Wappen-Bilder-Lexikon der bürgerlichen Geschlechter Deutschlands, Österreichs und der Schweiz* (Munich: Battenberg, 1992).

Schrot, Martin. *Wappen-Buche des hohen geistlichen und weltlichen Stands der Christenheit in Europa* [...] (Munich, 1576). urn:nbn:de:bvb:12-bsb11054888-4

Sibmacher, Johann. *New Wapenbuch, darinenn deß h. Römischen Reichs Teutscher Nation hoher Potentaten, Fürsten, Herren* [...] (Nürnberg, 1605). https://collections.thulb .uni-jena.de/rsc/viewer/HisBest_derivate_00006345/VD17-574579966_0001.tif.

Siebmacher, Johann. *Johann Siebmachers Wappenbuch von 1605. Herausgegeben und mit einem Nachwort von Horst Appuhn* (Dortmund: Harenberg Edition, 1994).

Siebmacher, Johann. *Johann Siebmachers Wappenbuch von 1605. Herausgegeben und mit einem Nachwort von Horst Appuhn* (Munich: Orbis Verlag für Publizistik, 1999).

Solis, Virgil. *Wappenbuch. Antzaigung deren wappen darauf des Heyligen Römischens Reichs grundtfeste gepflantzt und geordnet ist, sambt derselben Namen und Farben. Zu Ehren der Römischen Kay. Und Ku. My, auch Babstlicher Heyligkeit. Sambt andern der furnensten auslendischen Ronigreichen Churfursten, Fursten und gemeinen Stennden. Darauf des heyligen Romischen Rychs grundsveste gevflanket und geordnet ist. Solch Der selben Wappen zubethumen sind gewesen mit Iren namen und farben Durch Virgili Solis Maler und Burger zu Nermberg, mit sonderm fleys gemacht* (Nürnberg, 1555). https://digi.ub.uni-heidelberg.de/diglit/solis1555.

Tacke, Andreas. "Sibmacher, Hans." *Neue Deutsche Biographie* 24 (2010), 305 [online version]. https://www.deutschebiographie.de/gnd119546655.html#ndbcontent.

CHAPTER 9

Emblems in Motion: From the Altdorf Academy and the Nürnberg Town Hall to Sweden and the Colony of Pennsylvania

Mara R. Wade

1 Introduction: The Emblematic Prize Medals of the Altdorf Academy

The seventeenth-century political emblems in the Great Hall of Nürnberg's *Rathaus* [Town Hall] have a long history, reaching back to the founding days of the Altdorf Academy and the long tradition there of "emblematic oratory."[1] At the Altdorf Academy, the central institution of higher learning for early modern Nürnberg, established in 1575, emblems were central to both rhetorical instruction and corporate identity formation. One element of the pedagogy at Altdorf consisted of awarding an emblematic prize medal with an allegorical motif and motto to the top boy in each class, each of whom was required to elaborate in a Latin oration the relationship between the motto and the image on the medal. Taken together, the oration, the motto, and the image constitute a full emblem. The practice was fundamentally radical, presenting the emblem simultaneously in two media: in durable metal and in ephemeral speech. The emblem was cast as a three-dimensional artifact displaying the *inscriptio* and *pictura*, and the oration comprised a performative *subscriptio*. The Altdorf emblematic medals and orations shaped the culture of political emblems that informed several generations of pupils, many of whom descended from Nürnberg patrician families and later assumed leading roles in the city's civic administration.

The Altdorf practice of emblematizing political virtues is reflected in the painted emblems of the Nürnberg Great Hall. In the early seventeenth century (1613–1617), emblems from Altdorf, and variations thereof, were used to decorate the Great Hall. In some cases, the Town Hall emblems were identical to, or variations of, the Altdorf emblematic medals awarded annually to the best students. At the nexus between the town and the academy in the

---

1 Stopp was the first to recognize the awarding of medals at Altdorf as an emblematic practice; see Stopp, 1974: 17; Moedersheim, 2004: 29–54; and Wade, 2004: 55–78.

© KONINKLIJKE BRILL NV, LEIDEN, 2023 | DOI:10.1163/9789004682245_011

decades immediately after 1600, the learned humanist and jurist Georg Rem (1561–1625) is central to the connection between the Altdorf emblem medals and those later painted into the window embrasures of the Great Hall. From around 1600, Rem was a *Ratskonsulent*, a legal adviser to the Nürnberg town council, and also *Kurator* of the Altdorf Academy during the first quarter of the seventeenth century.[2] In 1624 Rem became the *Prokanzler* of the newly privileged University of Altdorf. After his death, in 1625, the practice of awarding prize medals and holding emblematic orations ended at Altdorf, while in Nürnberg emblems and emblem books continued to flourish, experiencing a revival during the waning years of the Thirty Years' War, in the 1640s, and thereafter. The political emblems were still in the window niches of the Great Hall when the splendid Swedish peace banquet was held there in September 1649,[3] and some of the emblems appeared in the table decorations for the feasts.[4] The emblematic messages proclaiming the ethical norms for good governance and the common weal echoed long thereafter, as evidenced by their appearance on ceremonial halberds commissioned in Nürnberg around 1650 by Carl Gustaf Wrangel (1613–1676), the Crown's governor of Swedish Pomerania and the lord of Skokloster Manor, in Sweden. In the final decades of the seventeenth century, the Franconian jurist Franz Daniel Pastorius (1651–1720/21), who had studied at Altdorf and can also be assumed to have seen the Nürnberg Town Hall emblems himself, compiled the first emblematic work in the American colonies, his "Emblematical Recreations" (ca. 1690–1700).[5] A great friend of William Penn, Pastorius was the founder of Germantown, Pennsylvania.[6]

2 Emblematic Prize Medals at the Academy at Altdorf

Based on the prize medals awarded annually to a select member of each class, the academy at Altdorf engaged in emblematic pedagogy—that is, the teaching, particularly of political ethics, through emblematic speeches. This

---

2 The word 'Kurator' as used in the sense at Altdorf has the meaning of a representative of the city of Nuremberg at Altdorf and in the German sense of the word *Vormund*, that is, a legal guardian. The Altdorf Academy had a pro-chancellor, while the town council of Nürnberg itself exercised the duties of the chancellor. The council appointed Kuratoren from among their midst, and Georg Rem served as one for the first quarter of the seventeenth century until he himself was appointed pro-chancellor, five days after Philipp Camerarius's death.

3 Klaj, 1651.

4 Harsdörffer, 1657.

5 Franz Daniel Pastorius, "Emblematical Recreations," emblematical manuscript, Germantown, Pennsylvania, 1680–1720. I am writing a more detailed study of this manuscript.

6 Häberlein, 2001: 97.

FIGURE 9.1   The Academy at Altdorf with Fountain of Pallas Athena (1575/76) by Georg
             Labenwolf, July 2019, author photo
             PHOTO COURTESY OF AUTHOR

emblematic practice began with the founding of the academy and continued
for nearly fifty years (Fig. 9.1). For purposes of clarity, I refer to the institution
throughout this paper as the Altdorf Academy, although it went through several stages, finally becoming a university in 1622.

Frederick John Stopp published the most comprehensive study of the
emblematic medals of the Altdorf academy.[7] He coined the term "emblematic oratory" to describe the practice of speeches interpreting the mottos and
allegorical images on the medals. Associating a Latin speech with the motto
and image of the prize medal thereby created the three constituent parts of a
canonical emblem—motto, *pictura*, and *subscriptio* (in this case the oration
itself). While the emblematic orations were themselves ephemeral performances, the medals were material objects. This represented a radical innovation in emblematic pedagogy.[8] The medals were awarded and collected; the

---

7   Stopp, 1974. The above information on the history of the academy is summarized from Stopp.
    Owing to Stopp's monumental research, Fischer and Maué, 2014: 21, did not include the
    Altdorf medals in their catalog of medals in Nürnberg.
8   Wade, 2021.

speeches were presented, archived, and later printed. Together with images of both the obverse and reverse sides of the medals, the speeches were published over the years in a variety of small school publications and, not long after, in the format of emblem books that integrated the three elements of the motto, image, and text as a single unit. Levin Hulsius published the compendium *Emblemata Anniversaria Academiae Altorfinae* ..., which recorded the medals and speeches of the Altdorf Academy from 1582 to 1597 (Fig. 9.2).[9] The introduction to the reader at the beginning of the volume states clearly that it does not include those from previous years, printed in 1581 under rector Johann Thomas Freigius, and refers the reader to that volume, published by Katharina Gerlach.[10] The title page of the 1597 publication emphasizes the pedagogical aspects of the emblems, specifically calling them "emblemata ... academiæ ...." This locution definitively shifts the focus from the medals and the orations as individual elements of the school program to the integrated emblematic practice. At the very latest, with the publication by Hulsius, in 1597, the Altdorf medals entered a new medium as a printed emblem book.

The entire record of the Altdorf emblems through 1616 was published as *Emblemata Anniversaria Academiae Noribergensis* ... in 1617 (Fig. 9.3).[11] The compiler and editor of this volume was Georg Rem, although he is nowhere named in the book. The copy preserved today at the Herzog August Bibliothek, Wolfenbüttel, bears Rem's manuscript dedication to the learned Duke August, thereby attesting to Rem's key role in the publication (Fig. 9.4). It is unthinkable that the humanistic jurist Rem would have personally dedicated a volume to the learned duke that he himself had not compiled and seen to press. At several points Stopp tentatively suggests Rem as the author/compiler, but retreats, saying there is no concrete evidence for this assertion.[12] Therefore I would like to confirm his suggestion and state that Rem was, in fact, responsible for the publication. The newly edited volume from 1617, reflecting the complete run of medals, aligns with Rem's philological bent and humanistic training to represent a full accounting of the academy's medallic production and emblems. As legal counsel to both the academy at Altdorf and the town council of Nürnberg, he would have been highly motivated to present the academy and the Free Imperial City at the apex of learning and good government. Moreover,

---

9   Hulsius, 1597. Engravings by J. Siebmacher (ca. 1561–1611) depicting sixty-four prize medals from 1582–1597, with the Latin orations delivered by their recipients, printers Levin Hulsius and Christoph Lochner. See http://emblematica.library.illinois.edu/detail/book /emblemataanniveroouniv.

10   Hulsius, 1597. For the early medals, see Freigius, 1581.

11   Stopp discusses the complicated record of emblem orations presented in the 1617 edition; see Stopp, 1974: 31–35.

12   Stopp, 1974: 100.

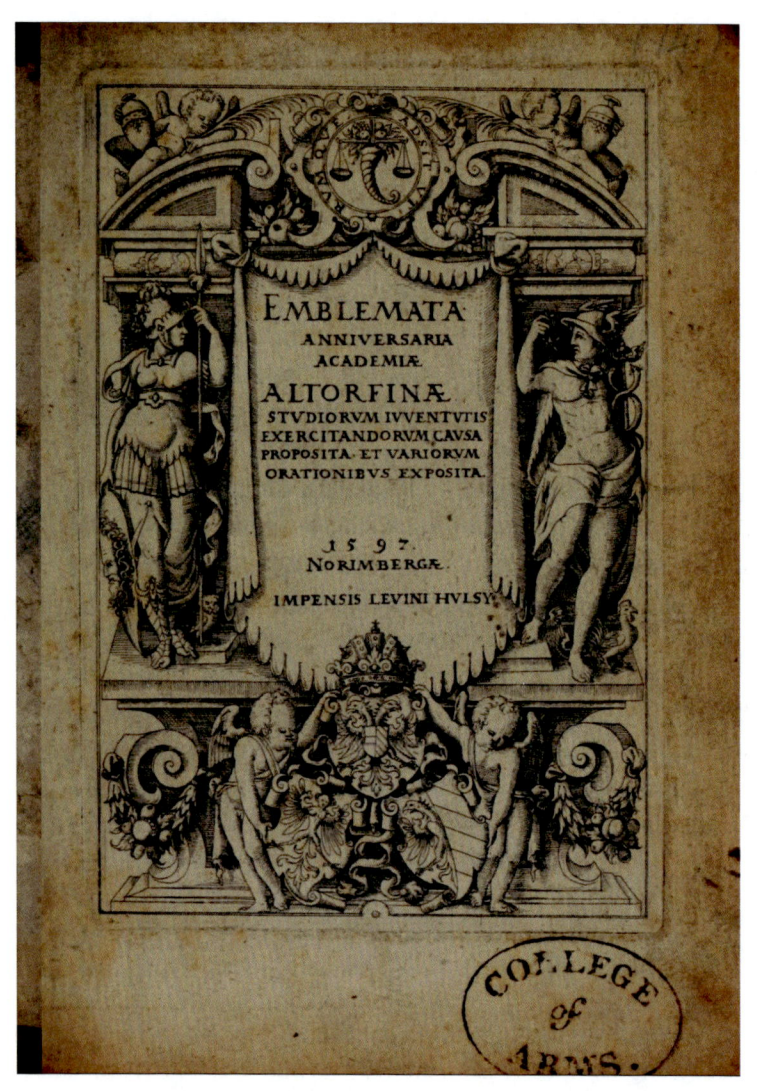

FIGURE 9.2 *Emblemata Anniversaria Academiæ Altorfinæ … Nürnberg 1597*
COURTESY OF EMBLEMATICA ONLINE, UNIVERSITY OF ILLINOIS
AT URBANA-CHAMPAIGN

he can be seen as a conduit between the academic emblems from Altdorf and the political emblems in the town hall. The wide circulation of the *Emblemata anniversaria Academiae Noribergensis* advertised both the town and the academy throughout Europe and was instrumental in positioning the academy for its elevation as a university in 1622. The Altdorf prize medals were minted,

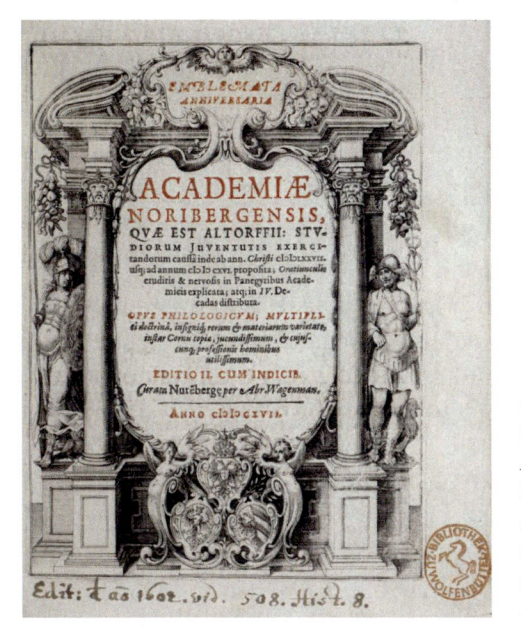

FIGURE 9.3
[Georg Rem], *Emblemata Anniversaria Academiæ Noribergensis ...*, Title page, Nürnberg 1617
COURTESY OF EMBLEMATICA ONLINE, HERZOG AUGUST BIBLIOTHEK: HTTP://DIGLIB.HAB .DE/DRUCKE/19-ETH-1S/START.HTM

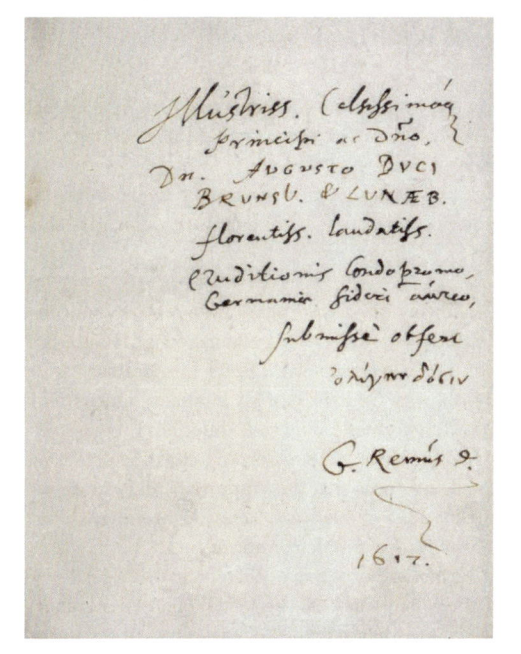

FIGURE 9.4
Georg Rem dedication of *Emblemata Anniversaria Academiæ Noribergensis ...*, to Herzog August Nürnberg 1617
COURTESY OF EMBLEMATICA ONLINE, HERZOG AUGUST BIBLIOTHEK: HTTP://DIGLIB.HAB .DE/DRUCKE/19-ETH-1S/START.HTM

stamped, awarded, circulated, and collected as material objects;[13] with their accompanying orations they were published in school programs and printed and reprinted as encyclopedic volumes of emblematica.

3   The Nürnberg Town Hall Emblems

Concurrent to the compilation and publication of the *Emblemata anniversaria Academiae Noribergensis* in 1617, the Nürnberg Town Hall underwent significant renovations. Matthias Mende has documented the extensive architectural and decorative renewal of the Town Hall through detailed archival research.[14] These renovations included painting thirty-two emblems into the sixteen window embrasures of the Great Hall (Fig. 9.5). In so doing, the city planners juxtaposed the compact ethical statements on good government of these emblems with the splendid allegories of imperial virtues as revealed in Albrecht Dürer and Willibald Pirckheimer's *Triumphal Chariot of the Emperor Maximilian*, painted in 1521 in the Great Hall (Fig. 9.6).[15] As chief legal counsel to both the town and the academy, who was simultaneously editing the Altdorf emblems for publication, Rem can with reasonable certainty be attributed with the oversight for the selection of emblems for the Great Hall.[16] When the engraver

---

13   One complete set and one nearly complete set of the Altdorf medals are held at the Germanisches Nationalmuseum, Nürnberg. I want to thank Dr. Matthias Nuding und Dr. Silvia Glaser for their kind assistance with my research there.

14   Mende, 1979: 38–95, 224–45, 333–62, provides a comprehensive documentation of the Town Hall during this period, including a detailed discussion of the allegories and emblems of the Great Hall.

15   Silver, 2008; Mende, 1974: 38–95.

16   Here I contradict Mende (and those following him), who, based on a remark in a contemporary Nürnberg emblem book, attributes the Town Hall emblems to the "Losunger" Georg Volckamer and Andreas Imhof, the chief financial officers for Nürnberg who were responsible for the town-hall renovations (Mende, 94). My argument asserts that these two men, Volckamer and Imhof, while formerly pupils at Altdorf and themselves emblematically inclined, would have had very little time to devote to the fine details of the emblematic decorations. There can be no doubt that they approved and encouraged these additional allegories, but the humanist and emblematist Georg Rem, who was compiling the encyclopedic publication of the Altdorf emblems concurrent to the extensive renovations, likely determined the selection and ordering of the emblems in the Town Hall. His editing and compilation of the final volume of Altdorf emblems, his authorship of the Latin *subscriptiones* published in Isselberg's book of engravings of the town-hall emblems, and his dedication, in the same year, of the published Altdorf emblems to Herzog August further support his central role. See Wade, forthcoming, and also Warnke, 2013: 43–50, here esp. 43–47; and Harms, 1982: "Einleitung."

FIGURE 9.5

The Great Hall of the Nürnberg Town Hall, window embrasures with emblems; the left-hand window depicts the helmet on a book with the motto "Utroque clarescere pulchrum"

COURTESY OF ZENTRALINSTITUT FÜR KUNSTGESCHICHTE, ZI2490_0058 DETAIL, PHOTO MÜLLER UND SOHN, 1943/1945. COPYRIGHT FOTO MARBURG & ZENTRALINSTITUT FÜR KUNSTGESCHICHTE, PHOTOTHEK

FIGURE 9.6A   The Great Hall of the Nürnberg Town Hall, Albrecht Dürer and Willibald Pirckheimer,
Triumphal Chariot of the Emperor Maximilian I. Z12490_0091, Detail, Photo, Müller und
Sohn, 1943/1944
COPYRIGHT FOTO MARBURG & ZENTRALINSTITUT FÜR KUNSTGESCHICHTE,
PHOTOTHEK

FIGURE 9.6B
Detail from above

Peter Isselburg (ca. 1580–ca. 1630) first viewed the emblems in their splendid architectural setting, he rushed to engrave and publish them, as he states in the introduction to the *Emblemata Politica* (1617).[17] Georg Rem wrote the Latin distichs for the printed emblems.

Published, as they were, on the eve of the Thirty Years' War, the Nürnberg Town Hall emblems, with their themes of mutual cooperation and good governance, resonated across the decades of war. In complete alignment with emblematic practices, Rem's colleague Johann Conrad Rhumelius (Rhumel, Rummel; 1574–1630) published the emblems as *emblemata nuda*, taking Rem's mottos and writing new Latin epigrams, in his *Emblemata curialia auctiora* (1629).[18] Rem and Isselburg's *Emblemata Politica* was published again in 1640.[19] In this imprint, the German translations of the epigrams appear on facing pages to Rem's Latin emblems. The republication of the Nürnberg Town Hall emblems, more than two decades after their first printing, can be interpreted as "Friedensarbeit"—as part of the peace process following long years of war. These concise messages advocating harmonious living under good laws belonged to the veritable explosion of emblems in Nürnberg during the decade leading up to the Treaty of Westphalia in 1648 and the peace congress at Nürnberg in 1649–1650.[20]

The Nürnberg Town Hall emblems were permanent fixtures on the walls of the venerable Great Hall of the city's Rathaus and widely available in various printings and adaptations throughout the Thirty Years' War. From the Altdorf Academy to the Nürnberg halls of justice, by the end of the war the emblems of good governance had been omnipresent for a period of over seventy years and inculcated into generations of the Altdorf scholars who later became the civic leaders of the Free Imperial City. The emblems were firmly embedded in the social imaginary of the town, its citizens, and their visitors. The emblematic ideal of the Common Good from the medals that were collected and preserved,

---

17 Rem and Isselburg, 1617. Several copies of the volume are available via Emblematica Online: http://emblematica.library.illinois.edu/detail/book/emblematapolitico0isel. Peter Isselburg also engraved the etching of the triumphal arch for the entry of Emperor Matthias into Nürnberg in 1612. See http://www.virtuelles-kupferstichkabinett.de/de/detail-view. See also Cholcman.

18 Nürnberg: Halbmayer, 1629. This edition is available online at the BSB: https://reader.digitale-sammlungen.de/resolve/display/bsb10522865.html. In the following year, Rummel expanded his emblem collection and published it as *Emblemata Miscellanea* (Nürnberg: Halbmayer, 1630). This edition is available online at the HAB: http://diglib.hab.de/drucke/217-10-quod-2s/start.htm. See also Schnabel, forthcoming.

19 Nürnberg: Endter, 1640. Available at the Niedersächsische Staats-und Universitätsbibliothek Göttingen: https://gdz.sub.uni-goettingen.de/id/PPN807277312.

20 Wade, 2020: 431–66.

the printed pages of the encyclopedias of the academic emblems that circulated throughout German-speaking lands and beyond, and the thirty-two paintings in the window niches of the Town Hall saturated the public imagination.

More than three decades after their publication by Rem and Isselburg, the emblems featured again during the Swedish peace banquet held in September 1649. While all manner of emblems were printed, painted, etched and engraved, and worked in metals during a blaze of emblematic activity in Nürnberg in the 1640s,[21] the political emblems comprised the themes and visuals of the festivities accompanying the peace negotiations held at Nürnberg in 1649–1650. While the emblems in the window embrasures surrounded the high-ranking guests and patricians at the Swedish Peace Banquet, some of the same emblems formed the table decorations (Fig. 9.7). As I have argued elsewhere, the emblems were not only a product of peace but an instrumentalization of existing cultural artifacts long embedded in the social imaginary to support the peace negotiations.[22] After Carl Gustaf (1622–1660), Count Palatine on the Rhine and, later, King Karl X Gustaf (Charles X) of Sweden, the field marshal Carl Gustaf Wrangel (1613–1676) served as one of the key representatives on behalf of the Swedish crown in Nürnberg.[23] The Swedes hosted the famous banquet that reset the course toward peace when the negotiations threatened to fall apart.

In Nürnberg, the Swedish commander-in-chief Carl Gustav Wrangel commissioned a set of ceremonial partisans emblazoned with emblems,[24] some of which are still preserved at his manor Skokloster in Sweden (Fig. 9.8).[25] These splendid weapons were intended to be carried by his ceremonial troops (or bodyguards) as a signal of his high rank in his new role as governor of Swedish Pomerania, a position he assumed following the peace negotiations in Nürnberg.

4   Emblems and the Commonplace

There are many variations of the emblem *pictura* showing a book and a sword, representing the concept that good rule is founded on both learning and

---

21   See Glaser.
22   Wade, 2020.
23   For more on the performance of emblematic musical pageants at the banquet, see Wade forthcoming (2).
24   https://en.wikipedia.org/wiki/Partisan_(weapon).
25   Rängstrom, 2006: 161–77; Rängstrom, 1975: 277–312; and Rängstrom, 1984.

FIGURE 9.7

Joachim von Sandrart, *Das Friedensmahl im großen Rathaussaal zu Nürnberg am 25.9.1649*, 1650, Öl auf Leinwand, 291,5 x 448 cm

MUSEEN DER STADT NÜRNBERG, KUNSTSAMMLUNGEN, INV.-NR. GM 0009. COURTESY OF MUSEEN DER STADT NÜRNBERG, KUNSTSAMMLUNGEN

FIGURE 9.8   Ceremonial partisans in the armory at the manor of Carl Gustav Wrangel,
Skokloster, Sweden
PHOTO BY MARA R. WADE

arms. This emblem of good governance is a commonplace that permeated the
Nürnberg tradition from its first appearance among the Altdorf prize medals in
1579. The fact that the final instance of the emblems investigated here is found
in Franz Daniel Pastorius's manuscript emblem miscellany from around 1700
speaks precisely to an important point. The examples presented here are all
emblems, whether they manifest with or without the epigram, with or without
a *pictura*. These emblem mottos and images elicited a completion (or *subscriptio*) from the well-educated viewer/reader/observer, who could recall a context
or invent one on the spot, alone or in conversation. The well-stocked mind could
follow the analogies and produce an existing or newly conceived epigram or
prose text. Conversely, provided with a motto, they could call to mind an image
depicting the concept. The humanist tradition from which emblems developed had its foundations in learning and education, with boys who from their
earliest school days kept commonplace books that combined pithy sayings for
use at a later time in constructing arguments, orations, legal cases, epigrams,

or commentaries. Emblems are the product of a well-furbished mind, and the numerous variations in combining mottos and pictures reflect the treasure trove of visual and textual learning typical of an early modern education. That emblems were part of the pedagogical program at many schools, including Altdorf, and apparently later used in this fashion by Pastorius in Pennsylvania, speaks to their suitability in educating the young: they are concise, they call to mind entire texts and images, and they illuminate possible trajectories of an argument for a speech or an epigram. They are memorable. The young men were trained in emblematic encoding and decoding, such that if they saw an Altdorf medallion or an emblem painted into the window niches of the Town Hall, they were well equipped to provide commentaries on the motto and *pictura*. In fact, such scenarios were meant to invite civil conversation—for example, at the Swedish Peace Banquet. These emblems were meant to be completed in performance, to be enacted, and they were reconstituted with each viewing. This idea speaks directly to the conceit of the emblem as a genre of intellectual play. As the examples below confirm, emblems are fugue-like variations on a theme, whereby meanings can be changed, new accents set, or a motto combined with a different image in a reciprocal interweaving of analogies, abstract reasoning, and symbolic thinking.

5   Arms and the Man at Altdorf and Nürnberg

A cluster of related emblems among the medals from the Altdorf Academy (re)configure the image of the book and the sword with a variation on the theme of *arte et marte*. In its third year, 1579, the Altdorf Academy created a medal of a mailed fist clenching a sword over the tablets of the Law with the motto "Lex regit, arma tuentur" [The law rules and arms protect] (AM 9) (figs. 9.9A–B).[26] This image is well known from classical antiquity, and it became a staple of emblem literature and appears in many variations. The image of the medal and the accompanying oration were printed in the school pamphlet commemorating the end-of-year event held annually on the Feast of Saints Peter and Paul, when awards and degrees were conferred, pupils

---

26   Stopp, 1974: 116–17. The information concerning the Altdorf medals is based on Stopp. I also use his translations of the mottos throughout, occasionally adding a variant in my own translation. In the notes I also refer to the Altdorf Medal (AM) by Stopp's numbering for those working with this standard reference work. "Lex regit" is AM 9 and the oration held by the pupil Albert Kewitz.

FIGURE 9.9A
"Lex regit, arma tuentur," Prize Medal, Altdorf Academy 1579
IMAGE COURTESY OF THE GEMANISCHES NATIONALMUSEUM,
NÜRNBERG, MEDK176, FOTO: CAROLIN MERZ

FIGURE 9.9B
"Lex regit, arma tuentur," Prize Medal, Altdorf Academy 1579
IMAGE COURTESY OF THE GEMANISCHES NATIONALMUSEUM,
NÜRNBERG, MEDK176, FOTO: CAROLIN MERZ

promoted to the next class, plays staged, and the emblematic orations were held.[27] The emblem refers to both arms and the book as foundational for the education of a man. Over the years this emblematic medal appeared in various iterations at Altdorf: The version from 1582 shows a sword on an open book that rests on a cushion with the motto "Virtutum doctrina parat" [Training of the mind is the foundation of Merit] (AM 19), alluding to how Alexander the Great slept with his copy of Homer and a dagger under his pillow (Fig. 9.10). As Stopp points out, the emblem refers to the education of a ruler: "Not only arms but the study of letters can be an ornament for King."[28] The Altdorf medal from 1588 depicts a sword resting on a book upon a globe with the motto "His nititur orbis" [The world of men on these] (AM 43), alluding to the fact that the laws of the state and the arms of princes govern the affairs of men (Fig. 9.11).[29] The final example from Altdorf depicts a somewhat greater variation on the medal from the following year, 1589, which shows a sword held upright entwined by ivy with the motto "Utroque clarescere pulchrum" [Distinction in both fields is attractive; or Beauty shines with both] (AM 48) (Fig. 9.12).[30] As the first point

---

27   Stopp, 1974: 17–44.
28   Stopp, 1974: 122; AM 19, the oration held by the pupil Philip Rieter.
29   Stopp, 1974: 134–35; AM 43, the oration held by the pupil Leonhard Dürnhöfer.
30   Stopp, 1974: 136–37; AM 48, the oration held by the pupil Jakob Geuder.

FIGURE 9.10A
"Virtutum doctrina parat," Prize Medal, Altdorf Academy 1582
IMAGE COURTESY OF THE GEMANISCHES NATIONALMUSEUM,
NÜRNBERG, MEDK186, FOTO: CAROLIN MERZ

FIGURE 9.10B
"Virtutum doctrina parat," Prize Medal, Altdorf Academy 1582
IMAGE COURTESY OF THE GEMANISCHES NATIONALMUSEUM,
NÜRNBERG, MEDK186, FOTO: CAROLIN MERZ

FIGURE 9.11A
"His nititur orbis" Prize Medal, Altdorf Academy 1588
IMAGE COURTESY OF THE GEMANISCHES NATIONALMUSEUM,
NÜRNBERG, MEDK210, FOTO: CAROLIN MERZ

FIGURE 9.11B
"His nititur orbis" Prize Medal, Altdorf Academy 1588
IMAGE COURTESY OF THE GEMANISCHES NATIONALMUSEUM,
NÜRNBERG, MEDK210, FOTO: CAROLIN MERZ

of serious academic training for Nürnberg's civic figures, the Altdorf Academy employed political emblems and oratory to train their future leaders.[31]

The Altdorf emblematic variation on the arts of war and learning can be readily traced in the Nürnberg Town Hall. Four of Rem and Isselburg's political emblems can be seen to have derived directly from Altdorf: numbers 14, 19, 20,

---

31　The printed, paper versions of the Altdorf medals discussed here, together with their respective orations, can be found in [Rem], *Emblemata Anniversaria Academiæ Noribergensis ... 1617*, on pages 35, 72, 158, and 166.

FIGURE 9.12A
"Utroque clarescere pulchrum," Prize Medal, Altdorf Academy 1589
IMAGE COURTESY OF THE GEMANISCHES NATIONALMUSEUM,
NÜRNBERG, MEDK215, FOTO: CAROLIN MERZ

FIGURE 9.12B
"Utroque clarescere pulchrum," Prize Medal, Nürnberg Town Hall
IMAGE COURTESY OF THE GEMANISCHES NATIONALMUSEUM,
NÜRNBERG, MEDK215, FOTO: CAROLIN

and 32, which are discussed in order in the following.[32] The motto "Vtroq[ue] clarescere pulchrum" from the Nürnberg Town Hall echoes the motto of the Altdorf emblem from 1589 and varies the image by portraying a helmet on a book (Fig. 9.13). In the complex world of emblematic analogies and parallels, the helmet replaces the sword, thereby also recalling the emblem of the bees swarming into an open helmet used as a hive. The substitution of the open helmet for the sword pictorially cites the emblem of "Ex bello pax" [From war, peace] and subtly shifts the meaning toward peace—one of the most repeated themes in the Nürnberg Town Hall emblems (Fig. 9.14). While the threat of armed conflict does not disappear, the emphasis centers more directly on peace and learning. These shifts in accent would have been readily discernable to the members of the Nürnberg town council, most of whom were educated at Altdorf and who themselves numbered among the medals' recipients. The viewers of these emblems were also a predominantly male audience in the Great Hall.

"Lex regit, arma tuentur" from the Nürnberg Town Hall repeats the Altdorf medal from 1582 exactly and displays the mailed arm holding a sword in front of the tablets of the Law (Fig. 9.15). "His nititur Orbis" likewise echoes the sword and book on a globe at Altdorf (Fig. 9.16). The final example from the Nürnberg Town Hall offers a significant variation. In this case, the image of the sword entwined by ivy, while visually similar to the Altdorf *pictura*, is interpreted as

---

32   The images in this article depict the painted versions from the Nürnberg Town Hall, while the printed emblems, according to their numbering (14, 19, 20, 32) as published by Rem and Isselburg, can be viewed on line at http://emblematica.library.illinois.edu/search /books?Query.Keywords=emblemata%20politica&Skip=10&Take=10.

FIGURE 9.13   "Utroque clarescere pulchrum," Emblem in the window niche, Great Hall of
the Nürnberg Town Hall, Z12490_0022, Photo Müller und Sohn, 1943/1945
COPYRIGHT FOTO MARBURG & ZENTRALINSTITUT FÜR
KUNSTGESCHICHTE, PHOTOTHEK

Ex bello pax.

En galea intrepidus quam miles gesserat, & quæ
    Sæpius hostili sparsa cruore fuit.
Parta pace, apibus tenuis concessit in usum,
    Alueoli atque fauos grataq́; mella gerit.
Arma procul iaceant, fas sit tunc sumere bellum,
    Quando aliter pacis non potes arte frui.
                              D

FIGURE 9.14   Andrea Alciato, "Ex bello pax," *Emblematum Libellus.*
               Paris 1534
               COURTESY OF EMBLEMATICA ONLINE, GLASGOW
               UNIVERSITY LIBRARY. HTTP://EMBLEMATICA.LIBRARY
               .ILLINOIS.EDU/DETAIL/EMBLEM/E030129

FIGURE 9.15   "Lex regit, arma tuentur," Emblem in the window niche, Great Hall of the
Nürnberg Town Hall, Photo Müller und Sohn, 1943/1945, ZI2490_0028
COPYRIGHT PHOTO MARBURG & ZENTRALINSTITUT FÜR
KUNSTGESCHICHTE, PHOTOTHEK

FIGURE 9.16   "His nititur Orbis," Emblem in the window niche, Great Hall of the Nürnberg
Town Hall, Photo Müller und Sohn, 1943/1945, ZI2490_0027
COPYRIGHT FOTO MARBURG & ZENTRALINSTITUT FÜR
KUNSTGESCHICHTE, PHOTOTHEK

FIGURE 9.17   "Rigorem clementia temperet," Emblem in the window niche, Great Hall of the
Nürnberg Town Hall, Photo Müller und Sohn, 1943/1945Z12490_0070
COPYRIGHT FOTO MARBURG & ZENTRALINSTITUT FÜR
KUNSTGESCHICHTE, PHOTOTHEK

the sword entwined by olive branches (Fig. 9.17). The new motto directs the
new interpretive trajectory: "Rigorem clementia temperet" [Severity tempered
by mercy]. As printed in Rem and Isselburg's *Emblemata Politica*, the accompanying Latin and German epigrams interpret the image as the clemency of
the ruler.[33] In both the Altdorf and the Nürnberg *picturae*, a naked hand, not a
mailed fist, grips the sword, suggesting a shift from the bellicosity of the "Lex
regit" emblems to a focus on the mercy of the ruler.

Owing to the emblematic orations at Altdorf, the medals cast to commemorate the awarding of prizes and promotions, and the circulation of these images
and texts in various printed editions, the ruling patricians would have immediately recognized the concise messages in these compact texts and images
and would have been in a position to discern and articulate both small and
great variations.

---

33   Rem and Isselburg, 1617: emblem 32; Rem and Isselburg, 1640: emblem 32.

6   The Mobility of the Nürnberg Town Hall Emblems

After the Treaty of Westphalia, which concluded the long decades of the
Thirty Years' War, there remained a peace to be negotiated, including the matter of disbanding troops as well as various political dealings. The so-called
Friedens-Exekutions-Kongress, held in Nürnberg from spring of 1649 through
the summer of 1650, provided the path forward in these delicate proceedings.
Banquets and other festivities punctuated the cumbersome diplomacy and
brought the formerly warring parties together, paving the way for the final conclusion of the peace. The Swedish Peace Banquet given by the Count Palatine
on the Rhine Carl Gustav, a cousin of Queen Christina who succeeded at her
abdication, was a fabulous dining event, including a figure of the Swedish lion
dispensing red and white wine to the general populace, musical performances,
the sumptuous meal consisting of many courses, an allegorical play, and
fireworks. The banquet took place in September of 1649, at a moment when
the negotiations had threatened to founder. It was held in the Great Hall of the
Nürnberg Town Hall, where the rich allegories of the Triumphal Chariot of the
Emperor Maximilian decorated the wall and the emblems of good government
the window embrasures. Emblems also embellished the tables in the form of
allegorical centerpieces for the banquet (Fig. 9.18).[34] Carl Gustav Wrangel was
one of the chief Swedish participants at Nürnberg.

Upon successful completion of the final peace treaty at Nürnberg, in 1650,
Wrangel assumed a new dignity on behalf of the Swedish crown as the governor general of Swedish Pomerania. For this new political and administrative role, Wrangel had made for himself thirteen partisans emblazoned with
emblems.[35] Several of these ceremonial weapons bear emblems that derive
directly from the Nürnberg Town Hall—among them ones displaying the
sword or helmet with a book. Seven of these weapons are preserved in the
armory at the castle of Skokloster, Sweden, and offer rich testimony to the circulation of emblematic ideals of good governance. The ever-popular emblem
of the mailed sword arm and the tablets of the Law is one of the emblems
that Carl Gustav chose to adorn his weapons and had inscribed with his personal motto: "Non est mortale quod opto" [I choose that which is not mortal]
(Fig. 9.19). This motto also appears on the reverse of every one of the preserved

---

34   Harsdörffer, 1657: Kupfertitel zu Teil IV. The "Schaugerichte" (table decorations) are
      described on 242–56. A digital copy of the edition from 1665 can be found at the SLUB
      Dresden: http://digital.slub-dresden.de/id405302673.

35   Rangström, 2006: 161–77. My thanks are owed to Professor Elisabeth Wåghäll-Nivre,
      Stockholm University, and the staff at Skokloster Museum, for procuring these images.
      Skokloster inventory no. SKO_DIG25440.tif.

FIGURE 9.18   Georg Philipp Harsdörffer, Titlepage to Part 4, "Von den Schaugerichten."
Vollständiges und von neuem vermehrtes Trincir-Buch. Nürnberg: Fürst, 1665
COURTESY OF THE SLUB DRESDEN HTTPS://DIGITAL.SLUB-DRESDEN.DE
/WERKANSICHT/DLF/102245/247#

partisans, where it is paired with an image of Ganymede captured in the talons of Jupiter's eagle, just as the boy is snatched to the heavens (Fig. 9.20). In this instance, the emblem can be interpreted to suggest Wrangel's proximity to the gods and heavens, to the highest reaches of Swedish nobility and the crown itself. It is therefore striking to find the motto repeated with a new image on the obverse of one of the weapons. The educated viewer of the mailed sword arm would have expected the motto "Lex regit" and would have paused to consider the new combination. Repetition in variation is typical of emblematic practices, and here the amplification of the motto with the image of the sword arm and tablets of the Law emphasizes its centrality to Wrangel's self-fashioning. As one of the most powerful officers of the Swedish state and representative of the crown in newly annexed German territories after the war, Wrangel chose emblems to demonstrate his own learning and rank, as the commander-in-chief of Swedish forces during the long years of war. The gilt partisans, the attributes of his governance, were put on display, Law backed by military might. The emblem flashing on the hilt of the halberd, glinting in

FIGURE 9.19
"Non est mortale quod opto."
mailed sword arm
COURTESY OF SKOKLOSTER/
PHOTO: JENS MOHR,
SKOKLOSTER CASTLE/SHM
(CC BY), SKO_DIG25440

FIGURE 9.20
"Non est mortale
quod opto." Ganymed
Courtesy of Skokloster
PHOTO: JENS MOHR,
SKOKLOSTER CASTLE/
SHM (CC BY),
SKO_DIG25436

FIGURE 9.21
"Utroque clarescere pulchrum."
Courtesy of Skokloster
PHOTO: JENS MOHR,
SKOKLOSTER CASTLE/SHM
(CC BY), SKO_DIG25439

golden highlights, would not have been visible to many, yet its message was nevertheless omnipresent.

Another emblem, well known from Altdorf and Nürnberg, that Wrangel chose for his ceremonial partisans features the motto "Utroque clarescere pulchrum" (Fig. 9.21).[36] In a familiar configuration, the *pictura* portrays the helmet on an open book. On the crosshilt at the blade's base, the rondel of the emblem is flanked by the attributes of war, while above the rondel, on the blade of the weapon, Pallas Athena leans on her shield and holds a banner with the motto "Prudentur" [Wisely]. This particular partisan has the remnants of the Swedish blue and yellow tassels that once decorated all of them. The theme of learning and weapons, the balance between the knowledge of the ancients and the art of war, emphasizes in the abstract the qualities of a leader who achieves immortal fame. The ceremonial weapons at Skokloster customize the emblems in the articulation of Wrangel's identity: the erudition symbolized by the book and the military might by the sword and helmet characterize Carl Gustaf Wrangel, the man who commissioned the partisans. His yeomen carried these weapons as they accompanied him on his official duties in Swedish Pomerania. They were portable insignia of the balance between *arte et marte*. They also sent a clear message to recently subjected German-speaking lands. While other contemporary partisans often were decorated with engraved coats of arms and/or allegorical female figures, only Wrangel's ceremonial weapons featured emblems.[37] The Wrangel partisans went beyond the heraldic; their emblematic embellishment distinguished Wrangel as a cosmopolitan man of learning. That the partisans are preserved among the other weapons in the castle's armory, which is near Wrangel's library, physically and spatially maintains the proximity of military might and learning that characterized the lord of Skokloster. Both learning and arms adorned him.

7   Emblems in the Colony of Pennsylvania

In the late seventeenth century, Franz Daniel Pastorius (1651–1719/20) translated the emblematic pedagogy of the Altdorf Academy to the American colonies. On 20 June 1683, he arrived in the colony of Pennsylvania, established by a land grant to William Penn in 1681.[38] One of the founders of the German

---

36   Skokloster inventory no. SKO_DIG25439.tif.
37   Rängstrom, 2006: 176.
38   https://en.wikisource.org/wiki/Dictionary_of_National_Biography,_1885-1900/Pastorius,
     _Francis_Daniel. See also Learned, 1908; Schweitzer, 1982: 1–6; and Lambert, 2007.

overseas emigration movement,[39] Pastorius, a former pupil at Altdorf,[40] compiled his "Emblematical Recreations," as it is titled in his own hand on the cover, in Pennsylvania (Fig. 9.22).[41] The manuscript, preserved at the Newberry Library, Chicago, has received scant attention, either from scholars of early Americana or from the emblem community.[42] The identification of the author Pastorius with the founder of Germantown, Pennsylvania, provides an important new context for the first emblem book made in colonial America. Trained as a lawyer at Altdorf, Pastorius certainly was acquainted with the emblematic practices of both the Altdorf emblematic medals and the Nürnberg Town Hall emblems. Writing mainly in English, he created an emblematical commonplace book, the "Emblematical Recreations," which in systematic fashion lists iconographic topoi—much in the manner of the emblem encyclopedia by Henkel and Schöne[43]—adding mottos in English, Latin, German, and French to accompany the images described. Pastorius's work is not illustrated.[44] This manuscript has been catalogued at the Newberry Library and also appears in Sandra Sider's catalogue of emblem manuscripts, although its importance as an emblem manuscript by the founder of Germantown and its connection to Altdorf was not remarked upon.[45] William E. Engel cites Pastorius's definition of the emblem as "speaking pictures," thereby acknowledging this important manuscript as part of the emblematic corpus.[46]

Section 22 of Pastorius's emblematic commonplace book deals with "Books" and suggests emblematic *picturae* for this topos. Among them are examples from Altdorf, where Pastorius received his law degree. The first example depicts "an Emperour [sic] portrayed with a book in one hand and a sword in the other" with the motto "Dignior est qui præstat utroque" [More worthy is he who offers

---

39   Pastorius, 1700.

40   Steinmeyer, 1912: 416: "Pastorius, Fr. D. Sommerhausen. 1668 (73). 10916. 11311." Note 15 gives more information about him: "1651–1719, Bürgermeister und Richter in Germantown ... 1670 IX. 2 als Stud. Phil. in Strassburg imm. 1676 Lic. Jur. (als Winshemio-Fr., Windsheimensis beziechnet.") See also 357, item 10916: "Franciscus Daniel Pastorius Sommerhusanus"; and 375, item 11311: "1673, 16. April, Franciscus Daniel Pastorius Sommerhusâ-Francus."

41   Pastorius, "Emblematical Recreations."

42   Pastorius has, however, been included in the seminal reference work on German Baroque literature. See Dünnhaupt, 1991, vol. 4: 3075–79). Since Dünnhaupt records only printed works, the manuscript under discussion here is, of course, not listed.

43   Henkel and Schöne, 1966.

44   See also the digital resource for Pastorius's extensive manuscript preserved at the University of Pennsylvania, his "Beehive": Digital Beehive, https://kislakcenter.github.io/digital -beehive/.

45   Sider, 1997: item 340. As in many other English works, he is called here "Francis Daniel Pastorius" and not at all associated with the famous founder of Germantown.

46   Engel, 2002: 46.

FIGURE 9.22   Franz Daniel Pastorius, "Emblematical Recreations," title page cover
                IMAGE COURTESY OF THE NEWBERRY LIBRARY, CHICAGO. CASE
                MS 1025.656 AUTOGRAPH MANUSCRIPT. PHOTO BY AUTHOR

both]. Another emblem represents a slight variation on this theme: "A Book
& Sword. Ex utroq[ue] Cæsar [from both the emperor], Legibus & legionibus
[Laws and legions], Hic regit, ille tuetur [This (the law) rules, arms protect],
and Arte & Marte [Art and War; by skill and by war)]" (Fig. 9.23).[47] Omitting
the ruler in the image, the motto of this variant refers to Caesar directly. The

---

47   These are on a verso page whose recto is numbered 205.

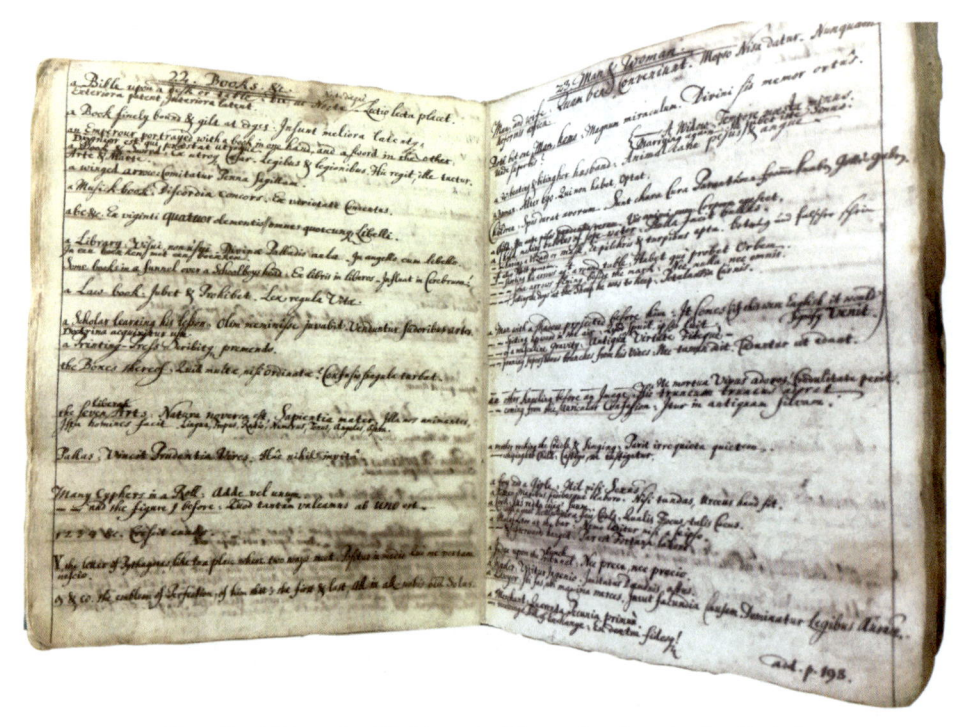

FIGURE 9.23   Franz Daniel Pastorius, "Emblematical Recreations," section "22. Books"
IMAGE COURTESY OF THE NEWBERRY LIBRARY, CHICAGO. CASE MS 1025.656
AUTOGRAPH MANUSCRIPT. PHOTO BY AUTHOR

reciprocal qualities suggested by the two emblems are noteworthy. In the first example, both learning and might characterize the personification of imperial dignity, while the second can be read as an expression of the notion that knowledge and arms create the idea of empire.

While Pastorius's book is unillustrated, his emblematic manuscript suggests in systematic fashion combinations of pictorial commonplaces and well-known mottos, referring to them in a kind of imagery shorthand, "a sword on an open book," with the knowledge that readers will understand the references at once. For many years, the energetic Pastorius, who was an author, poet, assemblyman, bailiff, court justice, and opponent of slavery, maintained a school in Germantown, which he temporarily removed to Philadelphia between 1698 and 1700. His emblematic manuscript might be understood as useful for pedagogical purposes. The fact that his widow gave it to their grandson when the boy Daniel was five years old suggests that the child received this little booklet when he started school, after the death of his grandfather: "A gift from Ann pastorius unto Daniel Pastorius wen [sic] he was fife [sic] years of age 1722"

FIGURE 9.24   Franz Daniel Pastorius, Emblematical Recreations, Dedication (top right) by his wife Ann
               Pastorius to their grandson Daniel
               IMAGE COURTESY OF THE NEWBERRY LIBRARY, CHICAGO. CASE MS 1025.656
               AUTOGRAPH MANUSCRIPT. PHOTO BY AUTHOR

(Fig. 9.24).[48] The title of the work, "Emblematical Recreations," also suggests
that Pastorius created these emblematic commonplaces as an activity for his
own nimble mind. The manner of compilation and the material condition of
the book suggest that it was excised from a larger work, and the practices of
compilation conform to those of his much larger work the "Beehive."[49]

8   Conclusion: Material Mobility, Semantic Stability

This survey of emblematic knowledge attests to the full geographic sweep of
the Renaissance texts and images known as emblems across a period of 150
years. From the academic prize medals at Altdorf to the emblematic primer in

---

48   Franz Daniel Pastorius, "Emblematical Recreations," [p. 1].
49   Grafton, 2012: 1–39.

Pennsylvania, the early modern social imaginary was fundamentally shaped by emblems. The geographic range of the emblems confirms personal networks of knowledge from Franconian Nürnberg and its academy at Altdorf to the Baltic littoral with the Swedish governor of Pomerania to his manor at Skokloster Sweden. Their literal translation to the American colonies and learned circles there—Pastorius was on excellent terms with William Penn—attests to enduring concepts of justice and learning, good government, and the Common Good. In 1688, Pastorius drew up a memorial against slave holding: a testimony to the emblems of justice and good government that resonates in the twenty-first century.

That these concise visual and textual adages were created in various media (cast from precious and weapon-grade metals, printed on paper, painted onto the walls of the town hall, and penned on manuscript paper) in various geographies (Altdorf, Nürnberg, Swedish Pomerania, Skokloster, and colonial Pennsylvania), and in various contexts (school prizes, political architecture, ceremonial weapons, commonplace books) attests to the flexibility of the form to adapt to various materials and to diverse intellectual and political settings. It is most striking that they began as emblematic orations by schoolboys and were compiled again in Pennsylvania as didactic lessons—those Pastorius himself taught in school and for his own grandson Daniel. Their mobility on so many levels—from the printed page and the walls of the Nürnberg Town Hall to the Swedish provinces along the Baltic and Wrangel's manor at Skokoster and, finally, to colonial Pennsylvania—is remarkable. The range of the material forms of these emblems is striking as well: prize medals, printed texts and images, beautifully colored paintings opposite Dürer's allegory of empire, confections for banqueting tables during the peace negotiations, engraved adornments on gilt ceremonial weapons, and a manuscript compendium of received visual and textual knowledge compiled by the founder of Germantown.

The dissemination of these compact messages across time, space, and media attests to the full integration of emblematic thinking and practices into the contemporary knowledge base. These concise packages of civic wisdom served to support good politics in diverse settings. Across these varied contexts and media of display, the message that both strength and learning were fundamental to good government endured.

Bibliography

Manuscript

Francis Daniel Pastorius, "Emblematical Recreations," emblematical manuscript, Germantown, Pennsylvania, 1680–1698. Newberry Library, Chicago, Case MS 1025.656, autograph manuscript.

Digital Resources

Francis Daniel Pastorius, "Beehive,": Digital Beehive, https://kislakcenter.github.io/digital-beehive/.

Emblematica Online, http://emblematica.library.illinois.edu/.

Printed Works

Cholcman, Tamar. "The Migration of Emblems through Nürnberg's History: From Triumph to Civic Memory." In *Emblems in the Free Imperial City: Emblems, Empire, and Identity in Early Modern Nürnberg*, eds. M. R. Wade, C. Fletcher and A. Schwenk. Intersections: Interdisciplinary Studies in Early Modern Culture, eds. K. A. E. Enenkel and W. S. Melion. Leiden & Boston: Brill, forthcoming.

Dünnhaupt, Gerhard. "Pastorius, Franz Daniel." In *Personalbibliographien zu den Drukken des Barock*, vol. 4 (Stuttgart: Hiersemann, 1991), 3075–79.

Engel, William E. *Death and Drama in Renaissance England* (Oxford: Oxford University Press, 2002).

Freigius, Johann Thomas. *Panegyres Altorfianæ, Una cum Natali Academiæ Altorfianæ, anno [1580] celebrato* (Altdorf: Gerlach, 1581).

Glaser, Silvia. "Emblems and Empire: *Emblematica Politica* in Early Modern Nürnberg: Some Examples of Applied Arts from the Free Imperial City of Nürnberg." In *Emblems in the Free Imperial City: Emblems, Empire, and Identity in Early Modern Nürnberg*, eds. M. R. Wade, C. Fletcher and A. Schwenk. Intersections: Interdisciplinary Studies in Early Modern Culture, eds. K. A. E. Enenkel and W. S. Melion. Leiden & Boston: Brill, forthcoming.

Grafton, Anthony. "The Republic of Letters in the American Colonies: Franz Daniel Pastorius Makes a Notebook." *American Historical Review* 117 (1) (2012): 1–39.

Häberlein, Mark. "Pastorius, Franz Daniel." *Neue Deutsche Biographie* 20 (2001), 97. https://www.deutsche-biographie.de/pnd12019323X.html#ndbcontent.

Harms, Wolfgang. "Einleitung." In *Emblemata Politica Nürnberg*. 1640. Rpt., Hildesheim: Olms, 1982.

Harsdörffer, Georg Philipp. *Vollständiges und von neuem vermehrtes Trincir Büchlein …* (Nürnberg: Fürst, 1657).

Henkel, Arthur, and Albrecht Schöne. *Emblemata: Handbuch zur Sinnbildkunst des XVI. und XVII. Jahrhunderts* (Stuttgart: Hiersemann, 1966).

Hulsius, Levin. *Emblemata anniversaria Academiae Altorfinae studiorum iuventutis exercitandorum causa proposita et variorum orationibus exposita* (Nürnberg: Hulsius, 1597). Copy used: University of Illinois at Urbana-Champaign, engravings by J. Siebmacher (ca. 1561–1611) depicting 64 medals used as prizes in 1582–1597, with the Latin orations delivered by their recipients. http://emblematica.library.illinois .edu/detail/book/emblemataanniveroouniv

Isselburg, Peter. see Rem.

Klaj, Johann. *Irene, das ist/ Vollständige Außbildung Deß zu Nürnberg geschlossenen Friedens 1650: Mit vielen feyrlichen Begengnissen/ Gastmalen/ Feuerwercken/ Musicen/ und andern denckwirdigen Begebenheiten/ nach Poetischer Reimrichtgkeit/ vorgestellet und mit nohtwendigen Kupferstücken gezieret / durch Johann Klai/ dieser Zeit Pfarrhern der evangelischen Gemeine zu Kitzingen und gekrönten Kaiserl. Poete* (Nürnberg: Endter, 1651).

Lambert, Margo M. "Francis Daniel Pastorius, An American in Early Pennsylvania 1683–1719/1720." Dissertation (Georgetown University, 2007).

Learned, Marion Dexter. *The Life of Francis Daniel Pastorius, the Founder of Germantown* (Philadelphia: Campbell, 1908).

Mende, Matthias. *Das alte Nürnberger Rathaus.* (Nürnberg: Stadtgeschichtliche Museen, 1979).

Moedersheim, Sabine "Duce virtute, comite Fortuna: Das emblematische Program des Goldenen Saals im Nürnberger Rathaus." In *Domänen des Emblems*, ed. Gerhard Strasser and Mara R. Wade. Wolfenbütteler Arbieten zur Barockforschung, 39 (Wiesbaden: Harrssowitz, 2004, 29–54).

Pastorius, Franz Daniel. *Umständige geographische Beschreibung der zu allerletzt erfundenen Provintz Pensylvaniae in denen End-Gräntzen Americae ...* (Frankfurt: Andreas Otto, 1700).

Rängstrom, Lena. "Partisans with Pictures." In *The Emblem in Scandinavia and the Baltic*, eds. Simon McKeown and Mara R. Wade. Glasgow Emblem Studies, vol. 11 (Glasgow: Glasgow Emblem Studies, 2006, 161–77).

Rängstrom, Lena. *Wrangel's Armory: The Weapons Carl Gustaf Wrangel took from Wismar and Wolgast to Skokloster in 1645 and 1653* (Stockholm: Livrustkammaren, 1984).

Rängstrom, Lena. "Bardisaner med Bilder." *Livrustkammaren* 13 (9) (1975), 277–312.

[Rem, Georg], *Emblemata Anniversaria Academiæ Noribergensis ...* (Nürnberg: Wagenman, 1617). Two copies of the volume are available via Emblematica Online: http:// emblematica.library.illinois.edu/search/books?query.keywords=Emblemata+Anni versaria+. The copy from the HAB contains Rem's manuscript dedication to Duke August.

Rem, Georg, and Peter Isselburg, *Emblemata Politica* (Nürnberg: n.p., 1617). Several copies of the volume are available via Emblematica Online: http://emblematica.library .illinois.edu/detail/book/emblematapolitico0isel.

Rem, Georg, and Peter Isselburg, *Emblemata Politica* (Nürnberg: n.p., 1640).

Rhumelius, Johann Conrad. *Emblemata curialia auctiora*. (Nürnberg: Halbmayer, 1629).

Rhumelius, Johann Conrad. *Emblemata Miscellanea* (Nürnberg: Halbmayer, 1630).

Schnabel, Werner Wilhelm. "Old and New Town Hall Emblems: Johann Conrad Rhumelius and the *Emblemata curialia auctiora* of 1629." In *Emblems in the Free Imperial City: Emblems, Empire, and Identity in Early Modern Nürnberg*, eds. M. R. Wade, C. Fletcher and A. Schwenk. Intersections: Interdisciplinary Studies in Early Modern Culture, eds. K. A. E. Enenkel and W. S. Melion. Leiden & Boston: Brill, forthcoming.

Steinmeyer, Elias von. *Die Matrikel der Universität Altdorf (1576–1809)*. 2 vols. Veröffentlichungen der Gesellschaft für Fränkische Geschichte, Vierte Reihe, Matrikeln fränkischer Schulen. (Würzburg: Kgl. Universitätsdruckerei H. Stürtz A. G., 1912).

Schweitzer, Christoph. "Introduction." In *Deliciæ Hortenses or Garden Recreations and Voluptates Apiniæ* (Columbia, SC: Camden House, 1982), 1–6.

Silver, Larry. *Marketing Maximilian* (Princeton: Princeton University Press, 2008).

Sider, Sandra, with Barbara Obrist. *Bibliography of Emblem Manuscripts*. Corpus Librorum Emblematum (Montreal/Buffalo: McGill-Queen's University Press, 1997), item 340.

Stopp, Frederick John. *The Emblems of the Altdorf Academy: Medals and Medal Orations; 1577–1626* (London: The Modern Humanities Research Association, 1974).

Wade, Mara R. "Von Schedels *Weltchronik* bis Birkens Friedensdichtungen: eine Nürnberger emblematisch-ikonographische Tradition im Kontext." In *Domänen des Emblems*, eds. Gerhard Strasser and Mara R. Wade. Wolfenbütteler Arbieten zur Barockforschung, 39 (Wiesbaden: Harrssowitz, 2004), 29–54, 55–78.

Wade, Mara R. "Emblematik als Friedensinstrument: Johann Klajs Friedensdichtungen." In *Johann Klaj (1616–1656). Friedensdichter, Poet, Theologe*, eds. Dirk Niefanger and Werner Wilhelm Schnabel (Berlin: De Gruyter, 2020), 431–66.

Wade, Mara R. "Teaching Ethics through the Emblem: The Academy at Altdorf (1577–1623) and Georg Rem's and Peter Isselburg's *Emblemata Politica* (1617)." In *Teaching Ethics in Early Modern Europe*, eds. Danilo Facca, Valentina Lepri, and Matthias Roick. Special volume of *History of Universities* XXXIV/2 (Oxford: Oxford University Press, 2021), 137–70.

Wade, Mara R. "'Inscriptiones picturæ et emblemata': How Nürnberg's Town Hall Emblems Came to the Newberry Library, Chicago." In *Emblems in the Free Imperial City: Emblems, Empire, and Identity in Early Modern Nürnberg*, eds. M. R. Wade, C. Fletcher and A. Schwenk. Intersections: Interdisciplinary Studies in Early Modern Culture, eds. K. A. E. Enenkel and W. S. Melion. Leiden & Boston: Brill, forthcoming.

Wade, Mara R. "Performative Emblematik: Der emblematische Friedensaufzug beim schwedischen Friedensbankett am 25. September 1649." In: *Theaterkultur der Frühen Neuzeit im Alten Reich*. Edited by Viktoria Gutsche, Jörg Krämer, Ernst Rohmer, und Werner Schnabel. (Forthcoming 2).

Warnke, Carsten-Peter. "Dürers größtes Werk. Zur Geschichte und Ikonologie der Ausmalung des grossen Nürnberg Rathaussaales. Ein Stiefkind der Forschung." In *Dürer und das Nürnberger Rathaus. Aspekte von Ikonographie, Verlust und Rekonstruktion* (Nürnberg: Imhof, 2013), 43–50.

PART 3

The Organization of Knowledge: Case Studies from the Herzog August Bibliothek, Wolfenbüttel

∵

"Mit vielen Concepten und sittlichen Lehren unterspickt": Bibliographic Approaches and the Ethics of Early Modern Literature

Matthias Roick

One outstanding feature of the current research landscape is the rhetoric of the new. It is rare to find research that does not claim to be innovative or even ground-breaking, introducing new ideas and methods to its field. Bibliographies such as Gerhard Dünnhaupt's *Personalbibliographien zu den Drucken des Barock*, normally simply referred to as *Dünnhaupt*,[1] rarely count among these innovative approaches, and this is both unfortunate and mistaken. In what follows I first argue that the bibliographical approach to literature has a great innovative potential and is essential to our understanding of past literary cultures. I then highlight a specific feature of seventeenth-century literature that becomes clearly visible in the *Dünnhaupt*: literature in the early modern period very often has a moral intent. Instead of seeing this feature as a liability, I maintain that the close relationship between literature and ethics is one of the most interesting aspects of early modern literary culture. To further my argument, I turn to the Ethica section in Wolfenbüttel, discussing its composition in the light of the early modern notion of virtue.

1   Bibliographic Backpacking

Bibliographies are useful tools, but in the end, they are tools. The bibliographer collects information, and the literary critic processes this information, putting forth innovative interpretations of the materials at her disposal. Despite the rise of book history and its reevaluation of bibliography, such an understanding is still common.[2] Let me challenge this perception with a counter-analogy and say that literary critics are like travelers who love to stick to the big cities. They do not have any qualms about writing yet another city guide, and that's

---

1   Dünnhaupt, 1990–1993.
2   For a concise summary of the development of bibliography as a field, see Levy and Mole, 2017: 10–16.

© KONINKLIJKE BRILL NV, LEIDEN, 2023 | DOI:10.1163/9789004682245_012

OK. After all, there is always something new and fascinating to see and describe in cities like London, Rome, or Berlin, just as there is in Dante, Shakespeare, and Goethe. What one misses, however, are the surroundings of the big cities, the countryside, or the far reaches. This is where bibliographers come into play. Far from being mere book keepers—pun intended—bibliographers are more adventurous than literary critics, backpackers instead of regular travelers, with a genuine interest to go beyond the great monuments and the grandiose architecture of the big cities. They like to visit the countryside and explore the far reaches of the *respublica litteraria*, and their work consists not so much in writing guides for the increasingly perplexed as it does in mapping uncharted territory.

The *Dünnhaupt* is a case in point. In his monumental work, the author thoroughly explores the difficult cultural landscape of seventeenth-century Germany, devastated by the Thirty Years' War and the negligence of later centuries.[3] As Dünnhaupt remarks, "[n]o other literary period—either before or since—suffered a similar decimation of books over the centuries."[4] Still, the *Dünnhaupt* contains an embarrassment of riches for anyone interested in German Baroque literature, revealing a distinct preference for literary cross-country travel. There is a personal note to this approach: Gerhard Dünnhaupt comes from a family of printers, publishers, and antiquarians based in Köthen, who were dispossessed after World War II, and the six volumes of his magnum opus are dedicated to his father and grandfather.

Notwithstanding Dünnhaupt's family history, the approach of the bibliographer can never be reduced to personal preferences. It is also a matter of historical method and heuristics. For one of the reasons that many literary historians prefer to study the "great" authors—in some cases, to the point of numbing overfamiliarity—is these authors' "timelessness," the perceived capacity of their works to reflect the problems and interests of the present in the mirror of the past. There is nothing wrong with this kind of presentism, especially since the concerns of the present will always shape our approaches to the past. Nevertheless, such a stance turns out to be unsatisfying from a heuristic point of view. By allowing ourselves to be led almost exclusively by the concerns of the present, we run dangerously close to seeing merely our own appearance in the mirror, and our involvement with the past turns into a largely pointless exercise. Moreover, we risk overlooking, misjudging, and dismissing aspects of the past that have become unfamiliar to us and that do not fit our expectations.

---

3   Dünnhaupt, 1990–1993, vol. 1: ix.
4   Dünnhaupt, 1990–1993, vol. 1: xx.

Bibliography and its field approach offers a natural remedy to this conundrum. The two basic "units" of the *Dünnhaupt* are person and print. Although both concepts involve a considerable amount of interpretation (Whom should one include as a person? What counts as a print, exactly?), they are quite inclusive. The term *person* does not specify that only authors, or "great" authors, should be part of the work. Dünnhaupt explicitly states his aim to take regional aspects into special consideration.[5] Likewise, the term *print* (*Druck*) does not automatically evoke the concept of a literary work, and all its modern connotations, thus giving preference to the general output of Baroque scholars, who, more often than not, crossed the lines of today's disciplinary boundaries. Think of a figure such as Matthias Bernegger (1582–1640), professor of history and rhetoric in Strasbourg. From our point of view, Bernegger has no clear disciplinary profile. Not only was he the editor of Tacitus, but he was also the translator of Galilei's Italian works into Latin, and a prolific commentator of Lipsius's *Politicorum libri sex* (1599).[6] Moreover, as Dünnhaupt remarks, scientific works often contained poetry.[7]

Dünnhaupt's bibliographical work ignores other boundaries as well, including translations and compilations in addition to "original" works. This is immensely important for a period in which, on the one hand, language societies such as the Fruchtbringende Gesellschaft promoted the use of German language as a literary language—not in opposition to but engaging with other vernaculars—and, on the other hand, compilatory habits structured and shaped much of the early modern culture of reading and writing. It is fascinating to see how lively the cultural landscape of Baroque prints is, and how European it is in its outlook, even at a time when the continent was rife with conflict and German lands were in a continuous state of war. As the *Dünnhaupt* clearly shows, seventeenth-century German literature was not yet part of a national culture, and its aim was to establish German vernacular not as distinct from, but as an equal to, other vernaculars.

Gerhard Dünnhaupt's bibliographical work highlights the transnational and transdisciplinary aspects of Baroque culture. Long before the material turn, he pioneered studies in early modern book history, bringing together literary history and the history of printing and publishing. Today, his research inspires many projects in the humanities. Of course, some aspects have radically changed—first and foremost, the accessibility of books. At the beginning of

---

5 Dünnhaupt, 1990–1993, vol. 1: x.
6 Dünnhaupt, 1990–1993, vol. 1: 490–533.
7 Dünnhaupt, 1990–1993, vol. 1: x. Dünnhaupt gives the example of Adam Olearius's *Muskovitische Reise*, containing the first printed edition of some of Paul Fleming's poems.

the 1990s, the sheer scale on which early modern books would be digitized was not foreseeable. Still, the *Dünnhaupt* has not become superfluous. On the contrary, it continues to serve as a key to German literature in the Baroque period, and, together with the bibliography in *Schriftstellerinnen, Künstlerinnen und gelehrte Frauen des deutschen Barock*, by Maria Fürstenwald und Jean Muir Woods,[8] it constitutes the nucleus for the complete digitization of the literature of the era.[9]

2   The Ethics of Baroque Literature

To thumb through the *Dünnhaupt* can make a strange impression on the modern reader. Think of a figure such as Aegidius Albertinus (1560–1620).[10] Albertinus, secretary to Duke Maximilian I of Bavaria, belongs to those writers who had huge success during their own time but are largely forgotten today. It is surprising to see, then, that Albertinus takes up almost fifty pages of bibliography in the first volume of the *Dünnhaupt*.[11] Albertinus certainly was a prolific writer, who published more than fifty works, among them no fewer than thirty-seven translations, but this is not the only reason he is so prominently represented. Many of his works went through multiple editions, attesting to the success Albertinus had on the early modern book market. Harsdörffer and Grimmelshausen were among his readers, and his translation/adaptation of Mateo Alemán's picaresque novel *Guzmán de Alfarache* (1599/1604) inspired the adventures of Simplicissimus.[12]

Albertinus's success was not limited to the novel, however. He was also well known for his anthologies and compilations, and while this kind of writing makes him deeply suspicious for a modern audience and its relentless demand for "originality," his *Buntschriftstellerei*, or eclectic writing in mixed forms, resonated strongly with early modern readers.[13] Among others, Albertinus translated and compiled the works of the Spanish chronicler and moralist

8   Woods and Fürstenwald, 1984.
9   See Dünnhaupt Digital at https://www.hab.de/en/duennhaupt-digital/ (20.06.2023).
10   For concise biographical information on Albertinus, see Dünnhaupt, 1990–1993, vol. 1: 191; and Gemert, 2019. For an extensive monograph study on Albertinus and his works, see Gemert, 1979.
11   Dünnhaupt, 1990–1993, vol. 1: 191–238.
12   For the relationship with Grimmelshausen, see Althaus, 2013.
13   For a discussion of the early modern forms of *Buntschriftstellerei*, see Schock, 2012; and especially Kühlmann, 2012: 21–42.

Antonio de Guevara (ca. 1481–1545), Charles V's court preacher, in German. He also converted the *Reductorium morale* of the Benedictine monk Pierre Bersuire (ca. 1290–1362), a moral dictionary based on the bible, into German.[14] Furthermore, he wrote the hugely successful *Hiren schleifer* [The brain whetter] (1618), an emblem book of his own pen.[15]

The pages on Albertinus in the *Dünnhaupt* show his versatility and many-sidedness, but they also reveal an important characteristic of early modern literature: the obvious moral intent driving so many works. Leafing through the *Dünnhaupt*, one encounters again and again titles that point out the moral dimension of their contents. When looking at seventeenth-century books, we are far from Charles Baudelaire's exasperation with his bourgeois and socialist critics' "missionary fervour" to "moralize" literature ("Moralisons! Moralisons! s'écrient toutes les deux avec une fièvre de missionaires").[16] Pierre Bordieu famously analysed the polemics around Baudelaire and Flaubert in terms of an emergent field of literature, autonomous in its outlook and bringing forth a rupture of the link between the ethical and the aesthetic.[17] Together with Balzac and Poe they pursued a literary style that William Olmsted has called "immoral moralism" and that still defines our contemporary notions of ethics and literature.[18]

When approaching the Baroque, however, we need to understand that what Baudelaire called the "chief modern heresy," teaching ("l'enseignement"),[19] was among the main tasks of early modern literature. Furthermore, and even more suspect for modern readers, ethics and morality were not secular but, rather, closely intertwined with religion and confession. Albertinus's interest in ethics and in the shaping of his readers into morally good persons was part and parcel with his Counter-Reformation stance. Another example is Abraham à Sancta Clara (1644–1709), the imperial court preacher at Vienna and member of the Order of Discalced Augustinians, a reform movement in the Catholic Church.[20] Like Albertinus, Sancta Clara was a compilatory genius, addressing both learned and a popular audiences. Among his works we find titles such as

---

14 Some of these translations were reprinted in modern editions: Albertinus, 1978; 1986. See also Walz, 1984.
15 On this work, see Larsen, 1985. See also Larsen's critical edition: Albertinus, 1977.
16 Baudelaire, 1954: 41. As Olmsted, 2016: 29 explains, Baudelaire attacks the Faucher decree that "aimed to encourage writers of moralistic and educational works."
17 Bordieu, 1996: 47–112.
18 Olmsted, 2016: 10.
19 Olmsted, 2016: 34.
20 On Santa Clara, see Eybl, 1992.

the *Geflügelter Mercurius* (1701), presenting "a number of entertaining pieces, however intermixed with ethical doctrine" ("worinnen zwar etliche kurtzweilige Sachen zu lesen seynd jedoch mit unter-mengter sittlicher Lehr"). Similarly, his *Heilsames Gemisch Gemasch*, published posthumously in 1717, contains a lot of "strange and wonderful stories, peppered with many concepts and ethical teachings" ("mit vielen Concepten und sittlichen Lehren unterspickt").

Protestant authors, too, took a moralistic approach to their works. In the pages of the *Dünnhaupt*, an interesting subset of these authors comes into view: composers and musicians. The Lutheran hymn composer Johannes Heermann (1585–1647) wrote an educational treatise (*Zucht-Büchlein*) with moral precepts and sentences.[21] And when the composer Heinrich Albert (1604–1654) published his song collection *Arien oder Melodeyen* (1638), the title indicated that the songs were both spiritual and secular, and served "for good morals and the delight" of the audience ("zu gutten Sitten und / Lust"). Johann Beer (1655–1700), who served Augustus, Duke of Saxe-Weissenfels, as musical director and librarian, wrote the novel *Teutsche Winternächte* [German winter nights] (1683) under the pseudonym Zendorius à Zendoriis. Again, the title proudly announces that the work not only contains many interesting "circumstances and discourses" but is also "peppered with useful moral teachings every now and then" ("Nicht allein mit allerley Umständen und Discursen ausführlich entworffen, sondern auch mit tauglichen Sitten-Lehren hin und wieder ausgespicket").[22]

The omnipresence of ethics and moral topics in both Catholic and Protestant authors is often seen through a confessional lens. It is possible, though, to reverse the argument and to read such omnipresence as a sign that ethics, or at least some of its elements, constituted a sort of neutral ground in the midst of confessional struggle. Georg Schmidt has made this point with regard to the *Fruchtbringende Gesellschaft* and its attempt to establish a new set of social and political values.[23] For although the *Fruchtbringende Gesellschaft*, founded in 1617, was a language society intent on the cultivation of German language, it also explicitly stated the "inculcation of decent mores" ("erbawung wolanstaendiger Sitten") as its aim.[24] When Johann Wilhelm von Stubenberg (1619–1663), the Unfortunate ("der Unglückselige"), translated the Venetian writer and politician Giovanni Francesco Loredano's *Scherzi geniali*

---

21   Dünnhaupt, 1990–1993, vol. 3: 2077.
22   Dünnhaupt, 1990–1993, vol. 1: 478.
23   Schmidt, 2001: 34. Regarding the more general argument for historical subjects and processes that were not confessionalized, see Lotz-Heumann, 2001: 104–5.
24   Anhalt-Köthen, 1992.

(1632) as *Geschichtreden*, the title of the work reflected the twofold aim of the Fruitbringers, stating that it had been rendered in German "for laudable virtues and morals as well as graceful eloquence" ("zu löblichen Tugenden und Sitten/ auch zierlicher Wohl-redenheit").[25] Likewise, Stubenberg's translation of Francis Bacon's *Essays* (1597) highlighted the work's practical dimension and its pertinence to the fields of ethics, politics, and economics ("die Sitten-Regiments- und Haußlehre betreffend").[26]

Among the many ways in which the importance of ethics and morality comes to the fore in the *Dünnhaupt*, paratexts provide a particularly clear illustration of the importance of morality for Baroque culture. The third edition of the Jesuit teacher Jacob Masen's *Speculum Imaginum veritatis occultae* (1650), a key work for the visual culture of the period, for instance, contains not only an "Index historicus," to help navigate the book, but also a thirty-six-leaves-strong "Index moralis," whose entries range from "abjectio muliebris," referring to the story of the Byzantine general Narses and empress Aelia Sophia, to "Zoilus," a Greek grammarian known for his harsh and malignant criticism of Homer.

The list could continue, but the message is clear. Different from our own sensibilities, early modern culture did not shy away from the moralizing impetus of literature. Indeed, the *Dünnhaupt* strongly suggests that authors and publishers alike sought to actively address and publicize the moral dimensions of their works. Moreover, they did not see their appeals to morality as detracting from the artistic significance or entertainment value of their creations.

3 The Ethica Section in Wolfenbüttel

The propensity toward ethics highlighted by the entries in the *Dünnhaupt* is also reflected in other parts of the early modern book culture. The Ethica section in Wolfenbüttel, part of the book collection of August the Younger (1579–1666), Duke of Braunschweig-Lüneburg, is a case in point. The duke started collecting books early on, and his library took shape in the 1610s and 1620s, when he resided in Hitzacker, a small island on the river Elbe.[27] As the seventh and youngest child in the ducal family, he stood little chance of taking up a ruling position in the Brunswick lands, and his position in Hitzacker was indeed marginal, holding little political prestige. August's identity as a learned

---

25 Loredano, 1661: title page.
26 Bacon, 1654: title page.
27 For August's first book acquisitions, see Katte, 1978. For his early years and his time in Hitzacker, see Katte, 1979a; 1979b.

collector of books and other interesting objects was one of the few venues open to him to build cultural capital. Of course, this situation dramatically changed in 1635, when August inherited the Wolfenbüttel principality. Despite his new political clout, however, he continued to show great personal interest in his library and intensified his activities as a collector, with a network of agents spread throughout Europe. At the end of his life, his library comprised around 100,000 volumes and was among the largest book collections in Europe.

The collection is remarkable not only for its size but also for the duke's personal and intellectual involvement in its contents. A clear sign for this involvement is the book-wheel catalogue ("Bücherradkatalog"), consisting of six huge folio volumes with 1,200 pages each.[28] August started it when he was still in Hitzacker, in 1625, and the first two volumes contain an overview of all the books the duke had collected up to this point, divided by rubrics or sections, devised by August himself.[29] His rubrics are based on various traditions, such as the seven liberal arts, the three high faculties, and humanistic disciplines.

Different from modern ideas of library management, the rubrics used by duke August do not reflect a well-defined classificatory scheme. As Ulrich Schneider has repeatedly emphasized, in designing the rubrics August did not employ a sophisticated epistemological or philosophical order—he did not use subrubrics, for example.[30] Instead, he followed a pragmatic plan that allowed him to label books swiftly and to set them up in an accessible manner. As a result, authors, works, and themes are spread over the whole collection. Different editions of Justus Lipsius's fundamental work *De Constantia* (1584), for instance, are filed under the rubrics Logica, Ethica, Politica, Theologica, and Quodlibetica.[31]

---

28   Herzog August Bibliotek, Wolfenbüttel, Cod. Guelf. BA I, 322–327. The digitized manuscript is available at the HAB.

29   The twenty sections are recorded in the duke's own hand as "Series dispositionis Librorum Bibliothecae secundum Materias" on the front pastedown of the first volume: "1. Theologica 2. Juridica 3. Historica 4. Bellica 5. Politica 6. Oeconomica 7. Ethica 8. Medica 9. Geographica 10. Astronomica 11. Musica 12. Physica 13. Geometrica 14. Arithmetica 15. Poëtica 16 Logica 17. Rhetorica 18. Gram[m]atica 19. Quodlibetica 20. Manuscripta." The same leaf also contains an alphabetical list of the sections, together with the pages.

30   Schneider, 2005a; 2005b. The only division within sections was into folio volumes ("in F.") and quarto and smaller volumes "in Quart."

31   A: 3.9 Log. (bound together with John Case, *Summa veterum interpretum in universam dialecticam Aristotelis*); A: 40.27 Eth. (with Lipsius's *Mellificium duplex ex media philosophia petitum*); A: 748.19 Theol. German edition (with Michael Sachs, *Arcana arrhae*); A: 135.6 Pol. French edition (as part of Lipsius, *Les politiques ou doctrine civile*); A: 163.3 Quod. 2° (with four other works, among them Wimpfeling's *Carolus Magnus Germanus*).

This seeming randomness and contingency might be misunderstood as a liability when applying our own understanding of ethics. The bibliographical approach suggests otherwise, however, and holds two important lessons. First, rather than indicating "errors" and "quirks," August's classification practice reveals the porous boundaries between different fields of knowledge in early modernity, requiring us to see the ethical in a different—more diffuse—light. Second, acknowledging that we do not move within our own contemporary conceptual and institutional framework, but within an early modern one, the section gives us the possibility to bracket our own ideas on ethics, and to let its composition sink in.

What makes the Ethica section interesting for us is not so much its size—the section is relatively small when compared to other sections—but its makeup.[32] Different from what might be expected, the section's emphasis does not lie on philosophical treatises or on ethics as a philosophical discipline but, instead, embraces a whole array of genres—novels, novellas, plays, emblem books, collections of proverbs, and conduct books, to name only a few. In general, the section's themes and topics are taken from a wide variety of geographical and cultural contexts, mirroring many of the most important developments in European thought from the fifteenth to the seventeenth century.

These reflections on the Ethica section complement the observations made regarding the *Dünnhaupt*: while the *Dünnhaupt* showcases the moral dimension of early modern literature, the Ethica section illustrates the literary dimension of early modern ethics. In fact, there is a significant overlap between the two sources. The Ethica section contains more than 200 works of at least fifty-seven authors mentioned in the *Dünnhaupt*, most prominent among them Georg Philipp Harsdörffer (1607–1658), Johann Balthasar Schupp (1610–1661), Johann Valentin Andreae (1586–1654), Johann Rist (1607–1667) and the above-mentioned Johann Wilhelm von Stubenberg.

The Ethica section also corroborates other findings in the *Dünnhaupt*. First of all, it confirms the strong European imprint of early modern litera-ture. Four languages—Latin, German, Italian, and French—have roughly the same presence,[33] while three other languages—Spanish, Dutch, and Ancient Greek—are much less common, but still have a significant presence in the collection.[34] Non-European languages are very rare exceptions, such as the

---

32   Regarding size, compare the Ethica section, with its 1,600 volumes, to the largest section, Theologica, which consists of approximately 11,000 volumes.

33   Based on the data in the Herzog August Bibliothek's OPAC: Latin 25%, German 23.7%, Italian 23.6%, French 22.6%.

34   Again, based on the data in the Herzog August Bibliothek's OPAC: Spanish 2%, Dutch 1.4%, Ancient Greek 1.3%.

1596 Jesuit translation of the *Imitatio Christi* into Japanese, presented to August in 1662 and included in the section only in 1690–1691, a quarter century after the duke's death.[35] Of course, the frequency with which a given language appears in the section does not directly indicate the cultural influence of works originally written in this language. Spanish works often found their way to Germany via Italian translations, as is the case with Alemán's *Guzmán de Alfarache*. The duke's original collection in Hitzacker contained only the Italian and German translations of the work.[36] Only later, between 1646 and 1647, did the duke write the catalogue entry for the Spanish original.[37] Furthermore, the section contains a whole selection of picaresque novels, among them also Francisco López de Úbedas *La picara Justina* (1604).

De Úbeda's work is an interesting case, as it invokes a second important similarity between the *Dünnhaupt* and the Ethica section: the compilatory habits of early modern culture. In the Ethica section, we find five volumes of de Úbeda's novel in Spanish, Italian, and German.[38] On a bibliographical level, then, the story of Justina was successful enough to be published in different editions and languages, and it illustrates the liveliness of so-called literary transfer in the European book market during the early modern period.[39] But the work also draws attention to the "sententious" character of seventeenth-century literature. As the first edition of the *Justina* states on the title page, the work's "amusing speeches" contain "useful pieces of advice" for the reader ("en el qual debaxo de graciosos discursos, se encierran provechosos avisos").[40]

---

35   Triplett, 2018. The volume contains a handwritten note to the duke, dated 1662. The entry in the *Bücherradkatalog* is on page 6943. According to Katte, 1972: 182, the entries in this part of the catalogue stem from 1690–1691, and are written in the hand of Johann Thiele Reinerding, ducal secretary since 1684.

36   A: 72 Eth.—Alemán, Mateo, *Della Vita Del Picaro Gvsmano D'Alfarace, Osseruatore della Vita Humana* (Venice: Barezzi, 1615); and A: 90 Eth.—Alemán, Mateo, *Der Landtstörtzer Gusman von Alfarche oder Picaro genannt, dessen wunderbarliches, abenthewrlichs und possirlichs Leben … hierin beschriben wirdt* (Munich: Henricus, 1615).

37   A: 107.13. Eth.—Alemán Mateo, *Vida del picaro Guzmán de Alfarache*, 2 vols. (Brucellas: Mommarte, 1604). The catalogue entry is on page 3558. For the date of the entry see Katte, 1972: 180.

38   A: 67.8 Eth.—López de Úbeda Francisco, Vita della picara Giustina Diez (Venice: Barezzi, 1624); and López de Úbeda Francisco, Vita della picara Giustina Diez (Venetia: Barezzi, 1625); A: 45.9 Eth.—López de Úbeda Francisco, *Libro De Entretenimiento, De La Picara Ivstina …* (Brucellas: Brunello, 1608); A: 67.1 Eth.—López de Úbeda Francisco, *Die Landstörtzerin Iustina Dietzin Picara genandt …* (Frankfurt am Main: Weiß, 1626); and López de Úbeda Francisco, *Die Landstörtzerin Iustina Dietzin Picara genandt …* (Frankfurt am Main: Ammon, 1627).

39   See Bodenmüller, 2001, for a discussion of literary transfers into Italian and English.

40   López de Úbeda, 1605: title page.

The Italian title page elaborates even more on these teachings, spelling them out for those interested in buying the book: "here you read weighty aphorisms, political precepts, moral examples, curious admonitions, and amusing and enjoyable tales" ("si leggono / Sentenze graui, / Precetti Politici, / Documenti Morali, / Auuenimenti curiosi, / e Fauole facete, e piacevoli").[41] The overarching moral theme is clear in the Italian subtitle of the *Justina*: "instruction for licentious minds" ("regola de gli animi licentiosi").[42] The German title page omits this subtitle, but it gives a German translation of the Italian description of the book.[43]

A look at these titles not only shows the sententious character of seventeenth-century literature but also reveals why in modern language use *sententious* means both "given to aphoristic expressions" and "abounding in excessive moralizing."[44] Regarding the second, derogatory meaning, it is interesting to see that Miguel de Cervantes referred to *Justina* as a botch ("librazo") and described it as "the ruin of our field" ("fue de nuestro campo la ruina"); likewise, a modern critic labeled the book as "a monument of bad taste" ("monument de mal gusto").[45] The moralizing character of de Úbeda's novel was certainly not helpful in this respect, and it is not by chance that reevaluations of the work often downplay the didactic character of the *Justina* or claim that the *picara* "reverses the forms of the didactic scholarly discourse."[46]

The Ethica section, however, underlines a view of literature that is both entertaining and didactic. It contains a considerable number of works that collect aphorisms, sayings, apophthegms, and proverbs. Some of these "florilegia" or "thesauri" collected aphorisms and sayings from a single author—for example, from Virgilius—others from a specific language, such as Hebrew, and still others from a whole range of authors and languages.[47] They are obvious signs that early modern culture was a "culture of dicta," organized in topics—not unlike the contemporary culture of memes. This is also one reason why *Buntschriftstellerei* was such a popular genre. All these works supplied

---

41 López de Úbeda, 1624–25: title page.
42 I translate "regola" as "instruction," following the definition of "regola" as "dimostramento della via dell'operare" in the first edition of the *Vocabolario della Accademia della Crusca* (1612).
43 The 1626 Frankfurt edition by Weiß reads, "Beneben allerley schönen Sprüchen/ Politischen Regeln/ Lehrhafften Erinnerungen/ trewhertzigen Warnungen/ und kurtzweiligen/ anmuthigen Fabeln."
44 See the entry in Merriam Webster's Dictionary: https://www.merriam-webster.com/dictionary/sententious (5 January 2020).
45 Both quotations in Bodenmüller, 2001: 6 and 8.
46 Ehrlicher, 2018: 78.
47 Rothmar, 1577; Buxtorf, 1648; Megiser, 1592.

readers with "morals stored and ready for use," as Ann Moss has written, putting moral maxims and sententious observations at their disposal.[48]

4   The Virtue of Literature

The intellectual wealth of the *Dünnhaupt* and the complexity of the Ethica section in Wolfenbüttel reflect the wealth and complexity of early modern ethics, a wealth and complexity we are only beginning to understand. In my opinion, the best way to develop such an understanding in the future is by focusing on one of the notions that is at the heart of early modern ethics as well as early modern moral culture: the notion of virtue.

Early modern virtue is not, as the writer Ursula K. Le Guin succinctly put it, "the virginity or monogamy of women"; it is much closer to the older sense of the "inherent quality and strength of a thing or person."[49] Furthermore, early modern virtue is mainly concerned with what is conducive to a good life. Therefore, a wider range of considerations comes under the notion of the ethical than we would nowadays assume.[50] Finally, early modern virtue is not the result of philosophical reflection only but of a process of habituation. We acquire virtues by exercising them. In the language of the time, ethics was less about understanding what is good than about becoming good.[51] Accordingly, virtue ethics aims at the emotive level of behavior and tries to inform our moral intuitions rather than our moral thought.[52] The variety of the literature in the *Dünnhaupt* and in the Ethica section reflects the variety of forms in which it was featured: in poems, stories, images, and representations of all types.

The *Dünnhaupt* and the Ethica section are very different in character and unalike in their histories. One is a modern compilation, based on decades of assiduous research, while the other is an early modern collection that came into being—and was largely completed—in the course of the seventeenth century. Still, as bibliographical sources for early modern literary history, they

---

48   Moss, 2013.

49   Le Guin, 1998: 110.

50   This point has been made in the context of present-day philosophy by Bernard Williams; see Williams, 2011.

51   Early modern authors often refer to Aristotle 2000, 10.9 1179^{b}1–2: "in practical studies the end consists not in contemplating and knowing about particular points, but rather in acting upon them. ... So knowing about virtue is not enough, but we must also try to attain and exercise it, or become good by any other route."

52   Contemporary moral psychology makes a very similar point regarding our moral behaviour. See, for example, Haidt, 2013, esp. part 1: "Intuitions come first, strategic reasoning second."

have a similar value. They help us, first, to recognize that our own point of view, our modern suspicion of the moral and didactic value of literature, hardly equips us to appreciate early modern notions of ethics and literature. Second, they clearly show that too narrow a focus on the "great" authors and on certain themes attractive to us not only leads to imbalances in the evaluation of early modern literature but also leaves in shadow large tracts of early modern ethical reflection. Third, they warn us against the tendency to base generalizations on the same restricted group of easily accessible texts—despite the wealth of materials that have become available online during the last two decades. Bibliographic approaches can encourage us to overcome this impasse, to rediscover the ethical imprint of early modern literature, and to recognize how the power of stories and imagination can mold our moral character. This is, after all, the virtue of literature.

Bibliography

Albertinus, Aegidius. *Institutiones vitae aulicae oder Hofschul* (Bern: Lang, 1978).

Albertinus, Aegidius. *Verachtung des Hoflebens und Lob dess Landtlebens* (Bern: Lang, 1986).

Albertinus, Aegidius. *Hirnschleiffer: kritische Ausgabe*, ed. Lawrence S. Larsen (Stuttgart: Hiersemann, 1977).

Althaus, Thomas. "Hirnschleiferei: die Umdeutungskunst des Aegidius Albertinus in der Perspektive auf Grimmelshausen." *Simpliciana* 35 (2013), 161–86.

Anhalt-Köthen, Ludwig von. "Kurtzer Bericht der Fruchtbringenden Gesellschaft Zweck und Vorhaben." In *Werke*, ed. Klaus Conermann, (Tübingen: Max Niemeyer, 1992), [7]–[10].

Aristotle. *Nicomachean Ethics*, ed. and trans. Roger Crisp (Cambridge: Cambridge University Press, 2000).

Bacon, Francis. *Francisci Baconis Grafens von Verulamio, weiland Englischen Reichscantzlers Getreue Reden: die Sitten=, Regiments= und Haußlehre betreffend …* (Nürnberg: Endter, 1654).

Baudelaire, Charles. "Les Drames et les romans honnêtes." In *Oeuvres complètes*, vol. 2, eds. Y. G. Le Dantec and C. Pichois (Paris: Gallimard, 1954), 38–43.

Bodenmüller, Thomas. *Literaturtransfer in der Frühen Neuzeit. Francisco López de Úbedas 'La picara Justina' und ihre italienische und englische Bearbeitung von Barezzo Barezzi und Captain John Stevens* (Tübingen: Max Niemeyer, 2001).

Bordieu, Pierre. *The Rules of the Art. Genesis and Structure of the Literary Field* (Stanford: Stanford University Press, 1996).

Buxtorf, Johann. *Florilegium Hebraicum. Continens Elegantes Sententias, Proverbia, Apophthegmata, Similitudines …* (Basileae: König, 1648).

Dünnhaupt, Gerhard. *Personalbibliographien zu den Drucken des Barock. Zweite, verbesserte und wesentlich vermehrte Auflage des Bibliographischen Handbuches der Barockliteratur.* 6 vols. (Stuttgart: Anton Hiersemann, 1990–1993).

Ehrlicher, Hanno. "Gender Trouble Without Subversion." In *Transgression and Subversion: Gender in the Picaresque Novel,* eds. Maren Lickhardt et al. (Bielefeld: transcript, 2018), 65–84

Eybl, Franz. M. *Abraham a Sancta Clara. Vom Prediger zum Schriftsteller* (Tübingen: Max Niemeyer, 1992).

Gemert, Guillame van. "Aegidius Albertinus." In *Literaturgeschichte Münchens,* eds. Waldemar Fromm et al. (Regensburg: Friedrich Pustet, 2019), 117–22.

Gemert, Guillame van. *Die Werke des Aegidius Albertinus (1560–1620). Ein Beitrag zur Erforschung des deutschsprachigen Schrifttums der katholischen Reformbewegung in Bayern um 1620 und seiner Quellen* (Amsterdam: APA, Holland University Press, 1979).

Haidt, Jonathan. *The righteous mind. Why good people are divided by politics and religion* (London: Penguin, 2013).

Katte, Maria von. "Herzog August und die Kataloge seiner Bibliothek." In *Wolfenbütteler Beiträge. Aus den Schätzen der Herzog August Bibliothek,* vol. 1, ed. Paul Raabe (Frankfurt am Main: Vittorio Klostermann, 1972), 168–99.

Katte, Maria von. "Die 'Bibliotheca Selenica' von 1586 bis 1612: Die Anfänge der Bibliothek des Herzogs August zu Braunschweig und Lüneburg." *Wolfenbütteler Beiträge* 3 (1978), 135–53.

Katte, Maria von. "Jugendzeit und Bildungsjahre, 1579–1603." In *Sammler Fürst Gelehrter. Herzog August zu Braunschweig und Lüneburg, 1579–1666,* ed. Paul Raabe (Wolfenbüttel: Herzog August Bibliothek, 1979), 49–70.

Katte, Maria von. "Fürst und Gelehrter in Hitzacker, 1604–1634." In *Sammler Fürst Gelehrter. Herzog August zu Braunschweig und Lüneburg, 1579–1666,* ed. Paul Raabe (Wolfenbüttel: Herzog August Bibliothek, 1979), 71–82.

Kühlmann, Wilhelm. "Polyhistorie jenseits der Systeme. Zur funktionellen Pragmatik und publizistischen Typologie frühneuzeitlicher 'Buntschriftstellerei.'" In *Polyhistorismus und Buntschriftstellerei: Populäre Wissensformen und Wissenskultur in der Frühen Neuzeit,* ed. Flemming Schock (Berlin: De Gruyter, 2012), 21–42.

Le Guin, Ursula K. "Notes." In Lao Tzu, *Tao Te Ching. A Book About the Way and the Power of the Way,* trans. Ursula K. Le Guin (Boulder: Shambhala, 1998), 105–25.

Larsen, Lawrence S. "Aegidius Albertinus's *Hirnschleiffer*: An Emblem Book?" *Daphnis* 14 (3) (1985), 547–58.

Levy, Michelle, and Tom Mole. *The Broadview Introduction to Book History* (Peterborough: Broadview Press, 2017).

López de Úbeda, Francisco. *Libro De Entretenimiento, De La Picara Ivstina …* (Medina del Campo: Christoval Lasso Vaca, 1605).

López de Úbeda, Francisco. *Vita della picara Giustina Diez*, 2 vols. (Venice: Barezzi, 1624–25.)

Loredano, Giovanni Francesco. *Geschichtreden: Das ist/ Freywillige Gemüts-Schertze Herrn Johann Frantz Loredano hochgelehrten vornehmen Venetischen Edelmannes* (Nürnberg: Endter, 1661).

Lotz-Heumann, Ute. "The Concept of Confessionalization: A Historiographical Paradigm in Dispute." *Memoria y Civilización* 4 (2001), 93–114.

Megiser, Hieronymus. *Paroimiologias, pars prima qua continentur sententiae insigniores, ex optimis et probatissimis, quibusque Graecae & Latinae linguae scriptoribus, tam poetis, quam oratoribus, desumtae, ... & cum Italorum, Gallorum, Germanorum, aliarumque Christiani orbis nationum, sententiosis proverbijs collatae* (Graecii Stiriae: Widmanstadius, 1592).

Moss, Ann. "Morals Stored and Ready for Use." In *Rethinking Virtue, Reforming Society*, eds. David A. Lines and Sabrina Ebbersmeyer (Turnhout: Brepols, 2013), 169–88.

Muir Woods, Jean, and Maria Anna Fürstenwald. *Schriftstellerinnen, Künstlerinnen und gelehrte Frauen des deutschen Barock: ein Lexikon* (Stuttgart: Metzler, 1984).

Olmsted, William. *The Censorship Effect. Baudelaire, Flaubert, and the Formation of French Modernism* (Oxford: Oxford University Press, 2016).

Rothmar Valentin. *Adagiorum Seu Proverbialium Versuum Ex Aeneide, Georgicis Et Bucolicis P. Vergilius Maronis Collectorum, Centuriae Quinque Et Decuriae Tres* (Ingolstadii: Weissenhorn, 1577).

Schmidt, Georg. "Die Anfänge der Fruchtbringenden Gesellschaft als politisch motivierte Sammlungsbewegung und höfische Akademie." In *Die Fruchtbringer—eine Teutschherzige Gesellschaft*, ed. Klaus Manger (Heidelberg: Winter, 2001), 5–38.

Schneider, Ulrich Johannes. "Der Ort der Bücher in der Bibliothek und im Katalog am Beispiel von Herzog Augusts Wolfenbütteler Büchersammlung." *Archiv für Geschichte des Buchwesens* 59 (2005), 91–104.

Schneider, Ulrich Johannes. "Repräsentation und Operation. Anmerkungen zu Augusts Bücherwelt." In *Bibliothek als Archiv*, eds. Hans Erich Bödeker and Anne Saada (Göttingen: Vandenhoeck & Ruprecht, 2005), 155–69.

Schock, Flemming, ed. *Polyhistorismus und Buntschriftstellerei: Populäre Wissensformen und Wissenskultur in der Frühen Neuzeit* (Berlin: De Gruyter, 2012).

Triplett, Katja. "The Japanese *Contemptus mundi* (1596) of the Bibliotheca Augusta: A Brief Remark on a New Discovery." *Journal of Jesuit Studies* 5 (2018), 123–27.

Walz, Herbert. *Der Moralist im Dienste des Hofes: eine vergleichende Studie zu der Lehrdichtung von Antonio de Guevara und Aegidius Albertinus* (Frankfurt am Main: Lang, 1984).

Williams, Bernard. *Ethics and the Limits of Philosophy* (London and New York: Routledge, 2011).

CHAPTER 11

Venice without Venice: Traces of Italian Printed Music in German Manuscripts during the Thirty Years' War

Jason Rosenholtz-Witt

1 The Context and Influence of Lodovico Viadana's *Cento concerti ecclesiastici*

Printed music before 1600 rarely included detailed instructions for performers. Customarily, they relied on rather formulaic laudatory prose addressed to a patron or public figure. Thus, Lodovico Viadana's lengthy preface to his 1602 *Cento concerti ecclesiastici* stands out as relatively novel (Fig. 11.1).[1] The composer includes extraordinarily specific details regarding matters of performance, instrumentation, and desired effect of his concerti. Among other details, the preface includes the first didactic passages on performing the new Italian *basso continuo*.[2] Whether or not this appraisal is accurate, the year 1600 is considered to be a watershed in the history of Western music, largely owing to publications such as this, as well as Giulio Caccini's 1602 *Le nuove musiche* and its corresponding essay.[3] Characterizing a turn from *cori spezzati*—a Northern Italian style of sacred music written for large, double-choir ensembles of at least eight parts—Viadana's *Cento concerti* consisted of small-scale motets for one to four voices with *basso continuo*. This genre of few-voiced sacred compositions had many names, though I will use the widely adopted term *concertato* motet.[4] In terms of influence, it is difficult to overstate the importance of Viadana's collection, along with his 1607 *Concerti ecclesiastici*, also for one

---

1 Viadana, 1602.

2 For a lengthier discussion of this preface, as well as a full translation see the introduction in Gallico, 1964. The term *basso continuo* refers to a group of instruments (or single instrument, such as an organ or viola da gamba) used to provide the bass line in a musical work as well as to the notated line from which those instruments play. This practice was a marked shift in musical theoretical thought, as it implied a polarity between the melodic line and the bass.

3 Caccini, 1602. The focal point of Caccini's introduction surrounded ornamentation, as he was clearly frustrated by the ways in which Florentine singers were ornamenting solo song.

4 A sustained discussion of the contemporaneous etymology of *concertato* can be found in Bianconi, 1987: 33–36.

© KONINKLIJKE BRILL NV, LEIDEN, 2023 | DOI:10.1163/9789004682245_013

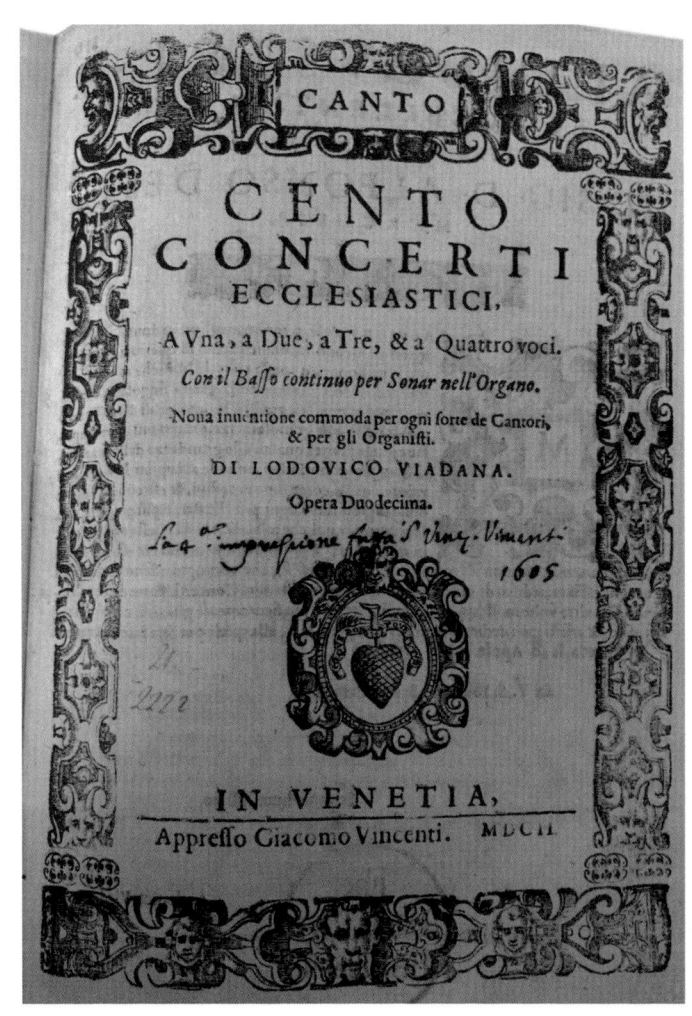

FIGURE 11.1   Title page, Lodovico Viadana, *Cento concerti ecclesiatici*
               (Venice: Vincenti, 1602). Biblioteka Jagiellońska, Kraków.
               The volume underwent numerous reprints in multiple
               cities, but the only complete specimen of the original 1602
               printing of which I am aware is held by the Biblioteka
               Jagiellońska in Kraków: PL-Kj, Mus.ant.pract. V 485

to four voices with *basso continuo*.[5] These publications would find especially
fertile ground in German-speaking lands; of the composer's twenty-seven publications of music (published between 1588 and 1619), fourteen of them saw

---

5   Viadana, 1607.

multiple editions.[6] *Cento concerti* and *Concerti ecclesiastici* went through seven and eight editions, respectively—a prodigious number compared to most contemporaneous examples—and were published in Germany as early as 1609 by Nicolaus Stein.[7] Stein's 1613 reprint of *Cento concerti* included a German translation of Viadana's lengthy preface to the performer, embellished to add that Viadana was the inventor of *basso continuo*, an erroneous attribution that persisted in music scholarship until the twentieth century.[8]

Venice dominated the printed-music market, and it was not uncommon for composers from across the Italian peninsula to seek out one of the Venetian presses for their work.[9] The physical material then spread in all directions thanks to the printed-book trade and found footholds in German-speaking lands through book fairs in Frankfurt and Leipzig.[10] Commonly, a number of Italian publications were bound together and sold in pre-packaged bundles known as *Sammelbände*. As Peter Wollny observes, this aspect of the music book trade is difficult to research, since very little information is available regarding professional music dealers working with Italian prints in Germany.[11] An inventory of items purchased by the Frankfurt Kapellmeister Johann Andreas Herbst offers rare evidence of the repertoire available during these book fairs.[12] Among the Venetian musical publications purchased by Herbst in 1625 are composers that feature heavily in the discussion of the German manuscripts that follows: Giovanni Priuli, Leone Leoni, Giovanni Gabrieli, Pietro Lappi, Giovanni Croce, Alessandro Grandi, Giacomo Finetti, Antonio Cifra, Gabriele Fattorini, Adriano Banchieri, Giovanni Valentini, and Giovanni Cavaccio. Venetian printing dominated the market to the extent that emerging musical styles came to be associated specifically with Venice, regardless of a composer's origin or place of work. Of the composers whose work Herbst purchased, only Gabrieli, Grandi, and Croce were directly associated with the city of Venice. Further cementing the association of the *concertato* motet

---

6   I rely on full subsequent publication details of Viadana's oeuvre from appendix I in Mompellio, 1967: 105–73. Mompellio's comprehensive appendix catalogues contemporary library holdings as well, and is often a more reliable source for the later Viadana printings than RISM.

7   The first German edition printed by Stein was *Centum concertum ecclesiasticorum*, in 1609.

8   For example, Paul Henry Lang refers to Viadana's *Cento concerti ecclesiastici* as the first publication to include thorough bass. Lang, 1941: 358.

9   For more on the Venetian music presses, see Bernstein, 2001.

10   Rose, 2005: 1–37.

11   Wollny, 1998: 53. Wollny cites here a 1653 catalogue published by the music shop of Paul Parstorffer in Munich.

12   Valentin, 1906: 263–66. My thanks to Dr Kertig-Meuleman, a librarian at the Goethe Universitätsbibliothek in Frankfurt am Main for bringing this source to my attention while examining one such *Sammelband*: D-F Mus 55.

with the city were didactic writings of Venetians such as Giovanni Bassano and Girolamo Dalla, and Venetian composers would continue to develop the *concertato* motet to a high level in the coming years.[13] The German reprints of Viadana's *Cento concerti ecclesiastici* played an outsized role in the dissemination of the genre. Through this publication, first printed in Venice, what came to be thought of as a distinctly Venetian style spread both north and south of the Alps, and yet Viadana himself never worked in Venice.

As Viadana states in his preface to *Cento concerti*, the motets were designed to cater to specific needs of churches and chapels in Rome. An itinerant cleric-musician, he worked at posts in Mantua, Cremona, Padua, Rome, Concordia, and Fano, composing music that was utterly practical.[14] At these locations, he encountered a lack of music that was both on a high artistic level and affordable to produce on a daily basis. It was not every church that had the resources—that is, the financial means and the requisite personnel—to pull off the expensive *cori spezzati* repertoire in the manner of Venice's San Marco. Viadana was not a radical, revolutionary composer looking to shatter the status quo; rather, he was offering a solution to the problem of small churches with small choirs unable to perform large-scale polyphony, a stylistic shift that was readily adopted in German-speaking lands amid economic and social turbulence brought on by the Thirty Years' War, which devastated the coffers of German churches. The circulation of printed editions and foreign reprints allowed these innovations to spread more quickly than would have been possible in previous decades, prior to growing international demand for Italian music. Viadana and his many foreign reprints emerge as an example of an interlocutor responsible for spreading a Venetian musical ethos without any specific association to the city; indeed, printers and scribes relied on the musical reputation of Venetian printing houses to broadcast the quality of their goods, whether or not the products themselves were "Venetian" in any real sense. Part commodification, part fetishization, I refer to this phenomenon as "Venice without Venice."

Viadana's influence north of the Alps, and the introduction of the *concertato* motet into German-speaking lands through agents such as Heinrich Schütz, is well documented; further elucidation here is unnecessary.[15] However, tracing this development invariably leads to questions surrounding music printing

---

13   Roche, 1984: 49.

14   Lacunae in the sources make reconstructing Viadana's biography rather difficult. The best source for biographical information on Viadana, as well as a detailed account of his twenty-seven publications, remains Mompellio, 1967.

15   There is a lengthy bibliography, but I would especially recommend the following selections: Arnold, 1985; Carver, 1988; Einstein, 1934; Federhofer, 1955; Kokole, 2000; and Roche, 1972 and 1998.

and publishing. Considering the large quantity of scholarship on early modern printed music, as well as the history of the book, there are a surprising number of fundamental questions with unsatisfying or non-existent answers. How did printing allow music and ideas to spread beyond the regional contexts in which they emerged, and who "read" and collected such texts? Fundamentally, how was printed music used? The musicologist most adroitly asking these questions is Kate van Orden.[16] For van Orden, an investigation into book history includes manuscript culture, which was very much alive for musicians and distinct from the model of a singular print culture developed by Elizabeth Eisenstein in her influential monograph *The Printing Press as an Agent of Change* (1979).[17] Harold Love's *Scribal Publication in Seventeenth-Century England* includes a sustained discussion of the scribal reproduction of music for viol consort, serving as a reminder that musicians continued to rely on handwritten dissemination in the era of print.[18]

Inspired by van Orden's nuanced and comprehensive examination of material aspects of sixteenth-century books of French chansons, I consider the contents and materiality of several fragmented manuscript music partbooks housed at the Herzog August Bibliothek, Wolfenbüttel, originating from churches in Helmstedt and Magdeburg from approximately 1616 to 1638.[19] I trace the printed sources of compositions by Italian composers to better understand the mediation and dissemination of Italianate music north of the Alps in the early seventeenth century. The results of this investigation demonstrate an increasing dependence on printed Italian musical sources, the role of German editors in curating the sources for a German audience, and the steady development of Venice into a type of musical commodity or marker rather than a fixed location. However, two of the featured "Venetian" composers in these documents had little to do with the city of Venice: the aforementioned Viadana and the Austrian-born, Regensburg-trained, Ljubljana-based composer Isaac Posch. Through print and manuscript networks, a new musical style was internalized and imitated by composers such as Posch and copied by scribes in Lower Saxony for church performances. One manuscript featuring both Viadana and Posch was deliberately designed to look and feel like a printed music book, utilizing a frontispiece from a prominent Venetian printing house. Studying the manuscripts and printed works chronologically, one can see the massive compositional changes that burst forth after 1600 in action, starting

---

16   Thoughtful questions for future research are posed in van Orden, 2014: 1–18; and thoroughly investigated throughout van Orden, 2015.

17   Eisenstein, 1979.

18   Love, 1993: 23–31.

19   The three manuscripts in the Herzog August Bibliothek are: Cod. Guelf. 322–324 Mus. Hdschr.

with equal-voiced Franco-Flemish polyphony, moving to a *cori spezzati* style of eight voices in two choirs, and, finally, tending toward mostly small scale *concertato* motets with connections to the Thirty Years' War. Through print and circulation, these examples represent a newly possible mode of musical mediation—Venice without Venice.

2   Cod. Guelf. 322 Mus. Hdschr.—Magdeburg, ca. 1616

In the early modern period, music was not displayed in scores, which bring all of the parts together, but in small individual books known as partbooks, with each voice or instrument printed separately from the others. Each musician used the partbook for his or her own voice or instrument, with no conductor.[20] One of the Wolfenbüttel manuscripts consists of three surviving partbooks (soprano, alto, and bassus) from Magdeburg, and was originally bound with the 1602 *Opus melicum* by Friedrich Weißensee, a German composer and Protestant minister who served as Kantor of the notable grammar school at Magdeburg and whose previous professors included Martin Agricola and Gallus Dressler. Dating the manuscript is difficult, and it is important to address possible errors in previous attempts. The Herzog August Bibliothek's records estimate the manuscript's date as ca. 1602–1605, and the RISM entry lists a 1605 date. The manuscript certainly was produced no earlier than 1602, the publication date of Weißensee's *Opus melicum*. The contents largely point to late sixteenth-century sources; however, there are three motets by Heinrich Grimm, who succeeded Weißensee for the Magdeburg post. Grimm was born in 1592/93, and it is highly improbable that a ten-year-old Grimm was behind the six and eight voice motets "Wie schön leuchtet der Morgenstern" and "Jauchzet dem Herren alle Welt."[21] Grimm studied at the University in Helmstedt before attaining the position of Kantor at Magdeburg's Altstädtisches Gymnasium in 1616 or 1617. Grimm began studies with Michael Praetorius in Wolfenbüttel before entering Helmstedt University in 1609, and likely concluded there in mid-1610s; the Magdeburg position was his first official post.[22] 1616 is therefore the earliest date Cod. Guelf. 322 could have been compiled.

The contents are intriguing because Weißensee was a significant Protestant composer and Magdeburg was a noted center of anti-Catholic sentiment. The music, however, is largely Catholic in origin, with sizable contributions from

20   For a longer, nuanced description of how early modern partbooks were formatted and produced, see van Orden, 2015: 8–25.

21   My thanks to Benjamin Dobbs for pointing to Grimm's presence in the manuscript as a reason to question the RISM-ascertained date of the manuscript.

22   Dobbs, 2015: 29–30.

FIGURE 11.2   Index, Cod. Guelf. 322 Mus. Hdschr., Herzog August Bibliothek, Wolfenbüttel

Orlando di Lasso, a major Counter-Reformation figure in music. The repertoire is mostly liturgical: either the Ordinary of the Mass or Vespers psalms and
their antiphons. While the majority of the music is set to Latin text, there are
German-language motets as well, by composers such as Praetorius, Melchior
Vulpius, and Grimm. In the late 1610s, Praetorius spent time in Magdeburg
working with Schütz and Samuel Scheidt in efforts to revise sacred musical
practices along more Italianate lines.[23] It is possible this manuscript was compiled as part of this effort, especially as Grimm was a former pupil of Praetorius
and would have been amenable to this musical agenda.

Regardless of confessional origin, the musical style is similar throughout,
and the newest trends from early seventeenth-century Venice have yet to be
felt here. The manuscript includes 116 indexed works for four to eight voices,
largely in a late sixteenth-century idiom of Franco-Flemish polyphony, with
a number of Italianate polychoral compositions (Fig. 11.2). The few Italian

23   Dobbs, 2015: 30.

composers represented in this manuscript point backwards rather than forwards. Ignoring emerging Northern Italian idioms, these Italians are working in the sonic world of the Franco-Flemish school, a musical lingua franca for much of the sixteenth century. There are single motets by Giovanni Pierluigi da Palestrina and Vincenzo Ruffo, as well as masses by Luca Marenzio, Giovanni Giacomo Gastoldi, and Vincenzo Ruffo. Most of the contents in this manuscript—including the few compositions by Italian composers—can be traced to German printed sources, though there is at least one Italian source. The Palestrina motet is "Viri Galilei" for six voices, liturgically the first antiphon at Second Vespers of Ascension. It originates from a book of motets published in Rome in 1569, reprinted in Venice in 1579, 1586, 1590, and 1600.[24] To the best of my knowledge, there is no German source for the motet, so one of the Venetian editions was likely the material for the scribe of the Wolfenbüttel manuscript. This manuscript source differs slightly from the 1579 Venice edition by Gardano in the notation of the breves; the notes are accurate, though a number of the rests spanning multiple measures are notated differently, plus there is some inconsistency in accidental markings.[25] There are enough of these small differences that the 1579 edition may be removed from consideration as a potential printed source for the Magdeburg scribe. Conversely, it follows perfectly the 1586 edition printed in Venice by the Scotto press, which therefore might have been the exact edition used by the Magdeburg scribe.[26] It also suggests that printed Venetian music was more readily available in and around Magdeburg than Roman publications (figs. 11.3 and 11.4).

In addition to Palestrina, several other Italian composers are represented in the manuscript's 139 compositions. An antiphon for Mary Magdalene composed by Ruffo was first included in a collection of masses printed in Venice in 1574.[27] The copy held by the Newberry Library, Chicago, contains far too many inconsistencies for it to have been the source for the Magdeburg scribe.[28] The antiphon is also found in a collection of mostly Italian composers printed in Nürnberg in 1588 and was far more likely to have been circulating in Magdeburg.[29] The two Gastoldi motets were translated into German ("Jesu wollst uns weisen" and "In dir ist Freude"). Gastoldi was based in Mantua but found immense popularity in the printed-music market north of the Alps during his lifetime. His *Balletti a cinque voci* (Venice: Amadino, 1591) was reprinted

---

24 Palestrina, 1569.
25 Palestrina, 1579.
26 Palestrina, 1586.
27 Ruffo, 1574.
28 US-Cn, Case minus VM 2011.R92m.
29 Eitner, 1963: 210–11.

FIGURE 11.3
Giovanni Pierluigi da Palestrina,
"Viri Galilei," in *Mottettorum,*
quae partim quinis, partim senis,
partim septenis vocibus concinantur
(Venice: Scotto, 1586)
SOURCE: GALLICA.BNF.FR

thirty times, both in Venice and in Germany.[30] Some of Gastoldi's sacred music found success in the German market—notably, his *Integra omnium solemnitatum vespertina psalmodia,* settings of psalm texts, reprinted as late as 1705.[31] Underscoring the popularity of this collection is the fact that no extant German translation exists; the scribe of Cod. Guelf. 322 evidently translated them or was working from a translated copy. Rather than a typical textual underlay linking each syllable to a specific note, three German verses are written below the music at the bottom of the page, supporting a theory of translation from Latin to German without special thought to textual-musical synchronization. Printed sources for the other Italian selections remain elusive, and the Marenzio masses appear to be unique sources, with no extant concordance. The Italian-sourced selections to Cod. Guelf. 322 Mus. Hdschr. were from composers who had gained a foothold in the German-speaking market for printed

---

30   Arnold and Fenlon, 2001.
31   Arnold and Fenlon, 2001.

E 11.4   Palestrina, "Viri Galilei," in Cod. Guelf. 322 Mus. Hdschr., Herzog August Bibliothek, Wolfenbüttel

music, though almost entirely through editions printed by German editors for
a German audience.[32]

3   Cod. Guelf. 324 Mus. Hdschr.—Helmstedt, ca. 1618–1620

An examination of the repertoire found in Cod. Guelf. 324 Mus. Hdschr.
reveals eight-voiced *cori spezzati* music and appears to be a repository for the
repertoire of the Stephani-Kirche in Helmstedt. The compiling of this manuscript took place when the church served as the university chapel. In 1620,
the approximate date of the manuscript, Helmstedt University was the third-
largest in German-speaking lands, with around five hundred students admitted annually.[33] Within a few years, however, the ravages of the Thirty Years'

32   For a more detailed discussion on the role of the editor in the German collections dis-
      cussed in this chapter see, Hammond, 2007: 13–44.
33   Havemann, 1857: 36.

War would reach Helmstedt, and a plague in 1625 killed one third of the city's population, leading to a complete cessation of activity at the university. Ignoring these events for now and instead focusing on 1620, we can see an example of the musical repertoire chosen to sustain the university's religious life before the effects of the war ended it.

The adoption of *cori spezzati* music in Cod. Guelf. 324 is a departure from the Franco-Flemish polyphony seen in Cod. Guelf. 322. Though it was once thought to be a regional practice particular to the cathedrals of Padua, Treviso, and Bergamo, new evidence has arisen in recent years showing that in the first half of the sixteenth-century, the genre was by no means confined to Northern Italy, so there is serious need for historiographic revision of the genre's development.[34] Nonetheless, eight-voiced *cori spezzati* maintained a strong connection with the city of Venice—namely, through the Frankfurt Book Fair, where the products of Venetian music printing houses were commodified and reified as superior objects.[35] Book fairs were particularly active in the 1600s and 1610s, when the catalogues list more books than in any other period before the 1760s.[36] As previously discussed, evidence is scant, though extant catalogues dating from between 1613 and 1628 list partbooks mainly from Venice, while other Italian cities are only nominally represented (Florence, Milan, Rome). One known copy of the 1615 catalogue is heavily annotated and bears Michael Praetorius's initials on its title page, which he perhaps used to research Italian music for his *Syntagma musicum*.[37]

Cod. Guelf. 324 Mus. Hdschr. consists of three surviving partbooks (tenor, altus, bassus), all incomplete, plus loose sheets from a fourth missing partbook. There are approximately 522 compositions indexed, and they were compiled during the first half of the seventeenth century, around 1618–1620. Composers are almost never mentioned, though most of the pieces have been ascertained.[38] The vast majority of composers in this collection are German-speaking Lutherans, especially Vulpius, Praetorius, and Grimm. Italian composers are not well represented here, but there are single motets by Viadana, Fattorini, and Bassano, and two by Ruggiero Giovannelli. Although they make up only five items in a very large collection, examining these pieces and their correspondence reveals the primary form of dissemination of Italian sacred music in Germany at this time. Rather than through single-composer Venetian

---

34 Morucci, 2013: 21.
35 Designated book fairs were held twice yearly at both Frankfurt and Leipzig, attracting sellers and buyers from all over Europe.
36 Rose, 2010: 5.
37 Schaal, 1974: 15.
38 Garbe, 1998, vol. 2: 34–90.

prints, these compositions were edited and printed in Germany in large, multi-authored collections representing composers from both sides of the Alps.

Giovannelli was active in the post-Tridentine reform of the gradual in Rome. "Jubilate Deo," one of his two motets included in Cod. Guelf. 324, was first printed in a multi-author collection in Rome in 1592.[39] However, it was reprinted in Germany in 1603 and was arranged for keyboard in a number of German sources as well.[40] Giovannelli, possibly a student of Palestrina, was frequently reprinted both in Italy and abroad perhaps because of his post as *maestro di cappella* at the Collegio Germanico in Rome from 1591 to 1594. German clerics frequently came to study there and the institution maintained a rich musical tradition, with Tomàs Luis de Victoria the most prominent of its former *maestri*. The other Giovannelli motet in Cod. Guelf. 324, "Laudate Dominum in sanctis ejus," was included in a 1603 collection printed in Leipzig: *Florilegium Selectissimarum*.[41] This was part of the series *Florilegium Portense* and was a project of German Kantor Erhard Bodenschatz; it provides a valuable cross-section of the German and Italian motet composition around 1600.[42] Bodenschatz released multiple editions of *Florilegium Selectissimarum*, to which he added new works. The 1617 printing has four additional compositions included in the manuscript.[43] One of the new motets included in a 1618 edition was "Repleator Os Meum" for eight voices by Fattorini, and it was also included in the manuscript.[44] It appears that multiple editions of the first part of *Florilegium Selectissimarum* were sources for the Helmstedt scribe of Cod. Guelf. 324. The second part of *Florilegium Portense*, from 1621, reverses the emphasis of the first, since Italian composers predominate—Giovanni Gabrieli and Viadana among them. The complete absence of any motets from the 1621 collection, coupled with the inclusion of selections from multiple previous editions, suggests the manuscript was compiled in 1618–1620.

Another Italian motet in the manuscript is by Giovanni Bassano, "Dic nobis Maria," for six voices. Giovanni was part of the Venetian branch of the famous Bassano family of musicians with Jewish origins, many of whom emigrated

39 *Psalmi motecta, magnificat, et antiphona, salve regina*, 1592.

40 Eitner, 1963: 418.

41 *Florilegium selectissimarum*, 1603. A complete specimen can be found at the British Library: GB-Lbl B.67.

42 See Riemer and Gottwald (2001): "Notwithstanding the predominance of Latin motets and the absence of chorale variations, it affords a clear view of the compositional activity of the early 17th-century German Kantor."

43 *Promptuarii musici*, 1617. The four compositions included in Cod. Guelf. 324 from this edition are Iacobus Gallus, "Dominus Jesus in qua nocte," and three anonymous works: "Audite me divini fructus," "Laudate nomen domini," and "Jubilate Deo."

44 The British Library record is GB-Lbl B.67b.

to England and made names as royal consort musicians and instrument makers. Giovanni was part of the doge's personal *piffaro* ensemble in Venice and published an influential treatise on wind playing.[45] The motet in question, "Dic nobis Maria," was printed in a 1598 collection for five to twelve voices.[46] It is improbable that the Helmstedt scribe selected this motet directly from Bassano's publication, since it is also found in a 1600 collection printed in Nürnberg.[47] The question remains, however, of why this specific piece was selected for the Nürnberg edition above others from Bassano's original publication. The answer lies in the cross-confessional possibilities of the text.

Bassano, like Giovannelli and a number of the other Italian composers occupying these manuscripts, was active in the musical Counter-Reformation. The choices of what works to include in German editions—and what was left out—show careful consideration of cross-confessional potential for specific Latin-texted pieces. "Dic nobis Maria" is a sequence prescribed for the Roman Catholic Mass and liturgical Protestant Eucharists of Easter Sunday. It is taken from *Victimae Paschali Laudes*, which is one of only four medieval sequences that were preserved in the *Missale Romanum* published in 1570, after the Council of Trent; it would have had a place in both a post-Tridentine Catholic service and a Lutheran one.[48] Looking to Bassano's 1598 Venetian print, the selection immediately following "Dic nobis Maria" is the Magnificat antiphon "Gabriel Angelus locutus est Mariae," sung at Vespers of the Annunciation feast. Textual selections so closely associated to Marian devotion were deliberately avoided by editors aiming for a Protestant/Lutheran audience.

The one Viadana motet in this manuscript, "Hodie nobis," can be found in the first volume of a four-part anthology of motets, *Promptuarium musicum*, intended for school and church use, edited by Abraham Schadaeus (Fig. 11.5).[49] The anthology comprises works for five to eight voices, and no fewer than thirty-six of its composers were leading exponents of the *cori spezzati* style in Italy. This is not the only source to include this specific Viadana motet, though I am convinced it was present in Helmstedt and was the source for the scribe of this manuscript.

---

45 Bassano, 1585.
46 Bassano, 1598.
47 *Sacarem symphoniarum continuatio*, 1600.
48 This particular sequence is also among the earliest to be given a vernacular text and to be adapted for non-liturgical use ("Christ ist erstanden," which predates the Lutheran Reformation). This is one of the earliest tunes to be so important—and probably textually contested—across the confessional divide.
49 *Promptuarii musici*, 1611.

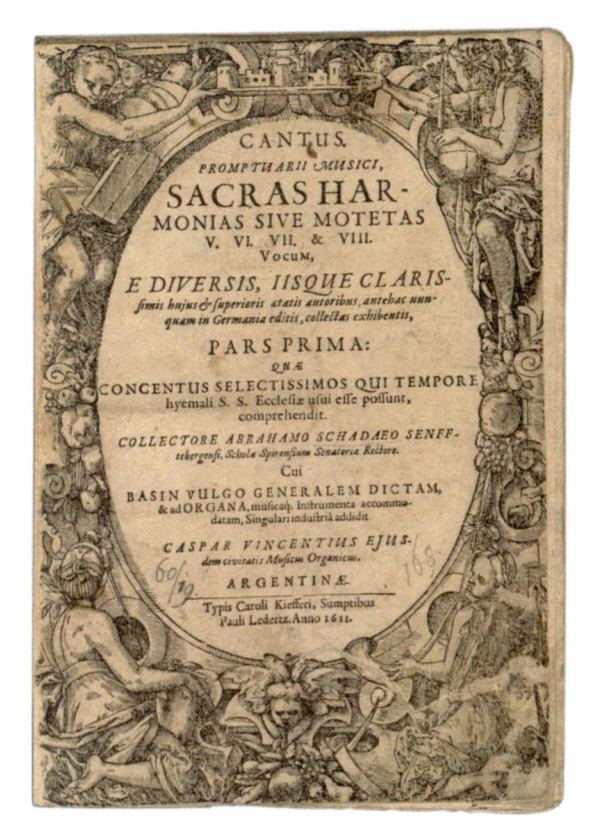

FIGURE 11.5
Promptuarii musici sacras harmonias sive motetas (Argentinæ [Strasbourg]: Pauli Ledertz, 1611). Bayerische Staatsbibliothek, Munich. 4 Mus.pr. 450–1/4, Cantus title page, urn:nbn:de:bvb:12-bsb00077792-3

The most glaring clue is the adjustment to black-note notation during two short triple-time sections of the music (*note nere*) (Fig. 11.6). There are multiple ways to indicate triple time in early modern notation, though *note nere* is a less common choice. A few pages later, the scribe notates an identical musical shift to triple time using open note-heads, a more frequently employed notation for such a musical shift (figs. 11.7 and 11.8). Details such as this help confirm the existence and reliance on the precise notation found in specific partbooks, as well as the location of at least one copy.

This evidence is especially beneficial since so few early modern partbooks survive as complete specimens. First-edition pressruns for partbooks and choirbooks generally averaged around five hundred.[50] Survival rates for these items are extremely low, as can be deduced form van Orden's table of print runs and extant copies.[51] The paucity of surviving contracts and ledgers from Venetian

---

50   van Orden, 2015: 92.
51   van Orden, 2015: 93–94.

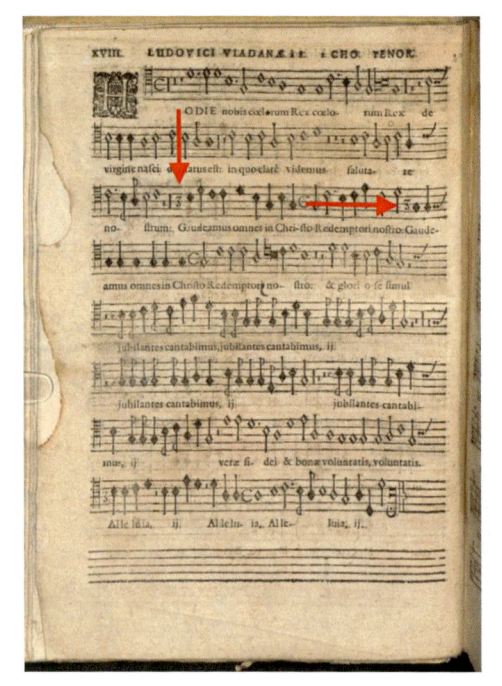
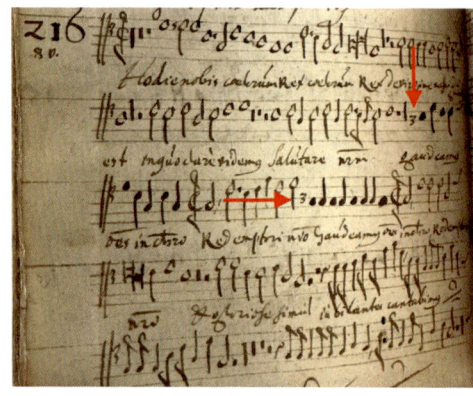

FIGURE 11.6   Note nere notation from print to manuscript. Left: Viadana, "Hodie nobis," in *Promptuarii musici*. Bayerische Staatsbibliothek, Munich. 4 Mus.pr. 450–1/4, Tenor, XVIII, urn:nbn:de: bvb:12-bsb00077792–3. Right: Viadana, "Hodie nobis," no. 216 in Cod. Guelf. 323 Mus. Hdschr. Herzog August Bibliothek, Wolfenbüttel

FIGURE 11.7   Detail, note nere notation in triple time. Cod. Guelf. 324 Mus. Hdschr., no. 216. Herzog August Bibliothek, Wolfenbüttel

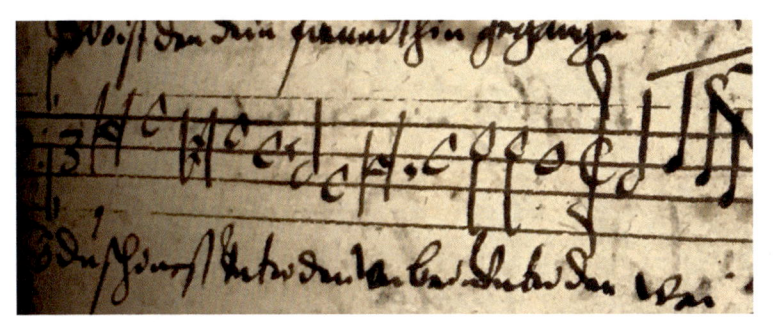

FIGURE 11.8   Detail, open note notation in triple time. Cod. Guelf. 324 Mus.
Hdschr., no. 283. Herzog August Bibliothek, Wolfenbüttel

music-printing houses makes it difficult to say with certainty how many copies of any Venetian printed work ever existed, let alone offer specific information regarding the impetus behind the inception and subsequent circulation and use of said printed musical.[52] Additionally, as many frustrated scholars of early modern printed music are well aware, certain partbooks can only be pieced together by visiting multiple libraries and archives in several countries. The Viadana motet "Hodie nobis" represents a rare example of unambiguous evidence of circulation and transmission, from a 1598 Venetian edition to the 1611 Nürnberg collection to the Helmstedt manuscript currently housed at the Herzog August Bibliothek, Wolfenbüttel. Through the Wolfenbüttel manuscripts, tracing printed sources of manuscripts emerges as a valuable tool for understanding the circulation of early modern music.

4   Cod. Guelf. 323 Mus. Hdschr.—Helmstedt, 1638

A third Wolfenbüttel manuscript is also from Helmstedt. Compiled in 1638, the bassus voice is the sole surviving partbook, which includes 130 compositions and a full index of 221 compositions and their composers. Compared to the previous two manuscripts, there is a sudden and drastic shift in contents, the vast majority consisting of motets in the newer *concertato* style. Notably, there are many solo motets, which was one of the most radical developments at the turn

52   There are fewer than a dozen references to sizes of print runs in sixteenth-century Venice, the undisputed center of the music printing industry. For an example of one of the very few surviving contracts from the Scotto printing house, see Agee, 1986: 59–65.

TABLE 11.1   Contents of Cod. Guelf. 323 Mus. Hdschr.
              by number of voices

1 voice	58
2 voice	51
3 voice	41
4 voice	30
5 voice	11
6 voice	12
7 voice	13
8 voice	5

of the century.[53] More than half of the works are for fewer than four voices (table 11.1). There are twenty-eight known composers represented—seven Italianate and twenty-one Germanic. There are also a number of pieces written anonymously. Two composers in particular represent Venetian musical transmission without the benefit of Venetians or Venice as an interlocutor: Lodovico Viadana and Isaac Posch.

Viadana is heavily represented, with twenty-four individual works. Many, but not all, of these originated in *Cento concerti* (1602) and *Concerti ecclesiastici* (1607). The main impetus behind publishing, as explained by Viadana, was to provide suitable sacred music for smaller ensembles. Much of the reason this caught on so strongly in Germany was that the personnel requirements so well suited the needs of impoverished German chapels. This new way of writing sacred music, for one or two voices with continuo, was widely imitated, with composers active around Venice—such as Claudio Monteverdi and Alessandro Grandi, both of whom are represented in Cod. Guelf. 323—becoming particularly proficient and developing the style to a high degree, thereby cementing abroad the association of this style with Venice. One composer outside of Venice to be influenced by these developments was the Austrian-born, Regensburg-trained Posch, who settled in what is now Slovenia. As far as we know, he never made the relatively short trip to Venice, yet his three published collections display strong Venetian influences. Posch was a typical example of a musician working both for official Catholic ecclesiastical authorities and for the secular, Protestant elite. Despite zealous efforts, many aristocratic families in Carniola, Carinthia, and Styria remained largely faithful to Lutheran teachings, and this coexistence of official Catholic and private Protestant worship encouraged patrons to foster the new Italian style of *concertato* motets, ideal

---

53   Roche, 1984: 56.

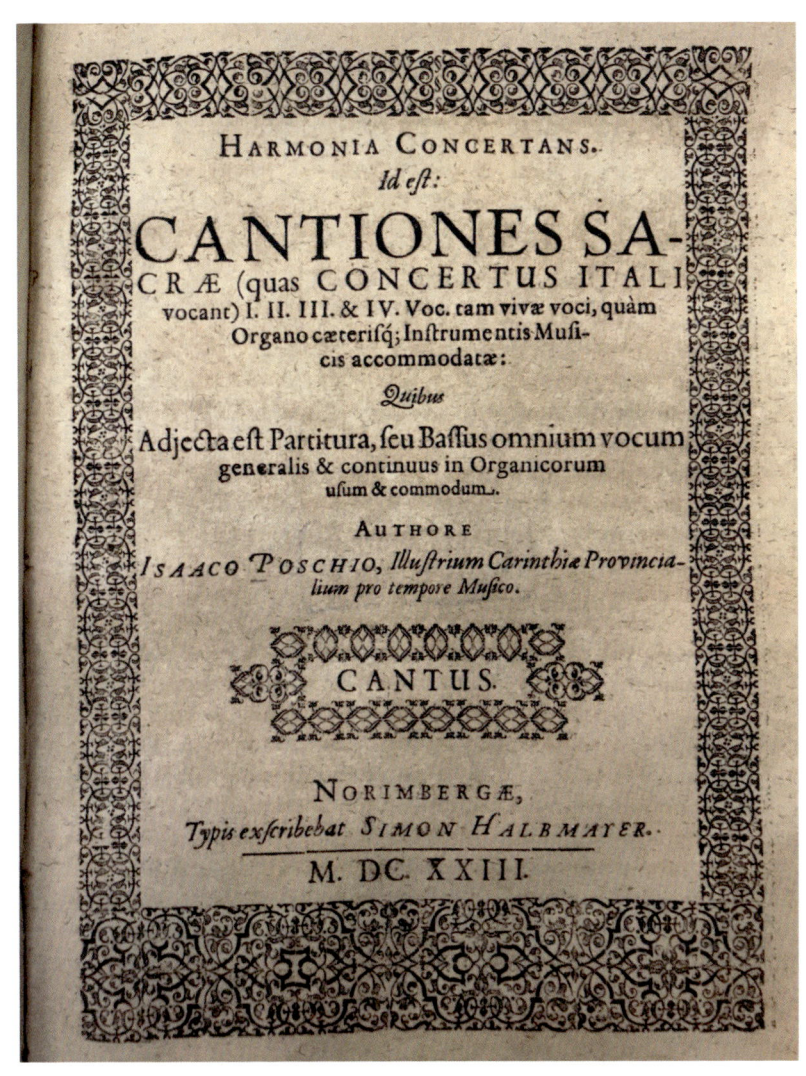

FIGURE 11.9   Title page, Isaac Posch, *Harmonia concertans* (Norimbergæ
[Nuremberg]: Simon Halbmayer, 1623). Universitätsbibliothek Johann
Christian Senckenberg, Goethe Universität, Frankfurt am Main.
D-F Mus 55

for private devotions and services at smaller churches where only a limited
number of singers was available.[54] The most important and influential model
for these composers were Stein's editions of Viadana's *Cento concerti*, issued
from 1609 to 1626. Posch's solo motets stand out because they show the composer's familiarity with the cutting-edge *concertato* motet. There were twelve in

54   Kokole, 2000: 478.

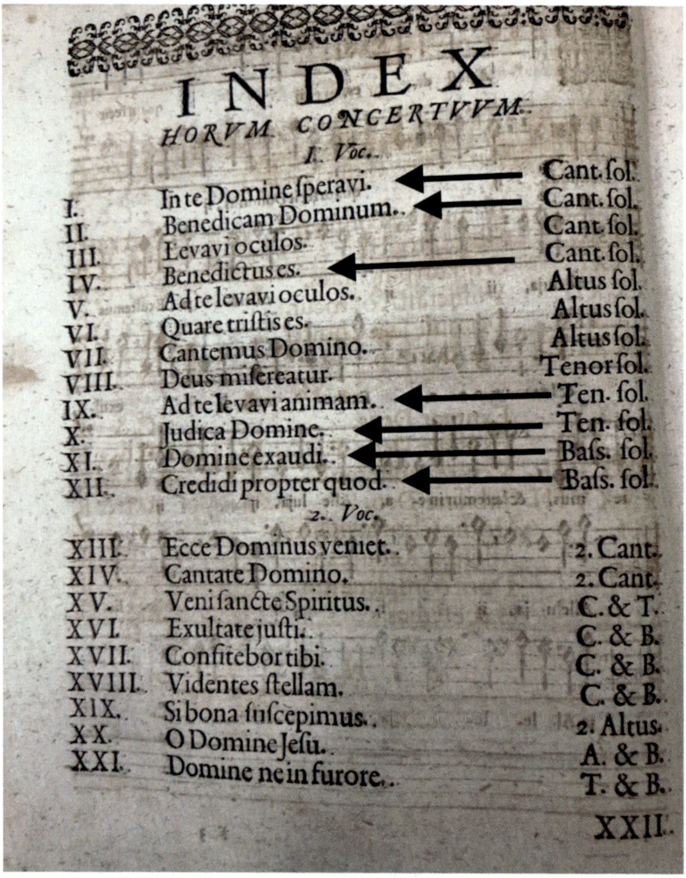

INDEX
HORVM CONCERTVVM.
I. Voc.

I.	In te Domine ſperavi.	Cant. ſol.
II.	Benedicam Dominum.	Cant. ſol.
III.	Levavi oculos.	Cant. ſol.
IV.	Benedictus es.	Cant. ſol.
V.	Ad te levavi oculos.	Altus ſol.
VI.	Quare triſtis es.	Altus ſol.
VII.	Cantemus Domino.	Altus ſol.
VIII.	Deus miſereatur.	Tenor ſol.
IX.	Ad te levavi animam.	Ten. ſol.
X.	Judica Domine.	Ten. ſol.
XI.	Domine exaudi.	Baſs. ſol.
XII.	Credidi propter quod.	Baſs. ſol.

2. Voc.

XIII.	Ecce Dominus veniet.	2. Cant.
XIV.	Cantate Domino.	2. Cant.
XV.	Veni ſancte Spiritus.	C. & T.
XVI.	Exultate juſti.	C. & B.
XVII.	Confitebor tibi.	C. & B.
XVIII.	Videntes ſtellam.	C. & B.
XIX.	Si bona ſuſcepimus.	2. Altus.
XX.	O Domine Jeſu.	A. & B.
XXI.	Domine ne in furore.	T. & B.

XXII.

FIGURE 11.10 Isaac Posch, index of one and two voice compositions in *Harmonia concertans*. The arrows indicate the solo motets included in Cod. Guelf. 323 Mus. Hdschr

his 1623 *Harmonia concertans*, and they represent the earliest extant Protestant sacred monody. Posch explicitly refers to Viadana as his model in the collections' preface, and the two books are arranged in a similar fashion (Fig. 11.9).[55]

One key difference in Posch compared with his Venetian counterparts is a complete absence of Marian motets. This is hardly surprising from a Protestant composer. Instead, the majority of Posch's texts come from the Song of Solomon and are paraliturgical, for private devotion. *Harmonia concertans* was published posthumously by Posch's wife and dedicated to Melchior Putz, a Carinthian Protestant nobleman. Simon Halbmayer, an important

55 See appendix L in Kokole, 2009: 263.

Protestant printer, published it in Nürnberg. Included in *Harmonia concertans* are twelve solo motets for a variety of voice types, seven of which are found in Cod. Guelf. 323 (Fig. 11.10). After comparing the manuscript to one of the three extant complete copies of *Harmonia concertans*, in Frankfurt, there is little doubt as to the print source for the Helmstedt scribe of Cod. Guelf. 323.[56]

Highly noticeable in the manuscript is the intermingling of Catholic and Protestant composers with Latin and German-language motets presented side by side. This is not especially rare, but one of the scribe's print sources was a cross-confessional collection that overtly alludes to the Thirty Years' War: *Fasciculus Secundus* and *Fasciculus Primus*, printed in Goslar in 1637 and 1638, respectively.[57] The title page mentions a long, sad war and encourages the practice of music by the youth amid the turmoil of conflict (Fig. 11.11).[58]

The music was compiled in Nordhausen, most likely by the local cantor Andreas Oehme, from the Collegium Musicum repertoire for the city.[59] Additionally, each composition concludes with a Latin couplet commenting on the music, almost like a textual antiphon. Some of these couplets also refer to war, such as a setting of "Verleih uns Frieden," a paraphrased text by Martin Luther based on the seventh-century hymn "O pace, Domine": Give us peace, Lord, in our time. The Latin couplet that follows is a plea to Jove for peace. Nineteen *Fasciculus* compositions are included in Cod. Guelf. 323: five from *Secundus* and fourteen from *Primus* (table 11.2). There is a conspicuous absence of Marian motets among the Italian works, which rely instead on psalms such as "O bone Jesu," Monteverdi's contribution. "Jubilate Deo" from Psalm 100, set here

---

56 The copy I consulted is part of a large, bound *Sammelband*: D-F, Mus W 55 Nr. 4.

57 *Fasciculus Secundus*, 1637; *Fasciculus Primus*, 1638.

58 Full German title page: *FASCICULUS | SECUNDUS | Geistlicher wolklingender CONCERTEN | Mit 2. und 3. Stimmen sampt dem Basso Continuo | pro Organis, | Aus den vornembsten und besten Com- | ponisten / von etlichen der edlen Music Liebhabern | fleissig comportiret in der Kayserlichen Freyen | Reichsstadt | NORTHAUSEN | und | Bey jetzigen langwerenden traurigen Kriegs-Pressuren | zu sonderlicher recreation unterweilen in ehrlichen zusammen | kunsten practiciret, | Jetzo aber | Undern Philomusus zu gefallen und der lieben Jugend | In Hierosophia ad praxin Musicam accedenti zum besten | Socialiter zum Druck ver- | fertiget ... Aut limos averte oculos, & comprime linguam: | Si potes, aut melius, Zoile, profer opus!*

    [Sacred melodious concertos for 2 and 3 voices, with the basso continuo for organ from the best and most distinguished composers, diligently compiled by several of the noble music lovers in the Imperial Free State of Nordhausen, sometimes practiced in genteel gatherings as a form of special recreation, to counteract the pressures of the present, long-lasting and sad war. Now put into print to please other music lovers [*Philomusus*] and to bring the beloved youth in schools to the practice of music. With the thanks and favor of His Highness, the Elector of Saxony. Either turn your eyes from the mud and hold your tongue: or, better, if you are able, Zoilus, advance this work!]

59 Engel, 1966: 38–39.

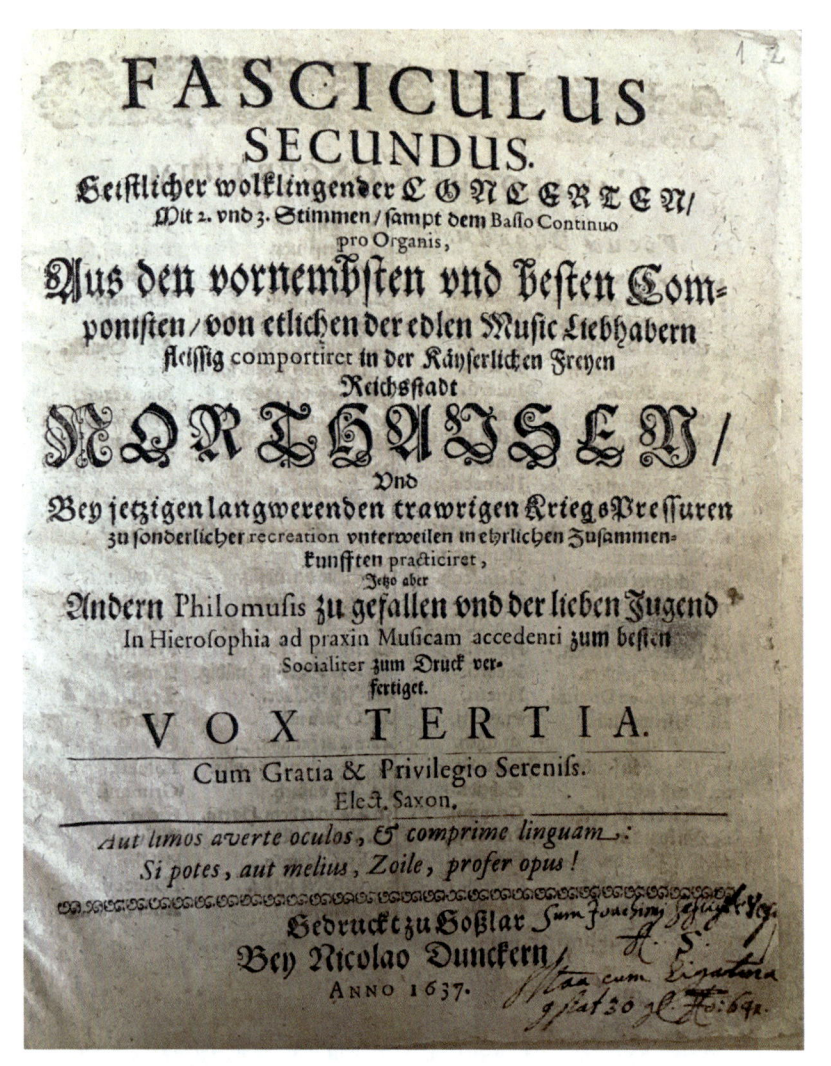

FIGURE 11.11   Title page, *Fasciculus Secundus* (Goslar: Nicolas Dunkern, 1637).
Biblioteka Jagiellońska, Kraków, Mus.ant.pract. D 600. The title page
to the 1638 *Fasciculus Primus* is identical, other than a different Latin
couplet at the bottom

by Giovanni Nicolò Mezzogori, calls for all lands to praise God with song. Nordhausen and Goslar were both imperial cities under the flag of the Emperor. Helmstedt was Protestant terrain and part of the principality of Braunschweig-Wolfenbüttel, bordering the Archbishopric of Magdeburg, which was also a Protestant territory since 1524. Notably, Magdeburg was the site of one of the worst catastrophes of the Thirty Years' War. Imperial forces besieged the city

FIGURE 11.12   Plate depicting the sack of Magdeburg from: Seth Henricus Calvisio,
*Das zerstöhrete und wieder aufgerichtete Magdeburg, oder, Die blutige
Belagerung, und jämmerliche Eroberung und Zerstöhrung der alten Stadt
Magdeburg* [The ruined and rebuilt Magdeburg, or, The bloody siege, and
the miserable conquest and destruction of the old city of Magdeburg].
Magdeburg: Christian Leberecht Faber, 1727. Newberry Library, Chicago

in 1631 after it allied with Sweden, eventually storming the walls (fig 11.12). The
result was the slaughter of over twenty thousand of the city's twenty-five thousand residents, and 1,700 out of its 1,900 buildings were completely burned
down.[60] A census taken the following year listed fewer than five hundred residents, and most of the city remained in rubble for nearly one hundred years.[61]
A new verb entered the German lexicon, *magdeburgisieren*, meaning to "make
a Magdeburg" of somewhere.[62] Over two hundred pamphlets describing the
city's fall appeared in 1632 alone.[63] This was a well-known event, and the two
Fasciculus publications must be viewed in this context.

---

60   Wilson, 2009: 469.
61   Wilson, 2009: 470.
62   Parker, 2001: 161.
63   Wilson, 2009: 470.

TABLE 11.2   Selections from *Fasciculus Secundus* and *Primus* included in Cod. Guelf. 323 Mus. Hdschr., with number of voices

Fasciculus Secundus (1637)	*Fasciculus Primus* (1638)
– Heinneccius, "Lobet den Herrn" à2	– Johann Dilliger, "O Herr hilff" à1
– Heinrich Grimm, "Wie bin ich doch" à2	– Johann Krause, "Herzlich lieb hab ich" à1; "Domine Iesu Christe" à1
– Claudio Monteverdi, "O bone Jesu" à2	– Lodovico Viadana, "Domine Dominus noster" à1; "O Domine Iesu Christe" à1;
– Johann Hermann Schein, "Kom heiliger" à3	Dulcissime Iesu Christe" à1; "Inclina Domine" à1
– Samuel Scheidt, "Dancket dem Herrn" à3	– Melchior Franck, "Das ist das ewige Leben" à1
	– Heinrich Baryphonus, "Wir glauben" à1
	– Andreas Oehme, "Wir glauben, pars 1" à1; "Wir glauben, pars 2" à2
	– Giovanni Mezzogori, "Iubilate Deo omnis" à2
	– Daniel Selich, "Wer unter dem Schirm" à2
	– Heinrich Schütz, "Lobe den Herzen" à2
	– Giacomo Finetti, "Domine inclina" à2

Two other references on the title page help support a reading of the *Fasciculus* publications as war-weary, cross-confessional products. Philomusus, translated in this context as "music lovers," was also the pen-name of sixteenth-century poet Jakob Locher, whose texts were used at the Nordhausen Gymnasium. Locher was a pupil of Conrad Celtis, a German humanist and founder of literary societies.[64] Hierosophia refers to Johannes Girbert, a grammatician and rector of the Gymnasium.[65] Locher, best known for his translations of Horace, remained faithful to the Catholic Church even after the Reformation. It is of course possible that the *Fasciculus* series was printed at a time when printers thought they had to add war references, though I consider it no accident that there are allusions to these two figures with connections to Nordhausen, one Catholic and one Protestant, on the title page of a collection incorporating such a fascinating mix of Catholic and Protestant composers. It certainly aligns

64   Tracy, 1980: 5.
65   My thanks to Barbara Dietlinger for helping me to identify this figure.

with both the cross-confessional ethos and the musical style of the Helmstedt manuscript. With this duality in mind, when the title page refers to Philomusus, it may signify not only music lovers but those who—like Locher—remained faithful to Catholic practice in war-torn Germany.

Finally, what stands out about this manuscript is its uncommon materiality, since it was carefully and deliberately designed to look and feel like a printed partbook. The size and layout are similar to what was pouring out of the Venetian printing houses, including a detailed index, arranged by number of voices. The most unusual and striking feature is the title page. The compiler of this manuscript partbook cut out segments from two different printed books, one from a color print for the ornamental border and one of a full frontispiece, with an added "Third Voice" [III Vox], inked by hand to indicate voice type, as this originally would have formed one part of a full set (Fig. 13).

The incorporation of curated printed imagery, carefully collaged into a new context was a deliberate act that broadcasts the customized manuscript as a Venetian commodity. The source of the frontispiece was one of the printer's devices used by the Scotto Press, in Venice, one of the most prolific music printers of the era. A printer's device, as Jane Bernstein states, not only acted as an advertisement for a music book but also attested to the quality of its contents.[66] Scotto used around twenty different devices, several of which adopted emblems specifically associated with Venetian iconography, including the one used here.[67] What kind of influence or thinking may have gone into the choice of Scotto's very Venetian device for this hybrid product?

While uncommon, the incorporation of printed material within a manuscript is not entirely without precedent. However, studying hybrid material such as this has certain obstacles, as manuscripts and printed books are not only treated as distinct archival categories but are often studied in separate rooms on different floors. I am inspired by a recent turn toward materiality in book history and print culture, including van Orden's *Materialities*, as well as a recent special issue of *The Journal of Medieval and Early Modern Studies* on the topic of the Renaissance collage.[68] The contributors to this issue ask how scholars can think about collaging as an intellectual gesture. Juliet Fleming points out that cutting and pasting has a long history, a refutation of art historical scholarship claiming this as a modern phenomenon.[69] The title page to Cod. Guelf. 323 is unmistakably a collage that goes a step beyond mere scribal

---

66   Bernstein, 1998: 79.
67   Bernstein, 1998: 79.
68   Fleming et al., 2015.
69   Fleming, 2015: 443.

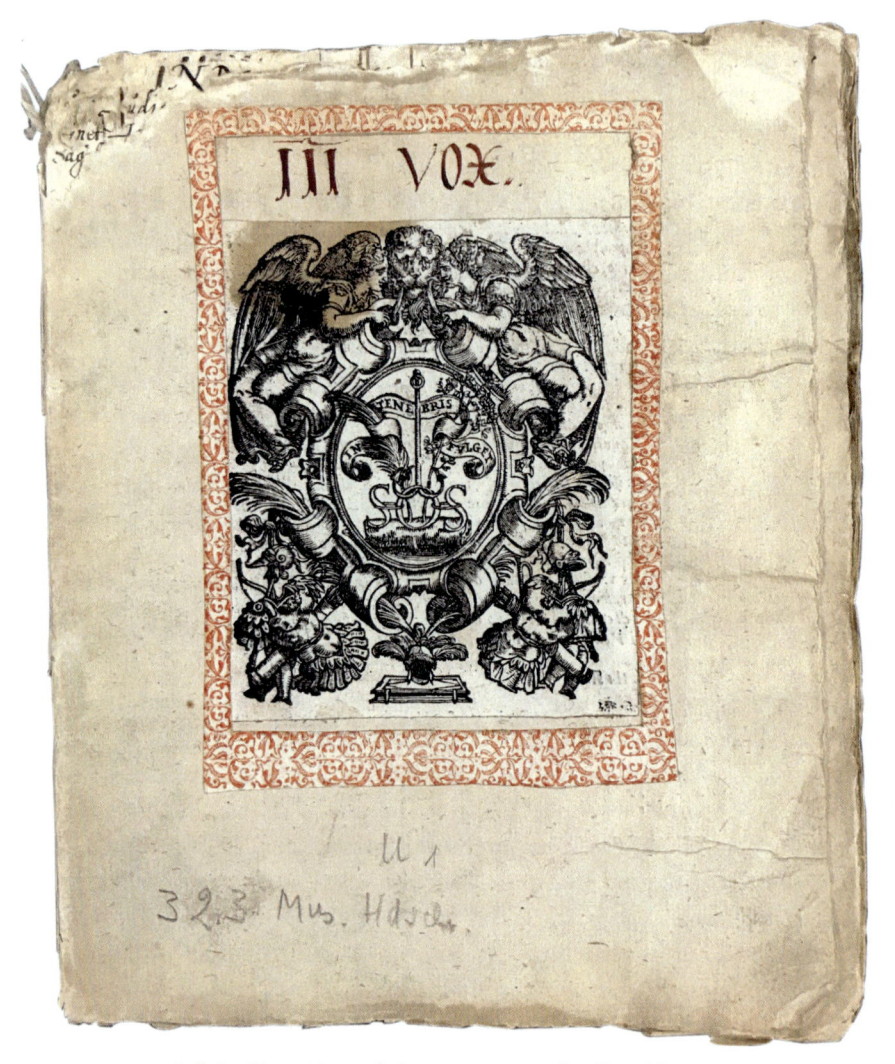

FIGURE 11.13   Cod. Guelf. 323 Mus. Hdschr., cover page with collaged frontispiece. Herzog
August Bibliothek, Wolfenbüttel

copying. It is an act of tactile intertextuality, one that emblematically connects
the contents of this manuscript to a Venetian musical ethos. The Scotto frontispiece acts as an emblem of Venetian musical quality, and is an image that a
trained musician would easily recognize. At the center of the Scotto device lies
an anchor surrounded by a palm frond and an olive branch above the letters
SOS, which stood for "Signum Octaviani Scotto" (Fig. 14). The banner reads,
"*In tenebris fulget*," or "In darkness he shines," the "he" referring to Scotto and
his products. Or, in its new context, the reference could be to music shining

FIGURE 11.14
Detail, Scotto press device

amid the darkness of war. The anchor and log joined together was specifically ascribed to Venetian iconography, symbolizing stability on both sea and land, a result of Venice's maritime prowess. The manuscript's curious materiality and its musical contents—curated from myriad printed material covering a wide swath of geography—epitomizes the early modern reality surrounding musical mediation and circulation: a complex, multimedia, interregional, and transnational network of communication.

5   Conclusion

Tracing the network of printed material, we see how quickly the *concertato* style spread throughout Germanic lands and how the scribes of the three Wolfenbüttel manuscripts relied on editors who had capitalized on the cultural cache of Venice as a musical commodity. By 1638, the *concertato* motet had supplanted a previous reliance on large-scale polyphonic motets in Helmstedt, as evidenced by the Venetian emblem in Cod. Guelf. 323, irrespective of its lack of Venetian musical content. The borders of the Venetian Republic turn porous thanks to the printed music book trade. The conception of Venice as an idea or commodity rather than a fixed locale deepens our understanding of musical mediation and circulation outside of Venice in the early seventeenth century.

Acknowledgments

Research for this chapter was made possible thanks to the Dr Gudrun Busch Stipendium für Musikwissenschaft, granted by the Herzog August Bibliothek for a residency from October to December of 2017. I am also grateful to the American Friends of the Herzog August Bibliothek for additional travel support, and to Matthais Roick for inviting me to present a preliminary version of this work in Wolfenbüttel in October of 2018. Additional research was supported by a Graduate School Research Grant from Northwestern University to consult sources at the Biblioteka Jagiellońska, Krakow, and the Palazzo Doria Pamphilj archive, Rome. The Northwestern Presidential Fellowship supported research at the British Library, London. I appreciate the assistance of my colleagues Anne Koenig, who helped me with certain German translations, and Barbara Dietlinger, who helped me identify an obscure reference in the *Fasciculus* title page.

Bibliography

Abbreviations

D-F: Frankfurt am Main, Stadt- und Universitätsbibliothek, Goethe-Universität
D-W: Wolfenbüttel, Herzog August Bibliothek

Manuscript Sources

D-F, Mus. 55
D-W, Cod. Guelf. 322 Mus. Hdschr.
D-W, Cod. Guelf. 323 Mus. Hdschr.
D-W, Cod. Guelf. 324 Mus. Hdschr.

Printed Sources

Agee, Richard J. "A Venetian Music Printing Contract and Edition Size in the Sixteenth Century." *Studi Musicali* 15 (1986), 59–65.
Arnold, Denis. "The Second Venetian Visit of Heinrich Schütz." *The Musical Quarterly* 71 (3) (1985), 359–74.
Arnold, Denis, and Iain Fenlon. "Gastoldi, Giovanni Giacomo." In *Grove Music Online*. Oxford University Press, 2001. https://doi.org/10.1093/gmo/9781561592630.article .10721.
Bassano, Giovanni. *Motetti per concerti ecclesiastici, 5–8, 12vv* (Venezia: Giacomo Vincenti, 1598).
Bassano, Giovanni. *Ricercate, passaggi et cadentie per potersi esercitar nel diminuir terminatamente con ogni sorte d'istrumento* (Venetia: Amadino, 1585).

Bernstein, Jane A. *Music Printing in Renaissance Venice: The Scotto Press* (1539–1572) (New York: Oxford University Press, 1998).

Bernstein, Jane A. *Print Culture and Music in Sixteenth-Century Venice* (Oxford: Oxford University Press, 2001).

Bianconi, Lorenzo. *Music in the Seventeenth Century*, trans. David Bryant (Cambridge: Cambridge University Press, 1987).

Caccini, Giulio. *Le nuove musiche* (Firenze: li here di Giorgio Marescotti, 1602).

Calvisio, Seth Henricus. *Das zerstöhrete und wieder aufgerichtete Magdeburg, oder, die blutige Belagerung, und jämmerliche Eroberung und Zerstöhrung der alten Stadt Magdeburg* (Magdeburg: Christian Leberecht Faber, 1727).

Carver, Anthony F. *Cori Spezzati: An Anthology of Sacred Polychoral Music* (Cambridge: Cambridge University Press, 1988).

Carver, Anthony F. *Cori Spezzati: The Development of Sacred Polychoral Music to the Time of Schütz* (Cambridge: Cambridge University Press, 1988).

Centum concertum ecclesiasticorum ... Auctore excellentissimo Lodovico Viadana (Francoforti: N. Stein, 1609).

Dobbs, Benjamin. *A Seventeenth-Century Musiklehrbuch in Context: Heinrich Baryphonus and Heinrich Grimm's Pleiades Musicae*, Dissertation (Music Theory, University of North Texas, 2015).

Einstein, Alfred. "Italienische Musik und italienische Musiker am Kaiserhof und an den erzherzoglichen Höfen in Innsbruck und Graz." *Studien Zur Musikwissenschaft* 1 (1934), 3–52.

Eisenstein, Elizabeth L. *The Printing Press as an Agent of Change* (Cambridge: Cambridge University Press, 1979).

Eitner, Robert, ed. *Bibliographe der Musik-Sammelwerke des XVI. und XVII. Jahrhunderts* (Hildesheim: Georg Olms Verlagsbuchhandlung, 1963).

Engel, Hans. *Musik in Thüringen* (Köln: Böhlau Verlag, 1966) [Mitteldeutsche Forschungen Band 39].

Fasciculus Primus Geistlicher wolklingender Concerten Mit 2. und 3. Stimmen sampt dem Basso Continuo pro Organis (Goslar: Nicolas Dunkern, 1638).

Fasciculus Secundus Geistlicher wolklingender Concerten Mit 2. und 3. Stimmen sampt dem Basso Continuo pro Organis (Goslar: Nicolas Dunkern, 1637).

Federhofer, Hellmut. "Graz Court Musicians and Their Contributions to the 'Parnassus Musicus Ferdinandaeus' (1615)." *Musica Disciplina* 9 (1955), 167–244.

Fleming, Juliet. "The Renaissance Collage: Signcutting and Signsewing." *Journal of Medieval and Early Modern Studies* 45 (3) (2015), 443–56.

Fleming, Juliet et al., eds. *Journal of Medieval and Early Modern Studies*, Special Issue: The Renaissance Collage. 45 (3) (2015).

Florilegium selectissimarum Cantiunum praestantissimorum aetatis nostrae autorum, 4. 5. 6. 7. & 8. Vocum ... Collectum & editum Studio ac labore M. Erhardi Bodenschatz (Lipsiæ: Abraham Lamberg, 1603).

Gallico, Claudio, ed. Viadana, Lodovico, *Cento concerti ecclesiastici: Opera duodecima 1602*, ed. Claudio Gallico (Kassel: Bärenreiter, 1964).

Garbe, Daniela. *Das Musikalienrepertoire von St. Stephani zu Helmstedt: ein Bestand an Drucken und Handschriften Des 17. Jahrhunderts*, 2 vols., Wolfenbütteler Arbeiten Zur Barockforschung Band 33 (Wiesbaden: Harrassowitz Verlag, 1998).

Hammond, Susan Lewis. *Editing Music in Early Modern Germany* (Aldershot: Ashgate, 2007).

Havemann, Wilhelm. *Geschichte der Lande Braunschweig und Lüneburg*, Band 3 (Göttingen: Dieterichschen Buchhandlung, 1857).

Kokole, Metoda. *Isaac Posch: "didtus Eois Hesperiisque Plagis"—Praised in the Lands of Dawn and Sunset* (Frankfurt: Peter Lang, 2009).

Kokole, Metoda. "Venetian Influence on the Production of Early Baroque Monodic Motets in the Inner-Austrian Provinces." *Musica e Storia* 8 (2) (2000), 477–507.

Lang, Paul Henry. *Music in Western Civilization* (New York: W. W. Norton, 1941).

Love, Harold. *The Culture and Commerce of Texts: Scribal Publication in Seventeenth-Century England* (Amherst: University of Massachusetts Press, 1993).

Mompellio, Federico. *Lodovico Viadana; musicista fra due secoli, XVI–XVII*, (Firenze: Leo S. Olschki, 1967) [Historiae Musicae Cultores Biblioteca 23].

Morucci, Valerio. "Reconsidering 'Cori Spezzati': A New Source from Central Italy." *Acta Musicologica* 85 (1) (2013), 21–41.

Palestrina, Giovanni Pierluigi da. *Liber primus motettorum, 5–7vv* (Rome: Eredi di Valerio & Aloysio Dorico, 1569).

Palestrina, Giovanni Pierluigi da. *Motectorum, qvae partim Qvinis, Partim Senis, Partim Septenis vocibus concinantur* (Venetia: Gardano, 1579).

Palestrina, Giovanni Pierluigi da. *Mottetorum, quae partim quinis, partim senis, partim vocibus concinantur* (Venetia: Scotto, 1586).

Parker, Geoffrey. *Europe in Crisis 1598–1648*, 2nd ed. (Oxford: Blackwell, 2001) [Blackwell Classic Histories of Europe].

Posch, Isaac. *Harmonia concertans* (Norimbergæ: Simon Halbmayer, 1623).

Promptuarii musici sacras harmonias sive motetas V. VI. VII. & VIII. VOCUM, ... pars prima, quae concentus selectissimos, qui tempore hyemali ss ecclesiae usui esse possunt, comprehendit (Argentinæ: Pauli Ledertz, 1611).

Promptuarii musici sacras harmonias V. VI. VII. & VIII. vocum, e diversis, clarissimis huius & superioris aetatis authoribus in Germania nusquam editis (Argentinae: Pauli Ledertz, 1617).

Promptuarii musici sacras harmonias V. VI. VII. & VIII. vocum, e diversis, clarissimis huius & superioris aetatis authoribus in Germania nusquam editis (Argentinae: Pauli Ledertz, 1618).

Psalmi motecta, magnificat, et antiphona, salve regina (Roma: Franciscum Coattinum, 1592).

Riemer, Otto, and Clytus Gottwald. "Bodenschatz, Erhard." In *Grove Music Online*. Oxford University Press, 2001. https://doi-org/10.1093/gmo/9781561592630.article.03360.

Roche, Jerome. "'Aus den berühmbsten italiänischen Autoribus': Dissemination North of the Alps of the Early Baroque Italian Sacred Repertory through Published Anthologies and Reprints." In *Claudio Monteverdi und die Folgen: Bericht über das internationale Symposium, Detmold 1993*, eds. Silke Leopold and Joachim Steinheuer (Kassel: Bärenreiter, 1998), 13–50.

Roche, Jerome. *North Italian Church Music in the Age of Monteverdi* (Oxford: Clarendon Press, 1984).

Roche, Jerome. "What Schütz Learnt from Grandi in 1629." *The Musical Times* 113 (1557) (1972), 1074–75.

Rose, Stephen. "The Mechanisms of the Music Trade in Central Germany, 1600–40." *Journal of the Royal Musical Association* 130 (1) (2005), 1–37.

Ruffo, Vincenzo Ruffo. *Il quarto libro di messe a sei voci … piene d'inusitata dolcezza, composte ultimamente con arte meravigliosa, conforme al decreto del … Concilio di Trento fra le quali e una de morti con la sua sequenza* (Venetia: Scotto, 1574).

Sacarem symphoniarum Continuatio (Noribergæ: Paul Kaufmann, 1600).

Schaal, Richard. *Die Kataloge es Augsburger Musikalien-Händlers Kaspar Flurschütz* (Wilhelmshaven: Heinrichshofen's Verlag, 1974).

Tracy, James D. "Against the 'Barbarians': The Young Erasmus and His Humanist Contemporaries." *The Sixteenth Century Journal* 11 (1) (Spring 1980), 3–22.

Valentin, Caroline. *Geschichte der Musik in Frankfurt am Main vom Anfange des XIV. bis zum Anfange des XVIII. Jahrhunderts* (Frankfurt am Main: K. Th. Völckers Verlag, 1906).

van Orden, Kate. *Materialities: Books, Readers, and the Chanson in Sixteenth-Century Europe* (Oxford: Oxford University Press, 2015) [The New Cultural History of Music].

van Orden, Kate. *Music, Authorship, and the Book in the First Century of Print* (Berkeley: University of California Press, 2014).

Viadana, Lodovico. *Cento concerti ecclesiastici, a una, a due, & a quattro voci. Con il basso continuo per sonar nell'organo* (Venetia: Giacomo Vincenti, 1602).

Viadana, Lodovico. *Concerti ecclesiastici a una, a due, & a qauttro voci, Con il basso continuo per sonar nell'organo* (Venetia: Giacomo Vincenti, 1607).

Wilson, Peter H. *The Thirty Years War: Europe's Tragedy* (Cambridge, MA: Harvard University Press, 2009).

Wollny, Peter. "The Distribution and Reception of Claudio Monteverdi's Music in Seventeenth-Century Germany." In *Claudio Monteverdi und die Folgen: Bericht über das internationale Symposium Detmold 1993*, eds. Silke Leopold and Joachim Steinheuer (Kassel: Bärenreiter, 1998), 51–75.

CHAPTER 12

Why Is Boccaccio's *Decameron* in the Ethica Section of the Herzog August Bibliothek, Wolfenbüttel?

Enrica Zanin

In the early modern era, Boccaccio's *Decameron* was considered an immoral text: it was condemned by the Roman index,[1] corrected and expurgated by its editors,[2] and regarded as dangerous reading for women and young men. Goethe famously wrote to his sister Cornelia that she could read any Italian book except Boccaccio's *Decameron*.[3] However, despite its supposed immorality, the *Decameron* is stored in the Ethica section of the Duke August Library in Wolfenbüttel. One might theorize that the *Decameron* was randomly assigned to the Ethica section, without any regard to its subject. But several pieces of evidence demonstrate that Boccaccio's collection of novellas was intentionally stored in the section, and thus was considered "ethical" material. First, the copies of the *Decameron* in this section are numerous: there are seven Italian versions, seven translations, and three anthologies, for a total of seventeen copies.[4] While there are four copies in other sections of the library, the reasons why they have been cataloged elsewhere are generally clear: one copy, placed in the Poetica section, is an epic adaptation of the *Decameron* by Brusantino; two other copies, in the Quodlibetica section, are bound with other texts. The majority of the copies of the *Decameron* are in the Ethica section.

In fact, not only Boccaccio's *Decameron* but many collections of novellas are in the Ethica section: I counted 114 collections of French, Italian, Spanish, and German novellas, among which are to be found books containing obscene material, which we would not expect to find in this section. Take, for example,

---

1 Bujanda, 1990: 384–90.

2 Chiecchi and Troisio, 1984.

3 "Ließ italienisch was du willst, nur den Decameron vom Boccaccio nicht": Letter from Goethe to his sister Cornelia Goethe, December 1765, quoted in Kocher, 2005: 13.

4 *Decameron*, 1492, 13.4 Eth. 2°(1); *Decameron*, 1498, 13.4 Eth. 2° (2); *Decameron* (French), 1537, 45.13 Eth.; *La Fleur des Nouvelles* (anthology), 1547, 139.11 Eth. (1); *Decameron*, 1549, 18.2 Eth; *Decameron* (Spanish), 1550, 13.2 Eth. 2°; *Decameron* (French), 1552, 149 Eth.; *Decameron*, 1552, 4.5 Eth.; *Decameron*, 1557, 12.3 Eth.; *Cento Novelle* (anthology by Sansovino), 1563, 101.16 Eth.; and 1571, 15.4 Eth.; *Decameron* (censored version), 1574, 8.5.1 Eth.; *Decameron* (censored version), 1587, 11.4 Eth.; *Decameron* (French), 1597, 159.1 Eth.; *Decameron* (English), 1620, 17.3 Eth. 2°; *Decameron* (Flemish), 1632, 24.4 Eth.; *Decameron* (German), 1646, 137.34 Eth.

Pietro Aretino's *Ragionamenti* (129.7 Eth), which relates the sexual initiation of a young woman, or Tabourot's *Escraignes dijonnaises* (127.9 Eth; 158.5 Eth, 162.3 Eth), a collection of scatological short stories told by a group of French peasants.

Novellas appear to be considered a genre in and of themselves and to have been intentionally placed in the Ethica section: among the first folios stored in the section, we find a copy of the *Heptaméron* by Marguerite de Navarre (4 Eth). Next to it, between 4 Eth and 5 Eth, a second well-known collection of novellas—Cervantes's *Novelas ejemplares* (4.1 Eth.)—and, later, a third one, Boccaccio's *Decameron* (4.5 Eth.). The principal models of the genre were placed together, among the first books of the section, showing that novellas were seen as a coherent genre and as useful "ethical" material.

1   Why Were Boccaccio's Novellas Considered Ethical Texts?

The *Decameron* was regarded as an immoral text, yet it was placed in the Ethica section. It seems difficult to understand why. One reason might be that what we now call "literature" was then considered part of ethics. According to Jean Buridan, poetry is a part of moral philosophy—namely, its "instrumental" part (*instrumentalem*).[5] Leonardo Bruni wrote in 1477 that poetry is a *doctrina vivendi*, a school of life.[6]

If literature was considered part of ethics, ethics itself was different from what we now understand as morality. Instead of prescribing moral rules, Renaissance ethics describes "forms of life,"[7] showing how the practice of virtue could lead to happiness. In particular, the exercise of prudence (*phronesis*) was believed to be crucial, since, according to Aristotelian ethics, only the prudent man (and the prudent woman) would know how to deliberate wisely, mastering the unexpected and reaching happiness. Renaissance ethics is eudaimonic and not deontological; when virtues are honored, societal

---

5   "Ipsa autem scientia, seu philosophia moralis, duas habet partes primas, unam principalem, aliam adminiculativam seu instrumentalem. [...]. Secunda vero pars quae hunc modum docendi docet, traditur in libris Rhetoricae et Poetriae"; "this science or moral philosophy, has two first parts: one principal, and the other ancillary or instrumental. [...] Now the second part, which teaches how to teach, is conveyed by the books of Rhetoric and Poetics": Jean Buridan, *Quaestiones in decem libros ethicorum Aristotelis ad Nicomachum*, (ca. 1361), quoted in Lines, 2002: 147 (all translations, unless otherwise stated, are by the author of the article).
6   "Poetas insuper ut legat et intellegat volo [...] eius poesim tota est doctrina vivendi"; "I want poets to read and understand [...] because all poetry is a teaching of life": Leonardo Bruni, *De studi et litteris* (1477), in Kallendorf, 2002: 111.
7   Quondam, 2010.

well-being improves.[8] From this perspective, Renaissance ethics is quite close to the poetics of early modern novellas.

Novellas are also described as forms of life: according to Pontano, novellas and jokes are "ad bonos mores institutae"[9]—made for improving manners and ethical habits—and Boccaccio should be praised because he teaches how to tell good stories and to contribute to the common merriment. Novellas not only provide solace, but they also exercise the reader's prudence. Boccaccio[10]—and, later, Bandello[11]—explains that novellas expound particular ethical situations. Each situation asks the reader to take ethical stands and to define possible strategies in order to resolve problematic issues. In this sense, the novellas impart a lesson of prudence, and are particularly useful

---

8   See Roick, 2017; Lines and Ebbersmeyer, 2012; Schneewind, 1998.

9   Pontano, 2008, book 6: 323.

10   "Cento novelle ... nelle quali piacevoli ed aspri casi d'amore e altri fortunati avvenimenti si vederanno"; [a hundred novellas ... in which pleasant and bitter cases of love and other fortunate events will be seen]: Boccaccio, 1980: 9.

11   "Ancor che tutto il dí si veggiano occorrer varii casi, cosí d'amore come d'ogn'altra sorte, e mille accidenti impensatamente nascere, non è perciò che di simil avvenimenti non si generi meraviglia in noi e che assai sovente non rechino profitto a chi gli vede od intende. E tanto piú è maggior la meraviglia e l'utile piú fruttuoso, quanto che le cose meno sperate avvengono. Per questo mi pare che ogni volta che cosa memoranda interviene, e che non sia con l'onor de la penna a la memoria de la posteritá consagrata, che veramente facciamo non picciola ingiuria a noi stessi ed anco a quelli che verranno dopo noi. Ché se i casi e strani accidenti e fortunevoli che la varietá de la fortuna produce si scrivessero, chiunque gli udisse o leggesse, se egli piú che trascurato non fosse, come potrebbe fare che qualunque ammaestramento non ci pigliasse e a se stesso con l'altrui danno non facesse profitto? Medesimamente i nostri figliuoli ed i nipoti e tutta la seguente posteritá con la lezione de le cose passate o emendarebbe gli errori suoi se in quelli fosse caduta, o vero megliore nel ben operare diverria, essendo commun proverbio che piú commoveno gli essempi che le parole"; "Even though all day long we see various events occurring, whether of love or of any other kind, and a thousand unthinkable incidents arising, it is not for this reason that we do not marvel at such events and that they do not often bring profit to those who see or understand them. And the greater the wonder and the more fruitful the profit, the more the less hoped-for things happen. For this reason it seems to me that every time something memorable occurs, and that it is not consecrated by the honor of the pen to the memory of posterity, we really do no small insult to ourselves and also to those who will come after us. For if we were to write down all the strange and fortunate events that the variety of fortune produces, whoever heard or read them, if he were not careless, could only learn from them for himself, drawing a lesson from the example of the damage done to others. In the same way, our children and grandchildren and the whole of the following posterity, by the lesson of things past, could either amend the errors into which they have fallen, or become better in doing good works, since it is a common proverb that examples move more than words": Bandello, 1928, vol. 2: II, 7, 349.

to young people, whose experience of the world is limited and who would learn from reading how to act in new and unforeseen situations.[12] That is why, according to Bandello, novellas should not be fictional but should relate historical facts, showing not only examples of successful characters but also cases of ineffective actions, bad deliberations, and vicious attitudes.[13] Each example would provide the reader with valuable strategies to improve his or her agency in civic life. In this sense, the *Decameron*'s vicious characters and immoral stories are ethical because they provide ethical cases and prompt a discussion on ethical values.

The novellas might be in the Ethica section for a second reason: because they are defined as useful texts. Boccaccio explains that the aim of his novellas is to provide not only pleasure (*diletto*) but also useful advice (*utile consiglio*),[14]—advice about how to pursue the good and avoid the evil. Boccaccio is here quoting a passage from Horace's *Ars poetica*, and thus gives his novellas the conventional scope of poetry: offering pleasure (*delectare*) and instruction (*prodesse*), combining business with pleasure (*miscuit utile dulci*).[15] Critics give different interpretations of Boccaccio's claim: according to some, the *Decameron* is an ethical and useful text, because it repurposes narrative material taken from the *exempla*;[16] for others, it only aims at pleasure, and the novellas draw material from the *exempla* in order to criticize and satirize

---

12 "Da questo senza dubio ne nasce che l'uomo, se si vede d'un diffetto macchiato il quale senta dagli scrittori vituperare, con l'altrui lezione diventa a se stesso ottimo pedagogo e maestro, e di cosí fatta maniera de stesso corregge"; "From this it undoubtedly follows that a man, if he sees himself tainted by a defect which he hears being reviled by writers, becomes an excellent pedagogue and teacher for himself through the lessons of others, and in such a way corrects himself": Bandello, 1928, vol. 3: II, 23, 106.

13 "Io non nego che non ce ne siano alcune [novelle] che non solamente non sono oneste, ma dico e senza dubio confesso che sono disonestissime [...]. Confesso io adunque molte de le mie novelle contener di questi e simili enormi e vituperosi peccati, secondo che gli uomini e le donne gli commettono; ma non confesso già che io meriti d'esser biasimato. Biasimar si deveno e mostrar col dito infame coloro che fanno questi errori, non chi gli scrive. Le novelle che da me scritte sono e che si scriveranno, sono e saranno scritte de la maniera che i narratori l'hanno raccontate"; "I do not deny that some [novellas] are not honest, but I say and I confess without doubt that many are dishonest [...]. I therefore admit that many of my novellas contain enormous and vituperative sins, according to what men and women commit them; but I do not think that I deserve to be blamed. It is necessary to blame and show with the finger those who make these sins, not those who write them. The novellas that I have written, and that will be written, are and will be written in the manner in which the narrators have told them": Bandello, 1928, vol. 2: II, 11, 349.

14 Boccaccio, 1980: 9.

15 Horace, 1997: lines 343–44.

16 Branca, 1996: 16–20; Battaglia Ricci, 2000: 31–53; Delcorno, 1989: 284.

them.[17] However, Boccaccio claims in his theoretical writings that fiction can be pleasing and useful at the same time, and that the pleasure of reading is closely intertwined with its usefulness.

Referring to the medieval theory of the fable seen as an *integumentum* [a veil],[18] Boccaccio explains that the story is the beautiful "chaff" of the novella, hiding its meaningful fruit.[19] The reader should interpret the text by going from the bark to the core. The more difficult the process of interpretation is, the more pleasurable it is as well. According to Boccaccio, pleasure is not aroused by the beautiful surface of the text but, rather, by the obstacles and difficulties of its interpretation. A difficult text would be "dearer" (*cariora*) to the reader than a simple one and would be easier to remember.[20] In his commentary on Dante, Boccaccio explains how pleasure and profit are closely intertwined: because of its multilayered form, a fable has a plurality of meanings (*polisena*).[21] The story does not convey a unique moral message but, instead, asks the reader to interpret its meaning, to discern different options, and to take a moral stand. In this respect, Boccaccio's novellas are ethical texts, since they conceal a multilayered moral message that the reader must unveil in order to enjoy the reading.

The novellas might be in the Ethica section for a third reason: because they provide solace and relief that are necessary for work and study. Indeed,

---

17   Neuschäfer, 1969; Küpper, 1993; Stierle, 1998; Picone, 2008.

18   See Dronke, 1974: chapter 1.

19   "Fabula est exemplaris seu demonstrativa sub figmento locutio, cuius amoto cortice, patet intentio fabulantis"; "The fable is an exemplary or demonstrative discourse hidden under the fiction. When its bark is peeled off, the narrator's intention appears": 1951: XIV, 9, www.bibliotecaitaliana.it.

20   Boccaccio, 1951: XIV, 12. See also Augustin, 1997: II. 6. 8.

21   "E perciò non si ramarichi alcuno, se da' poeti è sotto favole nascosa la verità, ma più tosto si dolga della sua negligenza, per la quale e' perde o ha perduto quello che il farebbe lieto, faticandosi d'avere ritrovata la cara gemma nella spazatura nascosa. E questo basti avere a questa parte risposto. Fu adunque il nostro poeta [Dante], sí come gli altri poeti sono, nasconditore, come si vede, di così cara gioia, come è la catolica verità, sotto la volgare corteccia del suo poema. Per la qual cosa si può meritamente dire questo libro essere poliseno, cioè di più sensi"; "So let no one complain if the truth is hidden by poets under fables, but rather be sorry for his negligence, for which he loses or has lost what would make him happy, struggling to find the dear gem hidden in the trash. And this is sufficient for answering this part. Therefore our poet [Dante], like other poets, was a hider, as we see, of such a dear gem, which is the Catholic truth, under the vulgar bark of his poem. For this reason, his book can deservedly be called polysemic, that is to say, of several senses": Boccaccio, 1999, www.bibliotecaitaliana.it. See also Dante Alighieri 2016, epistula XIII, 20.

recreation is not an "ethical" activity, but according to Boccaccio,[22] Bandello,[23] and Cervantes,[24] it is a necessary requisite for learning and ethical enquiry. To this extent, the novellas are a form of what Thomas Aquinas called *eutrapelia*. In his *Summa Theologica*,[25] he claims that in order to learn and to study difficult subjects, one should partake in some honest recreation, playing games, telling jokes, and playfully discussing pleasant subjects.[26] Therefore, even if the novellas do not teach moral knowledge, they provide a moment of playful rest that will allow the reader to regain the concentration needed to learn and to study.

Novellas are not "moral" texts, but they contribute to the ethical life of the reader because they help him or her to live more happily, fortifying his or her prudence, arousing his or her pleasure and providing recreation and solace. These may be the reasons that prompted librarians to place the *Decameron* and the collections of novellas, despite their apparent lack of morality, in the Ethica section of Wolfenbüttel library. But we may wonder whether early modern readers truly considered them ethical material, or whether they enjoyed reading them for other reasons.

2 Why Did Early Modern Readers Read the Novellas?

Early modern reading habits are difficult to assess given the general lack of documents that record them. But the marginal notes left inside books might provide some interesting insights, revealing how these works were read in the early modern period. Analyzing the marginalia in the collections of novellas

---

22 "Le donne, che queste leggeranno, parimente diletto delle sollazzevoli cose in quelle mostrate e utile consiglio potranno pigliare, in quanto potranno conoscere quello che sia da fuggire e che sia similmente da seguitare: le quali cose senza passamento di noia non credo che possano intervenire"; "the women, who will read these [novellas], will likewise be able to take pleasure in the amusing things shown in them and useful advice, inasmuch as they will be able to know what is to be avoided and what is likewise to be followed: which I do not believe they can do without passing boredom": Boccaccio, 1980: 9.

23 "Adunque voi, signor mio, quando da le gravissime occupazioni fastidio bramarete un poco di ricreazione prendere, questa mia novella per via di diporto potrete leggere"; "So you, my lord, when you are annoyed by your heavy occupations and yearn for a little recreation, you can read this novella of mine by way of entertainment": Bandello, 1929, vol. 3: 40, 405.

24 See the prologue of Cervantes *Novelas ejemplares*, 2001: 18.

25 See Thomas Aquinas, 2021: II, II[ae], 168, 2.

26 See on this subject Olson, 1982.

owned by the duke's library may indeed shed light on the purposes and aims of their readers.

In a beautiful folio (115.1 Quodl. Folio) printed in Venice in 1525, some erotic passages of Boccaccio's novellas have been underscored. Theses marks were probably left by the book's owner, who inscribed his name on the first flyleaf: "1542 // Lodovicho Horman". Lodovicho Horman is probably the Italianized spelling of Ludwig Hörmann, who, in 1542, was working for the Fugger Bank in Naples. He was the son of Georg Hörmann, a wealthy man of Gutenberg and one of the leaders of the Fugger Bank. We know that Ludwig came back to Gutenberg and got married in 1543.[27] We can assume that in 1542 he was a free, rich young man: the library owns one other book that belonged to him—a catalogue of harnesses (38.2 BELLICA) with beautiful engravings. We also know that the *Decameron* was then bound with *Le sorti*, by Francesco Marcolino da Forlì, a very precious engraved cartomancy book, now separated from the *Decameron* and probably lost. We can assume that Ludwig Hörmann bought both books, had them bound together, and used them in the company of his male friends. Sometimes he would play with *Le sorti* and tell his friends' fortunes; sometimes he would read with them the erotic and funny passages he underscored in the *Decameron*, or discuss harnesses and horses with them. In this case, the *Decameron* was read in company for pleasure and amusement.

In a German copy of the *Decameron*, published in Frankfurt by Schönwetter in 1646 (137.34 Eth.), all the passages satirizing the church and the clergy are underscored (Fig. 12.1). Long passages of the novellas depicting the lust and sexual incontinence of nuns and monks—such as III, 1 (Masetto da Lamporecchio) and III,10 (Rustico and Alibech)—are underlined and emphasized by vertical lines in the margins. This copy probably belonged to Rudolph August, son of August the Younger, as we can infer from the initials left on the frontispiece (Rudolph H[erzog] [von] B[raunschweig] U[nd] L[üneburg]) (Fig. 12.2).[28] Most emphasized passages are those that were censored in the Italian editions published after 1572. We can then suppose that the book was read either for philological or for polemical reasons: the owner might have wanted to restore the original passages that were removed in the Italian versions, or might have underscored passages that could be used as polemical arguments against the Catholic church.

More often, the *Decameron* was read to learn Italian. Boccaccio's book was considered a model of Italian prose, and it was commonly used as a reading

---

27   See Häberlein, 1998: 357–359.
28   I thank Matthias Roïck, who kindly helped me to decipher the inscription.

FIGURE 12.1

Boccaccio, Giovanni. *Ducento Novella: Zweyhundert newer Historien, welche von 3 Männern, und 7 Weibern, so zu Florentz ein groß Sterben geflohen zusammen geredt ...* Frankfurt: Schönwetter, 1646, p. 448

HERZOG AUGUST LIBRARY, WOLFENBÜTTEL, CALL NUMBER: A: 137.34 ETH

manual. In a copy of the *Decameron* published by Griffio in Venice in 1549 (18.2 Eth), a French reader translated into French the Italian words that he or she did not know. For example, where Boccaccio described the steep (*erta*) slope of a mountain (f. 5*r*), the reader overwrote *erta* with its French equivalent, *raide*. In the same copy, an Italian reader drew boxes around the words he or she did not know and wrote synonyms in the margin. Where Boccaccio explained that the marriage between Cassandra and Lisimaco had been postponed (*frastornato*) several times (f. 240*r*), the reader marked *frastornato* and wrote "tramisso" [delayed] in the margins.

The *Decameron* was read to acquire knowledge. Early modern readers would underline not only the Italian words they did not understand but also the maxims and the moral sentences they wished to learn and to use again in conversation. In the *Decameron* published in 1549 (18.2 Eth) and quoted previously, the Italian reader not only framed difficult words but also underlined useful or beautiful maxims. On the same page (96*v*), he or she emphasized the word *arringo* and underlined two lines: "bocca baciata non perde ventura, anzi rinnova come fa la luna" [Mouth, for kisses, was never the worse: like as the

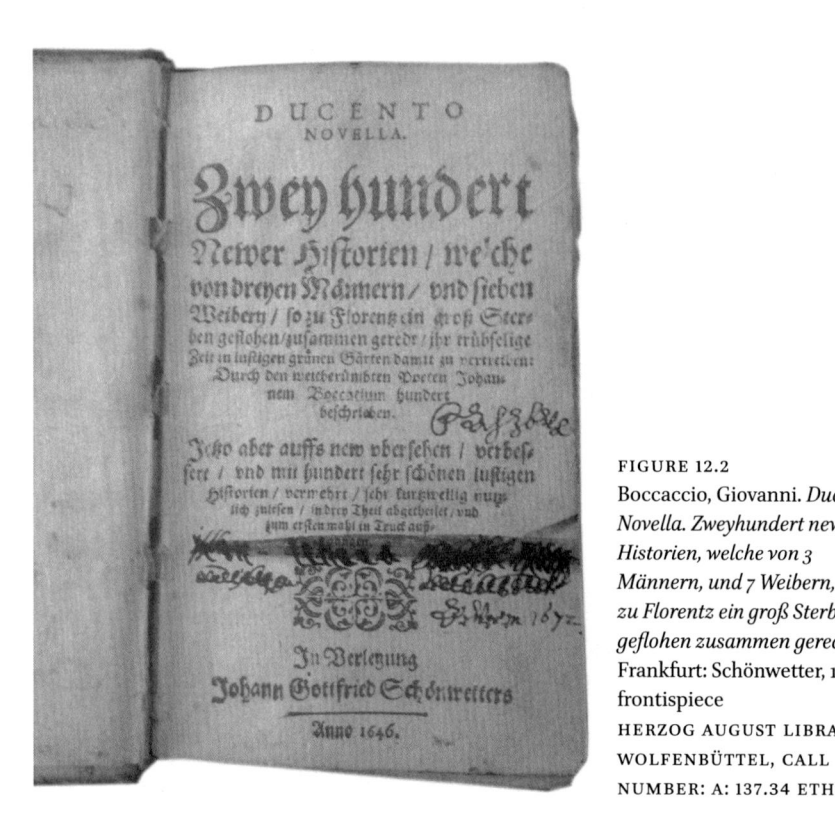

FIGURE 12.2
Boccaccio, Giovanni. *Ducento
Novella. Zweyhundert newer
Historien, welche von 3
Männern, und 7 Weibern, so
zu Florentz ein groß Sterben
geflohen zusammen geredt ...*
Frankfurt: Schönwetter, 1646,
frontispiece
HERZOG AUGUST LIBRARY,
WOLFENBÜTTEL, CALL
NUMBER: A: 137.34 ETH

moon reneweth her course] (Fig. 12.3). The *Decameron* thus functions as a conversational manual, contributing to the reader's linguistic and ethical training and thus improving his or her social skills.

Early modern readers often underscored ethical maxims in the *Decameron*. In a copy published in Brescia by Ludovico Britannico in 1536 (Li 34 Schulenburg), the first principle of natural law is underlined: every person is born with a fundamental will to fortify, preserve, and defend their own life ("Natural ragione è di ciascuno, che ci nasce, la sua vita, quanto può, aiutare e conservare e difendere,") (f 9r). We also learn that as the last degree of joy brings with it sorrow, so misery has ever its sequel of happiness ("Et si come la estremita della allegrezza il dolore occupa, cosi le miserie da sopravegnente letizia son terminate") (f. 4r). Early modern readers would have probably copied these maxims in their commonplace books. And indeed, on the flyleaf of a French collection of novellas (*Recueil des plaisantes et facétieuses nouvelles* [Lyon: Barricat, 1555] [154.28 Eth.]), some moral maxims drawn from the book were translated into Latin and recorded there (Fig. 12.4).

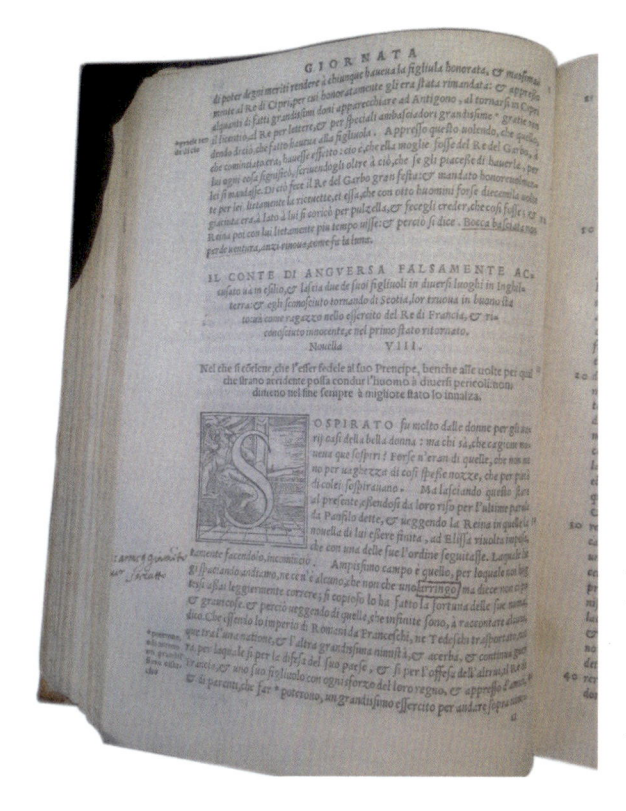

FIGURE 12.3
Boccaccio, Giovanni.
*Il Decamerone di
M. Giovanni Boccaccio, di
nuovo emendato secondo gli
antichi esemplari.* Venezia:
Griffio, 1549, f. 94*v*
HERZOG AUGUST LIBRARY,
WOLFENBÜTTEL, CALL
NUMBER: A: 18.2 ETH

The habit of underlining moral sentences and recording them in common-place books was quite common in the Renaissance.[29] Erasmus, in *De ratione studii* (1511), invited the readers to look for beautiful sentences and moral maxims, to record them in a notebook, and to learn them by heart.[30] However, this reading method generally applied to Latin texts and serious writings—it is interesting to see that the *Decameron*, a comic vernacular prose book, was also used for ethical and rhetorical training.

However, the maxims emphasized do not always seem "ethical" to us. For example, several readers underlined the proverb "Ch'elle femmine in ogni cosa sempre pigliano il peggio" [Women do ever and on all occasions choose the worst] in the tenth novella of the first day.[31] This sentence would be read today as a misogynist criticism of female understanding, but it was not regarded as

---

29   Moss, 1996.
30   See Desiderius Erasmus, 1971: 117–118.
31   This proverb is underlined in Boccaccio, 1536, f. 40r.

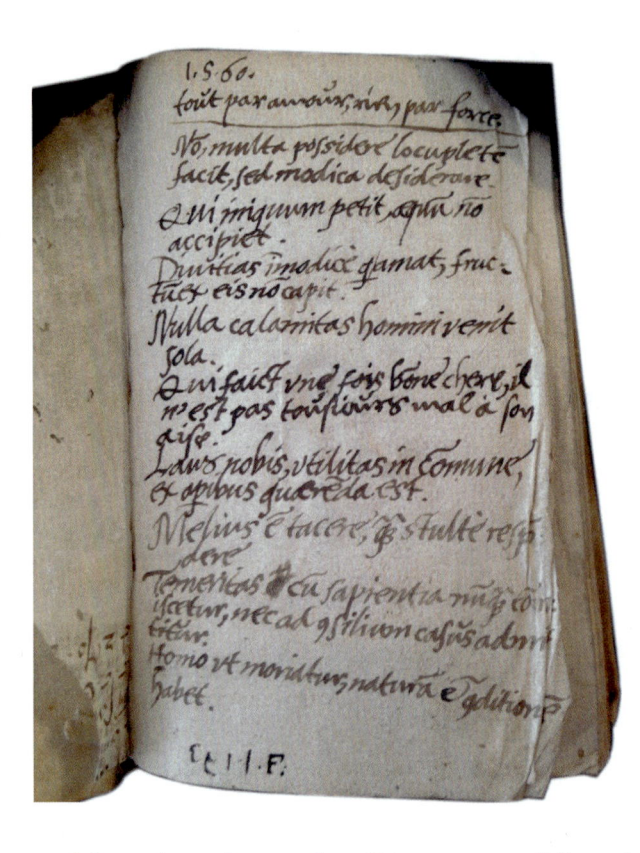

FIGURE 12.4
*Recueil des plaisantes
et facétieuses nouvelles
receuillies de plusieurs
auteurs reunies et
corrigees de nouveau.*
Lyon: Eustache Barricat,
1555, last flyleaf
HERZOG AUGUST
LIBRARY,
WOLFENBÜTTEL, CALL
NUMBER: 154.28 ETH

such by early modern readers. If it was so carefully underlined, it was because
the readers believed it provided useful information about the character and
nature of women. In this respect, the proverb was "ethical": it imparted practical knowledge and aimed to guide the reader in his or her social life, to
improve his or her prudence, and to orient his or her actions toward success
and happiness.

If we consider the collections of novellas within the frame of Renaissance
ethics, we can say that they were actually read as "ethical" books. Analysis of
the copies of the *Decameron* placed in the Ethica section shows that they were
used to improve conversational skills, to acquire knowledge, and to learn ethical maxims. Readers would thus know how to contribute fruitfully to civil and
courtly life. In this sense, we can agree with Pontano's assertion that the novellas were "ad bonos mores institutae": despite their apparent immorality, they
illustrate the language and pleasures of a refined society. Early modern readers
would look for Boccaccio's *Decameron* in the Ethica section because they knew
that the novellas were helpful in achieving the supreme goal of Renaissance
ethics: to make life happier.

Bibliography

Alighieri, Dante. *Epistole*, ed. Marco Baglio, Luca Azzetta, Marco Petoletti *et al.* (Roma: Salerno editrice, 2016).

Augustin. *De doctrina christiana*, ed. Madeleine Moreau (Paris: Institut d'études augustiniennes, 1997).

Bandello, Matteo. *Novelle* (1564), ed. Giochino Brognolino, 3 vols. (Bari: Laterza, 1928).

Battaglia Ricci, Lucia. "*Una novella per esempio* novellistica, omiletica e trattatistica nel primo Trecento." In *Favole, parabole, istorie*, ed. Gabriella Albanese, Lucia Battaglia Ricci, Rossella Bessi (Rome: Salerno, 2000), 31–53.

Boccaccio, Giovanni. *Decameron* (Brescia: Ludovico Britannico, 1536).

Boccaccio, Giovanni. *Decameron*, ed. Vittore Branca (Torino: Einaudi, 1980).

Boccaccio, Giovanni. *De genealogiis deorum gentilium*, ed. Vincenzo Romano (Bari: Laterza, 1951).

Boccaccio, Giovanni. *Esposizioni sopra la Comedia di Dante (1373–1374)*. In *I commenti danteschi dei secoli XIV, XV e XVI*, ed. Paolo Procaccioli (Rome: Lexis Progetti Editoriali, 1999).

Branca, Vittore. *Boccaccio medievale, e nuovi studi sul* Decameron (Florence: Sansoni, 1996).

Bujanda, Jesús Martínez de, ed. *Index de Rome, 1557, 1559, 1564, les premiers index romains et l'index du concile de Trente* (Geneva: Droz 1990).

Cervantes, Miguel de. *Novelas ejemplares* (1613), ed. Jorge García López (Barcelona: Crítica, 2001).

Chiecchi, Giuseppe, and Luciano Troisio. *Il* Decameron *sequestrato, le tre edizioni censurate del Cinquecento* (Milan: Unicopli, 1984).

Delcorno, Carlo. *Exemplum e Letteratura, tra Medioevo e Rinascimento* (Bologna: Il Mulino, 1989).

Dronke, Peter. *Fabula, Explorations into the Uses of Myth in Medieval Platonism* (Leiden: Brill, 1974).

Erasmus, Desiderius. *De Ratione studii*. In *Opera omnia, ordinis primi, tomus secundus*, ed. Jean-Claude Margolin (Leiden: Brill, 1971).

Horace. *Ars poetica*. In *Horace on Poetry*, vol. 2, ed. Charles Oscar, Brink (Cambridge: Cambridge, University Press, 1971).

Häberlein, Mark. *Brüder, Freunde and Betrüger, soziale Beziehungen, Normen und Konflikte in der Augsburger Kaufmannschaft um die Mitte des 16. Jahrhunderts* (Berlin: Akademie Verlag, 1998).

Kallendorf, Craig W., ed. *Humanist Educational Treatises* (Cambridge, MA: Harvard University Press, 2002).

Kocher, Ursula. *Boccaccio und die deutsche Novellistik* (Amsterdam: Rodopi, 2005).

Küpper, Joaquin. "Affichierte Exemplarität, tatsächliche A-Systematik: Boccaccios *Decameron* und die Episteme der Renaissance." In *Renaissance. Diskursstrukturen und epistemologische Voraussetzungen*, ed. Klaus W. Hempfer (Stuttgart: Steiner, 1993).

Lines, David A., ed. *Aristotle's Ethics in the Italian Renaissance 1300–1650* (Leiden: Brill, 2002).

Lines, David A., and Sabrina Ebbersmeyer, eds. *Rethinking Virtue, Reforming Society: New Directions in Renaissance Ethics, c. 1350 1650* (Turnhout: Brepols, 2012).

Neuschäfer, Hans-Jörg. *Boccaccio und der Beginn der Novelle* (Munich: Fink, 1969).

Moss, Ann. *Printed Commonplace-Books and the Structuring of Renaissance Thought* (Oxford: Clarendon Press, 1996).

Olson, Glending. *Literature as Recreation in the Later Middle Ages* (Ithaca, NY: Cornell University Press, 1982).

Picone, Michelangelo. *Boccaccio e la codificazione della novella* (Ravenna: Longo, 2008).

Pontano, Giovanni. *De sermone*, ed. Florence Bistagne (Paris: Champion, 2008).

Quondam, Amedeo. *Forma del vivere: l'etica del gentiluomo e i moralisti italiani* (Bologna: Il Mulino, 2010).

Roick, Matthias. *Pontano's Virtue* (London: Bloomsbury, 2017).

Schneewind, Jerome B. *The Invention of Autonomy. A History of Modern Moral Philosophy* (Cambridge: Cambridge University Press, 1998).

Stierle, Karlheinz. "Three Moments in the Crisis of Exemplarity: Boccaccio-Petrarch, Montaigne and Cervantes." *Journal of the History of Ideas*, 59 (4) (1998), 581–95.

Thomas Aquinas, *Summa Theologica*, ed. Albert Raulin (Paris: les Éditions du Cerf, 2021).

Index of Persons

Printed in the United States
by Baker & Taylor Publisher Services